The University of Michigan
Center for Chinese Studies

Michigan Monographs in Chinese Studies
Volume 59

The Mandarin and the Cadre: China's Political Cultures

by
Lucian W. Pye

Ann Arbor

Center for Chinese Studies
The University of Michigan

1988

ALJ 9546

Library of Congress Cataloging-in-Publication Data

Pye, Lucian W., 1921–
     The mandarin and the cadre : China's political cultures / by
Lucian W. Pye.
          p.   cm. — (Michigan monographs in Chinese studies ; no. 59)
     Bibliography: p.
     Includes index.
     ISBN 0-89264-082-0 : $19.50. ISBN 0-89264-083-9 (pbk.) : $12.50
     1. Political Science—China. 2. Political leadership—China.
3. Pragmatism. 4. Political culture—China. I. Title.
II. Series.
JA84.C6P94 1988   88-27727
306'.2'0951—dc19   CIP

Cover design by John Klausmeyer

Manufactured in the United States of America

6 5 4 3 2

To

Gabriel A. Almond

and

John King Fairbank

CONTENTS

PREFACE

No culture in the world matches China's in durability. Moreover, it is a culture long under siege. For two hundred years it has staved off a challenge from the West. Then for more than three decades Chinese culture has been brutally attacked and insulted, decried and denied from within by the extermination campaigns of the Chinese Communists. Yet China's cultural tradition persists and seems to be engulfing its Communist tormentors. The Deng Xiaoping leadership now holds that China is at a "primary stage of socialism," one that is "immature and imperfect," and that the eventual goal is to realize "socialism with Chinese characteristics"—suggesting a new respect for Chinese culture.

Indeed, the toughness of Chinese culture has forced a profound change in one of the most fundamental assumptions of Marxism-Leninism. By accepting the legitimacy of Deng Xiaoping's announced goal of "socialism with Chinese characteristics," the current Russian leaders have gone beyond Stalin's grudging acknowledgement of the possibility of different "roads to socialism"—roads that would lead to a common goal where there would no longer be cultural differences—and have now accepted for orthodox Marxism-Leninism the idea that when the end point of the promised land of Communism has been reached, cultural differences will still remain. Chinese culture has thus cracked the universalistic claims of scientific Marxism and forced its abstract, general categories to give way to parochial realities. If there can be "socialism with Chinese characteristics" then of course there will also be socialisms with Russian characteristics and the characteristics of other national cultures. Whereas noncommunists have long noted the enduring hold of culture in all the socialist countries, it is the exceptional

ix

vividness of the persisting Chinese culture that has made a modification in the dogma of orthodox Marxism unavoidable.

It is entirely fitting that Chinese culture should have forced this concession upon the dogma of Marxism-Leninism, because, long before such formal acknowledgment was made, the victory of Communism in China had already produced a distinctive political culture that deserves to be called Confucian Leninism. Whereas the Bolshevik version of Leninism was molded out of the revolutionary traditions of Russian political culture, the version of Leninism that triumphed in China, and also in North Korea and Vietnam, bears the stamp of the great East Asian, or Confucian, civilization. The result has been a distinctive version of what was supposed to have been a monolithic system. Confucian Leninism has its particular styles and practices that set it apart from the Leninism of the Soviet Union and Eastern Europe.

The secret of the survivability of Chinese culture lies in the intense self-consciousness of the socialization processes by which young Chinese are brought up by their families and guardians. Little is left to chance as Chinese children are taught correct behavior and the importance of loyalty to the group. The resulting intensity of group identity provides the basis for a virulent spirit of nationalism.

Just as the Chinese child is molded, so does the resulting culture hold Chinese political behavior in its grip. For all the turmoil of the past decades, the style of Chinese politics remains familiar. China's commitment to Marxism, and to the Four Principles, has not obliterated Chinese culture, but rather it has produced the distinctive culture of Confucian Leninism. China's modernization is going to take place in the context of that country's exceptionally resilient and distinctive culture. Just as a modernized Japan, for all of its dramatic changes, has remained surprisingly loyal to key features of its cultural heritage, so will China's past be a part of its future. Therefore, in trying to penetrate the uncertainties of China's future, one needs to seek out insights about Chinese cultural patterns. Moreover, as more students can now travel to China and see Chinese realities at first hand, teaching about China will have to deal less with the abstractions of ideology and policy and more with actual patterns of behavior.

The purpose of this book is precisely to facilitate such understanding of China's political cultures. Let us make it clear at the outset that in focusing on cultural considerations we have no intention of disparaging the importance of other approaches to the study of politics. Our need for knowledge is far too great to allow us the extravagance of slighting the advantages of multiple forms of analysis. At our current state of knowledge we truly need to allow "one hundred flowers to bloom." Readers who seek noncultural explanations for the points we will be making here will be wasting their time. Of course there are alternative explanations—there always are.

The book begins with a general discussion of the concept of political culture. The objective is not the hopeless one of converting zealous opponents of that approach, but rather to defend its value among other approaches and thereby possibly sway the undecided and strengthen the convictions of sympathizers. Following this discussion we try to explain how the same culture could have sustained both the ideological politics of Mao Zedong and the pragmatic politics of Deng Xiaoping. Some of the ideas in this chapter were presented in the Alexander Eckstein Memorial Lecture that I gave in 1986 at the University of Michigan. Chapter 3 explores the distinctive dimension of pragmatism in Chinese culture, and it is a revised version of the Contemporary China Institute annual lecture of 1985, given at the School of Oriental and African Studies at the University of London. Different versions of this chapter and of chapter 4 appeared first in the pages of the *China Quarterly*, and I appreciate the editor's permission to use them here. The book closes with a look at the importance of leadership in shaping Chinese politics and in providing the basis for legitimacy.

My thinking on many of the ideas in this work has benefited from the personal reactions of individuals who sought to pursue points further with me after my oral presentations at Ann Arbor, London, and the Universities Service Centre in Hong Kong. Donald Blackmer, Merle Goldman, Michel Oksenberg, Richard Samuels, Myron Weiner, and David Zweig made helpful comments on all or parts of the manuscript. Mary Pye was at all stages a close collaborator and helpful editor. I am most appreciative of the thoughtful editing by Michelle Paul, who, time and again, spotted problems I had not seen. Finally, my thanks go to Lola Klein for skillfully and patiently typing and retyping the various drafts.

Lucian W. Pye

CHAPTER I

EXPLAINING POLITICAL CULTURE

In preparation for his first visit to China as a cultural exchange lecturer, a distinguished professor of American studies decided he should read through a small library of books on contemporary China. On finishing the assignment he concluded that a peculiar form of racism seems to characterize the work of contemporary China specialists, in that they consistently describe the Chinese as a two-dimensional people who lack the deeper human qualities and seem to be motivated only by shallow rationalizations about their own public policy preferences. He found that, in contrast to the rich characterizations used to explain political behavior in America, to say nothing of France, England, or Germany, the characterizations of the Chinese described them as automatons programmed to battle over policy alternatives, rather than as people who give public expression to deeper human sentiments.

It is hard to quarrel with the professor's portrayal of much of the literature on the current scene in China, but his charge of racism is, I believe, off the mark. In fact, I suspect the exact opposite to be the problem. That is, many China specialists seem anxious to avoid any hint of offense to the Chinese; this has led them to the peculiar conclusion that they are elevating the dignity of Chinese politics by depicting Chinese political behavior as revolving around disagreements about policy alternatives, without considering deeper emotional and historical motivations. It is odd, but true, that many authors seem to believe that they are showing respect for the Chinese when they

1

describe them as people without the full range of human complexities. The fact that Chinese are often hesitant to expose their subjective worlds does not mean that they are devoid of inner feelings or that they do not appreciate the efforts of others to understand their feelings and cultural predispositions. It is, of course, true that many Chinese, like many individuals in other countries, are ambivalent about being culturally distinctive, and sometimes the Chinese do seem to long to be like everyone else. Yet the very essence of nationalism is the belief in one's own cultural uniqueness. Therefore, to take away the individuality of the Chinese is to strip them of their self-esteem and to debase their pride of national identity. Why is it that students of comparative politics see no problem in excepting the Chinese, alone among all peoples, from the application of Lasswell's insight that the motivating forces driving Political Man are private motives that are displaced onto public institutions and rationalized as being in the public interest? We are given an antiseptic view of the Chinese as mere pursuers of rationalistic policies, devoid of all the human elements of ambition, aggression, jealousy, pride, charity, dedication, pretension, scheming, fantasy, earnestness, frivolity, and general tomfoolery that, together with innumerable other passions and moods, produce the rich mixtures that fuel politics in civilized countries.

Even more puzzling is the fact that some historians of China, while knowledgeable about the rich and distinctive traditions of thought and practice of one of the world's greatest civilizations, nevertheless suggest that the Chinese are no different from Americans. They seem to believe that this is flattering to Chinese. They leave their students wondering why they should trouble themselves to learn about Chinese traditions if current Chinese politics can be understood by thinking of Chinese political behavior as the same as American.

In short, there seems to be some confusion about the propriety of noting cultural differences and the relevance of culture in explaining Chinese political behavior. On the question of the significance of cultural factors in general, the trends in the views of scholars and laymen cross in a perplexing manner. At the beginning of the behavioral revolution in the social sciences, it was academics who vigorously pushed the importance of appreciating cultural differences—the views of Margaret Mead, Ruth Benedict, Clyde Kluckhohn, and Erik Erikson were, for example, widely disseminated in classrooms—for it was assumed that Americans were by nature ethnocentric and insensitive to cultural relativism. At that time the American public was seen as too prone to expect others to behave like Americans. Sometime in the 1970s the lines crossed: scholars began to write as though we lived in a monocultural world, at least politically, while laymen increasingly recognized the importance of cultural differences. Theorists propounded universal models of rational actors, while laymen deduced that national differences abound and that, for example, Japanese ways may be superior in some spheres of industry.

In political science there was a lively interest in political culture in the late 1950s and early 1960s, when the concept seemed to beckon scholars to consider exciting new departures that would build upon the techniques of survey research and the insights of psychology and anthropology. Then suddenly there was an abrupt halt, largely because a rising tide of radical polemics stigmatized the notion of political culture, treating it as anathema. In the field of Chinese studies, those who sympathized with Mao's Cultural Revolution had no patience with any theory that suggested that the Chairman and his legions of Red Guards were not about to transform the Chinese people and their way of life instantly. In their view Mao was about to prove that ideological correctness and the liberating effects of political participation could wipe away deeply ingrained cultural traditions overnight. Elsewhere the glorified idea of revolution turned into a mindless belief that societies could be made over by the passionate chanting of slogans and the asserted willpower of true believers. Castro was said to be stripping the Cubans of their long-established Latin ways and making them into "New Men and New Women." Ho Chi Minh and his successors were proclaimed to have almost magical powers in changing the thoughts and attitudes of Vietnamese peasants. Some people claimed that the pseudo-revolutionary regimes of colonels, and even of sergeants and corporals, in Africa and Latin America were making awesome progress in eliminating old ways of thinking and producing model heroes. In such a politicized environment the concept of political culture became an unwanted challenge to propaganda about how dramatic changes were taking place. Those who were *au courant* with radical trends denounced the concept of political culture as being "conservative," if not reactionary, proving once again that the practice of putting political labels on scientific concepts usually produces results worthy of the theater of the absurd. (Note for example how the theories of sociobiology produced exactly opposite responses in two different political environments when they were politicized: in France sociobiology was hailed by the left as supporting their cherished neo-Rousseauian views about the desirable integration of man and nature, while in America it was denounced by liberals as "fascist" doctrine. Needless to say, on neither side of the Atlantic did the politically passionate trouble themselves greatly with ascertaining the empirical validity of the theories.)

In China the post-Mao era of "opening to the world" revealed the fact that while China had changed, there was still much cultural continuity. Indeed, the citizens of the Peoples' Republic of China and the people in Taiwan still seemed to have much in common, especially in their ways of responding to economic and political change. Today's Chinese have mixed feelings about their traditional culture and about what sort of people they would like to become as they strive for modernization. Chinese ambivalence about articulating national identity has made it tricky for others to confront contemporary Chinese political culture. Today the official line is that the national goal should be to "build socialism with Chinese characteristics"—but there is an awkward silence as to exactly what constitutes socialism and, even more embarassing, what exactly are Chinese characteristics. For nearly thirty years the Chinese authorities have fanatically tried to eliminate all "feudal remnants" and transform Chinese society into the mono-chromatic drabness of proletarian Communism. In the 1950s, after committing the desecration of tearing down the magnificent city walls of Peking, the Party made a survey and discovered that nearly five thousand ancient wonders still remained in the city; the decision was promptly made to preserve seventy-eight of these as "relics" and allow the rest to be destroyed.[1]* The object was to make Peking into another Moscow, a display place for heavy industry, filled with drab, smoking factories. Now, of course, the Chinese have discovered that they cannot awe foreign visitors by showing off run-down factories and that if they are to attract the much desired tourist dollars, they must play up yesterday's despised "feudal legacies," which are now being zealously restored, usually in even gaudier colors than before. In short, while the current generation is not entirely certain of what to be proud of, they do know that as Chinese they have a right to pride.

Chinese cultural inhibitions about psychological introspection do not make it easy to explore Chinese political culture. When the Chinese do look inward they are usually performing the rationalistic act of seeking self-improvement and self-cultivation in the Confucian tradition, and are not making deeper explorations into the dynamics of their own emotional development. Few societies have lurched about in such

---

*Notes are located at the back of the book. Those notes that contain textual material are indicated by an asterisk.

convulsions as has the Chinese in trying to achieve modernization, yet the Chinese have been unable to articulate what it has all meant to them. Americans, with their frustrations over Watergate and Vietnam, have compulsively poured out their soul-searching confessions of national flaws. When things have gone wrong in their national lives, as they certainly have, the Germans and the Japanese, the French and the British, have all debated about the weaknesses in their national characters.

In contrast, the Chinese, who have one of the great stories to tell of the travails of a major civilization struggling to cope with modernization and nation-building, have opened few doors into their collective subjective realm. This is ironic, partly because nearly all modern literature in China is politicized. Under the Communist regime Chinese authors have become political actors, criticizing or praising partisan views and addressing questions of national development. (Similarly, the May Fourth writers sought to mobilize the country against the corruption of the warlord leaders of their times.) Yet no Chinese writer has been able to take on the grand theme of what has happened to China's collective identity as the country's leaders have propelled it first in one direction, then in another, over the past decades. There has been no Chinese Tolstoy. Chinese critics, from the Reform movement of Liang Qichao to the Leftist writers of the 1930s, even including Lu Xun, have focused on political policy or social manners and not on deeper cultural dimensions. Because the levels of interpretation arrived at by the Chinese are, therefore, often superficial, outsiders are not provided with many useful clues to the psychodynamics of Chinese national life. Consequently, much of Western writing about China delves no more deeply than the Chinese would.

Chapter 4 examines the limited ways in which the Chinese have tried to explain to themselves how their culture could have unleashed the horrors of the Cultural Revolution. The Chinese, with their reticence about introspection, stand in contrast to other Asian cultures, such as the Japanese and Indian, in which a willingness to engage in critical self-analysis has greatly facilitated the study of their political cultures.[2]

Identifying Political Culture

The reasons for the temporary eclipse of political culture studies during the 1960s and 1970s range from legitimate confusion about how such a subtle and elusive subject should properly be studied to hostility from those committed to other approaches. Those hostile to the concept of political culture have been surprisingly intolerant of the diversity that traditionally characterized the social sciences—indeed, the very word "pluralism" seems to provoke rage in some scholars. In light of these difficulties it may be helpful to respond briefly to some of the more general criticisms before going on to our analysis of aspects of Chinese political culture.[3*] This is not an easy thing to do, because there has been no ongoing debate about political culture; rather, the critics have simply ignored or dismissed the concept as too tricky or simply as a residual category. Therefore it is necessary to argue against unstated or half-stated critiques. Consequently, one may sound more defensive than one would like to be.

As a start it must be granted that the analysis of political culture can be a ticklish undertaking. Critics may concede that cultural factors are present in any situation and that all actions are to some degree influenced by culture, but they still feel that the matter is too nebulous for systematic analysis. Some say that considering cultural factors invites imprecise and essentially tautological explanations—for example, "The Chinese acted that way because that is the Chinese way." This, it is said, opens the door to speculation about psychological states. This argument is both correct and irrelevant. It fails to recognize that politics is by its nature an elusive and highly subjective process, particularly with respect to motivations. The political arena is always filled with hidden agendas and actors with conflicting purposes. Political life is built upon speculations, subjective interpretations, hidden calculations, and strange blends of passion and morality. The political process is not something that can be grasped empirically in its totality. Rather it consists of observers and participants attempting to fathom the meaning of whatever objective hints and clues they can focus on in trying to explain what seems to be going on in public life. Political culture is therefore no more elusive or nebulous than is politics. If political culture seems devoid of hard data, and consequently easily susceptible to the subjective whims of the analyst, then so is most political analysis.

Champions of starkly objective political analysis run the dangerous risk of arriving at conclusions that err on the side of the obvious—for this is the common danger when the human dimension is ignored. The practice of elucidating the self-evident, too frequently followed in political science, is not the right road to greater knowledge; indeed, we do not need to train more graduate students to "prove" what their grandmothers already knew. In almost any form of political analysis, paying even modest attention to the workings of political culture and psychology can protect scholars from the sin of earnestly expounding banalities.

It is not true that the intangibles of politics can be ignored. Any form of political analysis—be it conducted by scholars, journalists, government analysts, or citizens—is inevitably premised upon fundamental notions about human nature and human society. Any attempt to analyze or discuss political life must involve psychological and sociological assumptions. The assumptions may be implicit in the analysis or they may be brought forward explicitly, but the implicit approach is just as dependent upon a psychology and a sociology as is the explicit. One's analysis can be based upon simplistic and superficial notions about human nature (and much of political analysis should probably be criticized for precisely this failing), or one can use the most sophisticated insights of psychology and sociology. Classical political philosophers, from Aristotle and Plato through Hobbes, Hume, and Locke, all sought to use the most advanced theories of the day about human nature—that is, psychology—in building their theories. Political science as a discipline has always been dependent upon psychology and sociology, even as it has sought to become more quantitative. Unfortunately, in retreating from the more advanced insights and theories of modern psychology, some political scientists have withdrawn to even more primitive views about human motivations than were used by the eighteenth- and nineteenth-century classical political theorists. The most common forms of political analysis are based on the method of "educated guesses" about the motives and intentions of public figures, but what is not clear is the kind of "education" on which these guesses are based: is it serious education about psychology, or is it education about what one's peers and the public will easily swallow? If it is the latter, then it can be no more than "conventional wisdom," which by definition would mean that such "educated" judgments can hold no hope for advancing knowledge.

The techniques of sample survey studies can provide an appropriate response to the concern for more "hard" data in the study of political culture. Systematic surveys generate the numbers that can serve as the basis for objective descriptions of cultural differences. Unfortunately, comparative national surveys have proved increasingly expensive, hard to organize, and at times fraught with methodological problems resulting from attempts to insure that the questionnaires in fact measure comparable concepts. This is not the place to go into the challenges of doing good cross-cultural surveys or the difficulties in arriving at scales that can in fact measure what they purport to measure. It is enough to say that, with respect to China, conditions do not permit national surveys, and more limited surveys are likely to produce results that would be no better than the judgments of thoughtful scholars.

At this point we need to address briefly the charge that political analysis that is not based on "hard" data opens the door to distortion according to the personal values and biases of the analyst, a charge to which it is often said that interpretive political culture studies are particularly vulnerable. It is true that in the social sciences much is made over the problem of value judgments—indeed, so much so that it is in fact a greatly exaggerated problem in the normal conduct of research. The notion that unstated values are in constant danger of contaminating the results of studies is a nightmare only for purist philosophers of science who have not engaged in real research. The issue is kept alive mainly because it seems to some people to be useful in polemical attacks on the results of studies they do not like, and therefore they find it gratifying to make essentially ad hominem criticisms. In practice the really serious problems of judgment are not those of value judgments but rather those of factual and analytical judgments. What are the facts that best describe the actual workings of the political process at any particular time and place? And, analytically, what should be understood as cause and what effect? What should be taken as the independent variables and what should be seen as intervening variables? How can we be sure that the theories we seek to build are realistic ones that focus on what is indeed decisive and not marginal in determining political developments? Once we face honestly these tough questions of judgment, it immediately becomes clear that it should be unthinkable to leave aside the human factor that is at the base of all political culture studies. To ignore the psychological dimension of behavior is to blank out far too many factual and analytical considerations that are manifestly central to political reality.

For some people the concept of political culture may be hard to grasp because its multiple dimensions require a juggling of a variety of approaches. Political culture involves both mass and elite attitudes; it includes barely articulated sentiments as well as the foundations of well-defined ideologies; it seems to call for the insights of depth psychology as well as hard-nosed analyses of political stratagems and operational codes. There is no escaping the fact that culture, since it involves the very essence of human nature, cannot be easily delineated or codified.

Geoffrey Gorer, the anthropologist and pioneer of national character analysis, once made a helpful stab in the direction of separating the different dimensions of culture, and thereby implicitly suggested the different methodologies appropriate for examining the various aspects of the phenomenon.[4] I believe that by analogy we can usefully stretch his suggestions about the dimensions of culture for our purposes of differentiating aspects of political culture that similarly call for different approaches. Gorer noted that language is a fundamental aspect of culture; he went on to observe that linguistic analysis has profitably separated language into three dimensions: phonetics, vocabulary, and syntax or grammatical structure—each of which has its distinctive characteristics and hence calls for particular analytical methodologies.

In the case of phonetics, differences in dialect sometimes require a sociological approach. At the same time, every individual's speech is unique. Indeed, people's "voice prints" are as distinctive as their fingerprints. By analogy, it at times becomes necessary in the study of political culture, especially in studying leaders, to focus on the unique personality; thus the techniques and insights of psychology are demanded. When the focus is on more than just an individual leader, it may be appropriate to study the analogue of a "dialect group"; that is, say, a generation of political leaders with a shared background. Instead of looking for the idiosyncratic character of the particular leader, the analysis broadens to identify shared orientations or what have been called operational codes.

Vocabulary is a group phenomenon, since the use of words varies according to the speaker's geographical region, class, educational attainment, and occupational jargon. Thus, when one is dealing with the functional equivalent of vocabulary in the study of political cultures, such as when one is analyzing group attitudes and values, the issue of representation becomes important. In the case of China, for example, there are obviously great differences in attitudes according to region, as well as lifestyle (rural and urban), degree of education, and level of political participation. It is at this level that the researcher would ideally turn to surveys based on demographically representative samples. Since this is impossible, it becomes necessary to use judgment in extrapolating from whatever evidence is available.

Finally, and maybe most important of all, there is the dimension of syntax, in which variation is of minor importance since nearly everyone who speaks a common language tends to follow much the same rules of grammar. A few native speakers can be adequate informants for the skilled linguist. The linguist needs, of course, to be on guard against grossly atypical informants, and this is why wisdom and sophistication are called for in doing any cultural analysis.[5*] In the case of political culture, "syntax" becomes the most basic shared orientation providing the sense of national identity and collective expectations about legitimacy and the role of power and authority. Gorer related the concept of national character to syntax. For our purposes, "syntax" becomes the rules of the game of national politics and the sentiments that give coherence to a national polity in spite of regional differences.

This analogy to linguistics is helpful, but it does not solve all problems. There is, for example, still the difficulty of determining what aspects of political culture are analogous to phonetics, vocabulary, or syntax, respectively. Fortunately, however, most scholars can generally determine which actions are appropriately attributable to the individual's unique personality, which call for sample surveys, and which are the basic aspects of political culture calling for interpretive generalizations.

Since there are no clear boundaries, different scholars will expand or contract the three domains. Some are predisposed to emphasize the scope of individual uniqueness and gloss over the extent to which observed behavior fits larger cultural patterns. Others will go to great lengths to try to quantify what some see as self-evident. Finally, there are those who find it plausible that broad generalizations can characterize political cultures. They see the making of such generalizations as the equivalent of the historian's practice of periodizing different ages. China scholars who feel comfortable distinguishing the dominant characteristics of the Tang, Song, or Qing dynasties should have no qualms about characterizing China's contemporary political culture.

The three dimensions of culture delineated above are also very helpful in understanding some of the problems of cultural change and continuity. Broadly stated, behavior at the level of "vocabulary" is more easily changed. Thus, attitudes that can be measured by sample surveys must be measured again periodically to determine whether they have changed, and to what extent. What each generation is cognitively taught can usually be readily changed. On the other hand, the deep structure or "syntactical" dimension is extremely slow in changing. This is because it is determined by the fundamental socialization process, in which the cultural "coding" is passed on from generation to generation intuitively and with little conscious awareness of what is taking place.

Scientific Imagination and the Fallacy of Premature Precision

Some political scientists have additional problems with political culture because of their uncompromising concept of what constitutes "science" in our multi-dimensional discipline. They are not amused that the term science is so elastic that it can be stretched to embrace both the doctrines of Mary Baker Eddy and Marx's "scientific socialism." Their notion of "science" is rather mechanistic, geared to a nineteenth-century Newtonian view of physics, and often seems to place little importance on the human imagination, which is, of course, the driving force of true science. Rather, they are obsessed with the importance of measurement. They fail to appreciate that science cannot be limited to the small domain in which banal ideas can be laboriously "tested" by elaborate measurement procedures. The imaginative hypothesis must come first. The thinking through of novel ideas and speculating about connections and causal relationships that others had not observed are the hallmarks of all great scientists from Galileo to Darwin and to Einstein, and for that matter to Adam Smith, Marx, and Weber.

Advocates of such a narrow version of science in political science have generally anathematized the concepts of intuition and reductionism, decreeing that they have no place in an enterprise that seeks to be scientific. In doing so they ignore essential features of contemporary, post-Newtonian physics, the discipline on which they frequently argue they are modeling their work. Anthony Zee has vividly described how beauty and simplicity, essentially aesthetic ideals, have been the driving force behind the breakthroughs of intuition and reductionism that have brought particle physics to the threshold of a new and elegant "grand unified theory."[6] Murray Gell-Mann's Nobel Prize was in recognition of his intuitive insistence that quarks had to exist as particles. C. N. Yang and Robert Mills built, in the 1950s, theories of symmetry that did not describe anything yet seen in nature, but in the 1970s their elegant theories were seen as describing perfectly what had to be the interaction of all fundamental particles. In physics the experimental "testing" of theories often comes long after the intuitive insights are appreciated— especially if experimentation must await advances in measuring equipment. In contrast, in political science it is usually assumed that instant tests should be possible. Worse still, in the social sciences it is standard practice to treat any single *apparent* disproof of a hypothesis as enough to discredit it entirely, while in contrast, physical scientists and engineers will stubbornly stick with their intuitive ideas as they ignore one experimental failure after another until they finally succeed in working out what they knew had to be right.[7*]

Those social scientists who glorify procedure and minimize the importance of imagination tend to dismiss intuition as being simplistic, untutored, naive, superficial, or worse. The fact is, as researchers at the forefront of artificial intelligence now know, intuition calls for tremendous amounts of observation, highly skilled judgments, sensitive appreciation of possible connections, and the extraordinary speed of the human mind in managing memory and calculations.

Let us make it clear that in the last analysis proof must lie in the evidence, for political science is an empirical discipline in which reality is sovereign. The analysis of political culture must follow the conventions of science and employ techniques open to anyone, at any time, anywhere, without any claims of secret faculties or hidden skills. Above all, facts must be respected and contrary arguments, as long as they are not offered in malice, must be taken into account. The standards may not be quite those of textbook sociology, but they are those that a Kaplan, or even more likely a Lakatos, would understand and accept. The slippery problem in the study of political cultures, however, is that of getting the right, or more correctly, the relevant facts for checking truly imaginative theories. Available data banks frequently are not appropriate sources for evidence with respect to subtle theories, but this should not mean turning our backs on developing such theories. Maybe in time we will have the means to test them. In the meantime it is important to uphold the main tradition of the discipline of political science, which insists that one must necessarily build theories using concepts that are not easily operationalized—concepts such as the state, legitimacy, justice, the polity, and the social system.

As for the charge of reductionism, it is usually made by those who have a very vivid but constricted view of what the boundaries of different fields of study are or should be. In particular, such critics tend to believe that the study of politics should be separated from, and uncontaminated by, the insights about human behavior provided by sociology, psychology, economics, or any of the other social sciences. For them political analysis can be faulted if economic, social, or cultural variables are included, for in their view politics and government can have lives of their own—as though the ideas and motivations of public life were somehow separate from the general human condition. There is something strangely contradictory in the position of some who use the charge of reductionism: on the one hand, they seem to wish to limit the definition of what is "political" to a small, precious domain—much like insisting that only sonnets should be classified as poetry—while, on the other hand, they will vigorously engage in trying to politicize the study of politics.[8*] To the extent that their criticisms are ideologically inspired, they should keep in mind the wise advice of the historian Gertrude Himmelfarb: "In the vicissitudes of ideological warfare, victory is uncertain, defeat unacknowledged, and the verdict of history unpredictable." Moreover, in the social sciences, as contrasted with the physical sciences, there can be no presumption that the latest paradigm is superior to what went before.

The goal of all sciences is to seek simplicity, ignoring some elements of reality in the search for basic explanatory connections. Reductionism is bad when the analysis seeks to explain phenomena at one level by introducing variables that belong to a level at which the phenomena do not exist—as would be the case if one tried, for example, to use particle physics to explain chemical processes. In political analysis, however, political culture exists at nearly all levels of analysis. The idea that reductionism is a bad thing, something scientifically unjustified, is possibly most frequently made against political psychology, which is the foundation of much of political culture analysis. Those who make this criticism tend to forget that in the modern social sciences the unit of analysis is the act, and all acts involve actors who are, ultimately, specific individuals behaving in particular situations. Thus considerations of individual psychology must come into play.

While critics of psychological interpretations tend to favor formal or rational theories based on a rational actor model, they are apt to overlook the fact that such theories are equally reductionist. To reduce the human element in politics to mere rationality is a strange way to advance science. We shall have more to say about the relationship between cognition and affect, but at this stage we can make the point that the controversy about the relative importance of the two for political behavior involves more heat than substance. While cognition and affect are distinct abstractions, in actual studies it is impossible to distinguish neatly between the two. In practice people's cognitions are colored by their feelings, and their feelings are influenced by their judgments; cognition and affect blend to produce motivations and rationalizations that are hybrids.

For our purpose of understanding political culture it is significant that a premature demand for precision nearly strangled the study of national character at the time of its inception. Alex Inkeles, quite unintentionally, brought the then growing field of national character studies to a sudden halt in the mid-1950s by calling for rigorous standards of precision in measuring national differences; many thought those standards were impossible to realize and that such studies should consequently be avoided.[9] Twenty-five years later Inkeles demonstrated his respect for the concept of national character by producing an exceptional study that proved, using contemporary sample surveys, that there has been a striking degree of continuity in the core values held by Americans from the time of De Tocqueville's penetrating observations.[10] The techniques he used in the late 1970s had been available in the mid-1950s, and therefore there had really been no need for others to have turned their backs on such research.

Gabriel Almond and Stephen Genco address the problems raised by an overly limited view of the meaning of "science" from yet another perspective.[11] They take note of Karl Popper's observation that the problem of determinacy and indeterminacy can be thought of as a continuum stretching from the high degree of regularity and predictability of "clocks" to the irregularity and indeterminacy of "clouds." When Newtonian physics became the ideal for science, "all clouds became clocks," but with the arrival of Heisenberg's principle of indeterminism "all clocks became to some degree clouds." Analogously, some social scientists see the social world as being "clock-like" and therefore composed of mechanical, law-like relationships, while others see the social world as being "cloud-like"; that is, composed of generally definable larger patterns, the individual components of which act in random ways. Many methodologists in the social sciences have tried to tilt all analysis toward the ideal of "clocks." When they find a single seeming exception to a generalization, they believe they have destroyed it. If medicine had operated with such a notion of science, germ theory would have been abandoned from the start for explaining the transmission of, say, colds. After all, cases could be readily found of people being exposed to cold germs and not coming down with colds themselves. Indeed, it would be hard to think of any theory about the transmission of diseases or the causes of internal disorders that could have stood up to a "clock" theory of medical science.[12*]

At the other extreme, there are, of course, people who focus only on the random movements of the molecules of gas that make up the "clouds." For such people the social world is essentially devoid of any possibility for generalizations about collective human behavior.

There are, however, regularities to be found in social and political life, but as Almond and Genco note, such regularities are "soft" and have a short "half-life." One of the great disappointments of the early version of behavioralism has been the realization that the findings of any systematic study cannot stand as permanent, universal "laws," but are bound by considerations of time and place. The idea that a highly "scientific" or "clock-like" study of political behavior in the United States might serve as a model for political behavior in general is only slightly more foolish than the assumption that such a study can provide a permanent explanation even for American behavior alone. Hypotheses about political behavior that were "tested" and "proven" valid at one moment in history need to be rechecked constantly against the changes of time and circumstances.

Inappropriate efforts at producing "clock-like" studies would be only foolishly harmless, were it not for the fact that the enormous investment of effort that has to go into such enterprises encourages the authors to exaggerate the sigificance of the findings, often to the point of glorifying the trivial.[13*]

The False Dichotomy of Rational-Nonrational

Beyond these methodological issues, the study of political culture has been hampered by theoretical problems that arise from a Western philosophical propensity to believe in the possibility of pure rationality in human affairs. The presumption is that behavior can be neatly divided between actions based on man's rational faculties and those based on his emotions. It is analytically possible to conceptualize behavior, as Talcott Parsons did, as involving the trinity of the cognitive, affective, and evaluative modes of action.[14] Neo-classical economists, of course, employ simplified models that are devoid of cultural considerations as they focus on what they believe to be the rational calculus that guides utility optimization. And neo-Marxists believe that by stressing "structure" they can ignore questions of values and personal predispositions.

The idea of "rational choice" is, however, an abstraction like all myths. There simply is no such thing as pure or universal rationality, for as Clifford Geertz observes, " . . . men unmodified by the customs of particular places do not in fact exist, have never existed, and most important, could not in the very nature of the case exist." Geertz goes on to point out bluntly that " . . . there is no such thing as human nature independent of culture."[15] Since all action is inevitably shaped by the influence of culture, no behavior can be classed as exlusively rational or nonrational; nor can rationality be considered a universal mode of cognition. It is not just anthropologists who are skeptical about the possibility of a "rationality" untouched by culture: a pioneer in artificial intelligence, a field that would seemingly have the strongest defenders of the concept of a pure and universal rationality, supports the anthropologist's view. Marvin Minsky has observed, "Our culture teaches us that thoughts and feelings lie in almost separate worlds. [But in fact,] beyond a certain point, to distinguish between the emotional and intellectual structures of an adult is merely to describe the same structures from different points of view."[16] Minsky also notes a paradox that should give pause to rational theorists: in Western culture we assume that something can and should be done if someone has emotional problems—that is, there is a universally accepted concept of normality—while if someone has trouble thinking straight nothing can be done about it. This seems to suggest that there are greater shared standards of normality for the psychological than for the rational dimension of behavior.

To make rationality hinge on the relationship of ends and means, as Mannheim did, is often not particularly helpful for political analysis; there are usually too many possible means for arriving at any one end for some actions to be considered "rational" on these grounds and others not. Even among technocrats there are heated debates as to what is the "best" policy. Furthermore, the test of efficiency in relating means and ends leaves the issue squarely in the domain of cultural considerations, since the question of what technologies and knowledge are available to the society for problem-solving at any particular time is, of course, an essentially cultural matter. Of course, if the test of whether particular means are rational for achieving specific ends becomes a question of efficaciousness, the cultural variable becomes even more critical, since undoubtably what works in one culture may not in another.[17*]

The notion of purpose helps to clarify somewhat the problem of rationality in social analysis. As Almond and Genco note, the introduction of purpose in human behavior does reduce the level of indeterminacy, bringing it to the level of what Popper calls "plastic control," as contrasted to the "cast-iron" control of "clocks." For example, once a student has made a purposeful decision as to what courses he or she will take during the next semester, it becomes possible to predict, but not with certainty, the precise places where that student will be at certain given times in the semester ahead. Similarly, the apparently random and totally unsystematic, patternless comings and goings of a peripatetic professor, who is seemingly footloose, turn out to be clearly "predictable" if one can get a peek into his calendar of commitments to meetings, conferences, guest lectures, and other professional activities. Indeed, with some people nearly every hour in the weeks ahead can be accounted for by the tyranny of their pocket calendars.

The existence of purpose, however, can also be the cause of difficulties, for analysts often falsely believe that they actually know the "purposes" of the public figures they are studying, or they confuse such "knowledge" with their own judgments as to what they would rationally do if they were in the other person's position of power. Much of normal political analysis thus takes the form of the observer making "predictions" based on the presumption that he has successfully "peeked into the calendar" of the public people being studied. That is, we like to convince ourselves that we know the commitments and priorities of leaders.

Yet in observing political behavior it is usually difficult to determine the precise motivations and purposes of the actors, especially given the "hidden agendas" that most politicians seem to have. The game of politics calls for all manner of tactics and stratagems, including deception and playing one's cards close to one's chest. Moreover, given the mixed motives resulting from the interplay of the active politicians' inner psychological drives and their need to respond to circumstances, it is usually hard even for them to know whether their articulated "purposes" are in fact serving as guides to their actions. Voltaire expressed much the same observation about rationality: "Men use thought only to justify their wrongdoings, and speech only to conceal their thoughts."

All of this adds up to the point that one of the most common pitfalls in political analysis is the seductive illusion that we can easily and accurately comprehend the purposes of the public figures we are studying. The payoffs in making predictions that derive from knowing the commitments of leaders are so great that we are all too easily deluded into confidently believing that we do in fact know their guiding purposes, and therefore we can go ahead and build elaborate explanations of what they have done or are about to do. Even worse, we tend to ignore any facts that might contradict how we expect them to behave. Once we presume to know the motivations of those we are studying, too much becomes emotionally and intellectually invested to permit changes in our judgments. Thus we tend to be quick to determine what must be the purposes of others, because the benefits for explanation are so great, but slow to recognize that we might be wrong, because the commitment involves the fusing of our own sense of identity with the subject of our analysis. Note, for example, how some students of Chinese politics were once so committed to the idea that Mao Zedong's goals were guided by sympathy for peasants that cognitive dissonance prevented them from perceiving the fact that Mao's policies, especially during the Great Leap, were anti-peasant and destined to create the worst rural famine in all of human history—some thirty million deaths. Nor did they perceive what the intellectuals sent down during the Cultural Revolution were to discover: Mao had indeed made the Chinese countryside a hell on earth. Similarly, many people were so convinced that Mao was guided by egalitarian principles that they were insensitive to the obvious fact that instead of working for a more equal society he was creating a caste society by giving everyone labels that derived from the status of their fathers or grandfathers. Moreover, by preventing people from moving freely to find better employment, he could not help but increase inequalities by preventing the development of a true labor market. The policy had to increase the gap between urban and rural conditions of life. Yet until Deng Xiaoping's reforms revealed these inequalities and the ways in which the Chinese peasantry had been mistreated, most Western observers continued to believe that Mao was a champion of peasants and of equality.

The point is not that we should avoid trying to understand the purposes of public figures in order to make better predictions, but rather that we should try to avoid superficial interpretations. There is no escaping the need for using the most sophisticated insights of psychology and cultural analysis in arriving at judgments as to what the real purposes of leaders are. Although it is true that in much of the popular press political analysis is, to paraphrase Samuel Butler, the art of drawing sufficient conclusions from insufficient premises and facts, this should not be the case in scholarly research. What we need to do is to transform the "insufficient premises and facts" into better theories and more accurate data.

Rational choice and formal theory, including game theory, have been powerful additions to our repertoire of techniques for analyzing political behavior. They become even more powerful, however, when not narrowly applied but expanded to take cultural predispositions into account. Indeed, there are two important reasons why it is inappropriate for political scientists to try to narrowly emulate economists by adopting their methods of microeconomic analysis.

First, we political scientists cannot operate as the economists do and hold that questions abut the sources of the preferences of those being analyzed should be treated as exogenous to our systems of analysis. The domain of political analysis is such that we cannot avoid the responsibility of trying to determine how people arrive at their preferences. As Aaron Wildavsky has convincingly argued, political scientists have an obligation to examine the sources of people's preferences.[18] Wildavsky, moreover, successfully demonstrates that people do not arrive at their preferences out of the blue but through interactions with others in social processes. "Cultural theory is based on the axiom that what matters most to people is their relationships with other people and other people's relations with them. It follows that the major choice made by people (or, if they are subject to coercion, made for them) is the form of culture—shared values legitimating social practices—they adopt." Thus preferences are a cultural matter that call for cultural interpretations.

Second, the economists can properly limit their analyses to objective, material factors, while political scientists have to include in their models the subjective domains of those being studied. Myron Weiner has, for example, noted that in political analysis, especially among public choice theorists who wish to follow the lead of economists, there is a tendency to treat the purposes of government policies as largely the maximizing of material objectives, in spite of the innumerable examples of governments acting in contrary ways. He takes as a telling example the well-established fact that immigrants almost without exception make positive contributions to the economy of the new country, but all governments act strenuously to inhibit or limit immigration.[19]

The notion that political leaders routinely engage in cost-benefit analyses in arriving at policies suggests that they are essentially bookkeepers, something they obviously are not. The reason that public policy programs have to go to such painful lengths to teach textbook methods of making cost-benefit analyses is precisely because it is such an unnatural approach in normal political life. In the messiness of politics there is often little room for systematic reasoning; as Abba Eban has noted, "Men and nations behave rationally and wisely only after they have exhausted all the alternatives."

Moreover, the very institutions of government place severe limits on the possibility of government by rationality. Yet faith in the sovereign place of reason in public affairs is rarely disturbed. Indeed, with every national election Americans display their unshakeable conviction that reason can and should guide our system of government. Thus, we demand to know what "programs" each candidate would carry out if elected, even while we congratulate ourselves over our unique system of separation of powers, which insures that no coherent program can be carried out in practice. We scold ourselves for allowing considerations of "character" to dominate over discussions of the "issues," even though we know that campaign talk about issues has little relationship to how things will actually work out in an administration that must confront an assertive Congress. Elections aside, we ceaselessly generate "rationally" coherent policies by establishing national commissions or paying out millions of dollars to think tanks and universities even though we know perfectly well that our revered system of checks and balances will insure that whatever comes out in the end will have little resemblance to what was planned. And of course the American ideal of the division of powers is not limited to just the three branches of government, but exists within each; within all administrations the various departments vigorously engage in hampering each other's work, Congress rejoices in its competing turfdoms, and two major parties work only by incoherent compromise. By standing in awe of both rationality in planning and diffusion of power, we end by having government by unintended consequences. Our political culture is strong enough to constantly rejuvenate our faith in the system and blind us to the dangers of impotence.

The Pointless Argument about Structure versus Culture

The debate over whether structure or culture provides the more useful explanations of political developments is really a matter of personal taste and ideological preference, not something that can be decided by testing the efficacy of the two approaches. All that can definitely be said on the issue is that each affects the other: What determines the particular character of structures? Why, of course, the culture involved. What shapes a culture? Why, of course, the structures involved. Which came first, the chicken or the egg? Given the current state of development of political science, it is pointless to argue that one approach is inherently superior; therefore, as serious followers of structural analysis would agree, the debate should be left to ardent fools. Good studies and bad ones can be found that stress either. The idea that the "right" choice of an approach will guarantee a superior research product is a denial of all that scholarship stands for in terms of individual creativity and skill. Ideally what would be called for would be multiple approaches that combine all the available techniques and theories. But this, of course, is unrealistic both because it would demand too much of the individual scholar and because it is natural that people's talents make them better at one approach or another. In practice, research must be a collective enterprise, with people working in different parts of the vineyard and all showing respect for the payoffs of others' styles of work.

Yet, in spite of this apparently self-evident truth, some of those who prefer structural considerations have tended to depreciate the utility of cultural analysis. There is, of course, nothing wrong in trying to push a structural analysis, or any other type of analysis, to its limits as a way of testing its utility. But to deny any role for cultural considerations becomes a form of reductionism that is as bad, if not worse, than the reductionism the proponents of a structural approach customarily charge more psychologically oriented scholars with employing.[20]

The dichotomy of culture and structure is further blurred, if not shown to be spurious, when advocates of structural analysis, such as neo-Marxists, treat ideology as a part of "structure."[21*] No serious analysis of ideology can go far without an examination of historical traditions and contemporary states of mind, factors that are the very essence of political culture. This peculiar position of the neo-Marxists is manifested in the Latin American *dependencia* literature, which ostensibly poses the argument that the "structural" features of the world capitalist system have prevented the economic and political development of the Third World, irrespective of cultural differences. However, any close reading of this literature will reveal it to be a cultural twin of the great Latin American tradition of "magical realism." If one looks beneath the Marxist surface trappings of the dependency theorists, one encounters soulmates of Gabriel Garcia Marquez, Jorge Luis Borges, Octavio Paz, Isabel Allende, and the host of others who take that uniquely Latin American approach to fiction. While the *dependencia* authors are not the literary peers of these novelists, they share the attitude, as Vargas Llosa has put it, that "Nobody can believe any more in real reality." Myth and fact are blended to produce magical realism. The inevitable result is Gabriel Garcia Marquez's conclusion: " . . . I consider journalism to be a literary genre" and therefore political analysis is not really very different from fiction writing, for although "The timing may be different . . . the experience is the same in literature and journalism."[22] *Dependencia* theory thus tells more about Latin American culture than it does about the realities of development.

In short, the attempt to make an issue over the relative explanatory powers of culture and structure has contributed little to the advancement of political science, and instead has undoubtedly impeded progress. Since we cannot place any precise weight on the relative importance of such variables as culture or structure, the debate has little significance for the generalized kinds of analyses that currently characterize interesting problems in comparative politics. To engage in such a debate is the equivalent of reviving the nineteenth-century debate of mind *versus* brain without the benefit of twentieth-century knowledge.

In the pages that follow, when we analyze dimensions of Chinese political culture in general terms, we will be skipping over considerations that are important in other approaches. Therefore, let us repeat here again that our purpose is not to dismiss other approaches, but only to demonstrate the value of treating seriously cultural and psychological factors.

Culture, not Race

Another criticism of the cultural approach is made by those who feel that it may be just a sophisticated way for authors to express their prejudices about other peoples. Some even raise the charge of racism.

This is a most unfair charge, because the very essence of traditional cultural anthropology is that everything must be explained by nurturance and nothing by nature or genetics. The tradition of cultural anthropology, which inspired the concept of political culture, was aggressively hostile to the suggestion that any aspect of behavior could be inherited. Franz Boaz, Margaret Mead, Ruth Benedict, Geoffrey Gorer, and all the other pioneers who advocated adopting Freud's insights into the discipline of anthropology were passionate in their opposition to racial or genetic theories. They grasped at the theories of psychoanalysis because these provided an answer to the most vexing questions in anthropology: Why do cultures persist? Why have people not easily borrowed from each other to the point of producing a more homogeneous world? Why is social change so often such a traumatic matter? They rejected the idea that the continuity of cultures could be a matter of biology—especially after the rise of Nazism and Hitler's racist doctrines. In Freud's work they found their answer. Personality and culture could now be seen as the opposite sides of the same coin and, according to the theory, personality was determined by the childhood experience of socialization. The reason for cultural persistence is that each generation of children is brought up in reaction to the same cluster of values. The stress should be put on reactions because the socialization process involves more than just being instilled with particular values; it also involves rebellion and the need for each generation to fight again the same battles. If the tradition of cultural anthropology is to be criticized, it should probably be on the grounds that its founders went too far in excluding genetic factors in explaining human development. Certainly recent developments in biology and linguistics suggest that genetic factors do play a greater role than the earlier anthropologists believed to be the case, but it is still, for good moral as well as scientific reasons, improper to consider the possibility of genetic differences in making political analyses.

Political culture theorists grasped at the view of culture as being a product of nurturance, but they then went further and developed the concept of political socialization, in which later and more cognitive learning experiences about politics could be acknowledged as being significant in shaping political orientations. This has, regretfully, led to another debate of ardent fools in political science, in which some have insisted that one stage of the socialization process is more important than any other. Although it may be possible to judge the crucial stages of development in a biographical study of an individual, it is pointless to argue the relative importance of family, school, peer group, or job in the socialization process of political cultures in general. Some scholars are more interested in studying family experiences, others are happier looking at school life; that is the way it should be, and there is no need to belie the importance of another's interest.

One of the reasons why I have followed the practice of explicitly taking child-rearing patterns into account in my work on political culture, thereby running the risk of being scorned as a Freudian, is precisely that I wish to make it clear that my explanations strive always to include only factors of nurturance and nothing biological or genetic. The assumption has to be that all humans start off essentially the same, but, given their plastic nature, they are soon molded by experience. This is the antithesis of racism.

It would seem that historians who routinely point to continuities of traditional patterns in countries, without specifying the mechanisms whereby those patterns are transmitted, would be more vulnerable than the proponents of political culture to the suspicion that they are implicitly attributing causation to biology and hence race. Yet fortunately, the conventions of historical explanations are sufficiently accepted by the academic world that nobody would be so rude as to suggest such a possibility. We should be most thankful for the tolerance with which historical explanations are accepted, and only wish that the courtesy could be extended to cultural explanations, which generally try to be more specific and rigorous in linking cause and effect in arriving at explanations. Indeed, the graceful ease with which intellectual historians trace lines of influence from thinker to thinker on the basis of who once read what authors is a matter of awe and envy for practitioners of political culture. (As a naive graduate student I used to think it not implausible that radical young Chinese students could have had their thinking permanently shaped from having read particular Western books; as a professor I find to my sorrow that students generally retain appallingly little of what they have supposedly read.)

Closely related to the charge of racism is the suggestion that cultural and psychological interpretations are biased toward presenting negative images of others, and therefore that the approach is essentially unsympathetic, and indeed hostile, toward the subjects of analysis. It is true that area studies got their great boost during World War II, when it was necessary to train many people as interpreters, interrogators, and specialists in the languages and cultures of the enemies. It was in that setting that anthropology came of age for studying advanced societies—indeed it seemed perfectly natural shortly after the war that Clyde Kluckhohn, an anthropologist with no previous background in Slavic studies, should have been appointed the first director of the Harvard Russian Research Center. Ruth Benedict's *The Chrysanthemum and the Sword* and Eric Fromm's *Escape From Freedom* were of course wartime attempts to understand Japanese and German behavioral patterns. It is also true that after the war some Japanese were uncomfortable with Benedict's analysis, but very soon Japanese scholars were hard at work on interpretations that on the face of it would seem to have been harsher. Indeed, in Japan there has developed a strong tradition of studying *Nihonjinron*, "theory of Japaneseness," led by such major figures as Muruyama, Doi, Nakane, Tazaki, and the team of Sato, Murakami, and Kumon, all of whom have probed the depths of the Japanese personality in ways that illuminate what moralistic critics would consider both virtues and vices. There is no reason to assume that psychological analyses will bring out only the dark side of personalities and cultures. The American public has long been mature enough to enjoy such efforts to explicate our national character as David Riesman's *The Lonely Crowd*, Margaret Mead's *Keep Your Powder Dry*, and David Potter's *People of Plenty*. Even the nationalistically sensitive Indians have found interest and value in such studies as Ashis Nandy's *At the Edge of Psychology*, S. Kakar's *The Inner World: A Psycho-Analytical Study of Childhood and Society in India*, D. Narain's *Hindu Character*, and K. M. Carstairs's *The Twice-Born*.

There is no reason why psycho-cultural studies should be seen as inherently unfriendly toward the societies that are their subjects. Probably the explanation for why some people suspect such studies to be unflattering is that there is a general human instinct to feel uncomfortable with the thought that we all have an unconscious dimension to our personalities, and therefore discussion of Freud's discoveries can be seen as threatening. If the problem is not an unreasoned fear of psychoanalysis, then it may be an equally unreasonable belief in the prevalence of reason in politics. In this case it is well to remember the words of Graham Wallas, a founder of political psychology, written in 1908: "Whoever sets himself to base his political thinking on a reexamination of human nature must begin by trying to overcome his own tendency to exaggerate the intellectuality of mankind."[23]

Culture and Change

Another criticism that is sometimes voiced against the theory of political culture is that it cannot account for change. Those who advance this view seem to assume that cultures are essentially static phenomena, capable only of responding to exogenous forces, and in which each generation essentially clones itself through the socialization process. The relationship between culture and change is in fact far more complex and calls for a considerably more sophisticated understanding of the human condition.

It is true, as we have just seen, that anthropologists were greatly attracted to a psychologically based understanding of culture because it helped to explain the baffling mystery of why cultural differences have persisted with such tenacity. The discovery of the relationship between culture and personality does not, however, mean that cultures cannot and do not change out of their own dynamics. On the contrary, the theory of culture opens the door to possibly one of the best ways of understanding and forecasting change. For it is culture that establishes both the parameters of likely change and the dynamics that drive and shape social and political change. Through the analysis of culture one can gain insights into the areas of stress and tension in any particular society, and thereby more readily determine the kinds of change that will be either easy or difficult according to the character of the people. The patterns of China's past are thus not frozen, to be changed only by outside forces, but rather continue to serve in shaping the course of China's modernization, which is not just a copying of the West.

The role of political culture in explaining change is extremely complex and subtle, for it governs, among other things, which of the appeals of contending leaders will attract a mass following, and which ones will not. Erik Erikson's theory about the relationship between personal identity and political ideology, for example, helps to explain why some ideologies have been able to command the loyalties of mass publics, while generally the words of false prophets fail to capture the spirit of the people, and hence fall on deaf ears. The successful leader is able to communicate a message that the public feels is true and gripping because he speaks out of his own psychological development, and in doing so he touches cords that resonate in the lives of the masses, who, in lesser degree, share with the leader common psychic reactions to being human. Purely rationalistic appeals generally fail, for they are usually seen as too clever to be the truth.

The psychological state of an individual can be the force that generates creativity, and so it is that features of a culture can bring about social and political change. Just as individual personalities are complex mixtures of numerous different ambivalences, so too are political cultures the product of contending themes, of mores and counter-mores, that are often in disharmony.[24] The shifting relationships of these themes generally become the dynamic forces determining change and continuity. Cultures, like individual personalities, can change, but they do so according to their character and not just randomly. In the next chapter we will be examining how it is possible for such apparently contradictory styles as the radical, ideological politics of Maoism and the pragmatic policies of Dengism to be thought of as being equally typical manifestations of Chinese culture. Indeed, the central thrust of the rest of this book is precisely the relationship of Chinese culture to the modernization of China, and therefore we shall be demonstrating how culture can explain change.

The Practice of Analyzing Political Cultures

Critics of political culture may accept the idea that culture and personality are significant factors in explaining political behavior but doubt whether we have appropriate methods for analyzing the psycho-cultural realm. Here again there seems to be some confusion not only about methodology but also about what is and is not properly involved in studying political cultures.

The first point is that individual skill does count. This is not a mystical matter of intuition but rather a recognition that people who have spent years working on understanding a particular society, reading extensively about it and reflecting on its characteristics, may in time become in effect finely calibrated "instruments" for "measuring" that particular culture. The capital investment of costly years of training should not be minimized. Just as with historical analysis, judgment counts.

The second requirement for analyzing political cultures is a clear sense of what it is that needs explaining. What are the questions that call for answers? Depending upon the question, the focus should shift towards the psychological dimension of an individual or toward the interpersonal dynamics of a group; toward generational traits or toward the longer-range matters of cultural continuities and discontinuities. Often it is necessary to hypothesize the existence of some cultural phenomenon that might explain the distinctive performance of the political system as a whole.[25] Such a problem may then call for a more detailed analysis of the phenomenon in order to illuminate its peculiar characteristics. For example, one might hypothesize that, since the 1920s, nationalism has been a key factor in shaping China's political development. We can advance this proposition even though we can say with almost total certainty that, if a national sample survey of China's 400 million people had been taken in the 1920s, it would have shown that only a small proportion of the population was aware of, to say nothing of being agitated by, explicit sentiments of nationalism. The hypothesis is legitimate because the behavior of only a small minority can and usually does determine the Zeitgeist of a period in history. (Consider how we label the various decades in American history in terms of the behavior of only a small minority of the population. How many flappers made the 1920s the "Roaring Twenties"? How many radicals did it take to make the Sixties the decade of upheaval?) Following the posing of this hypothesis, the analyst of political culture can proceed with identifying the distinctive character of Chinese nationalism. This calls for an analysis of how the Chinese understand in-groups and out-groups, how they respond to "family" as against "foreign," how they respond to perceived mistreatment—do they complain openly about "unequal" treatment (treaties) or are they prone to repress their sufferings?—and so on.

In the pages that follow, our central concern will be those dimensions of Chinese culture that have made both the era of Maoism (including the Cultural Revolution) and the era of Deng Xiaoping's reforms seem, in their totally different ways, equally "Chinese" in character. In doing this, we shall be advancing hypotheses for which the *available* evidence falls short of the *required* evidence for adequately "testing" our hypotheses. We could at each stage remind the reader of the unavailability of the evidence, and that we are proceeding with the judgment that if somehow the data could be obtained they would confirm our hypotheses. The constant repetition of such qualifications would, however, be most annoying. Therefore we can safely assume that readers have enough good judgment to understand what is taking place.[26] It might be noted here that often there is more evidence than people assume. This is particularly the case with regard to the evidence needed to make psychological interpretations of individual leaders. But sometimes the situation is exactly the opposite: major figures, such as Mao Zedong, have generally been closely observed and their behavioral patterns well-reported. Therefore the evidence available for understanding them is about as much as clinical psychologists customarily have available in making their diagnoses. In clinical work, time is taken up with the treatment, and the diagnosis may be made at an early stage. The key problem in political psychology is not usually whether adequate evidence is available, but rather whether the analyst possesses the skill necessary to relate the predictive theories of depth psychology to the available facts.

Another qualification that will apply throughout our study but should not require constant repeating is that our speaking of psychological and cultural factors does not mean we believe them to constitute the *sole* cause of historical developments. Of course there are other considerations and other variables, but the goal of scientific simplicity implies that one cannot talk about all things at the same time. We are acting in the same spirit of scholarship as historians do when they write about "France" doing this or that at a particular time, or of "Washington" expecting "Beijing" to do this or that. Among the wise it is unnecessary, indeed somewhat insulting, to clutter up analysis with the obvious qualification that such collectivities are not homogeneous entities.

When we speak of political culture "hypotheses" we are often dealing with generalizations that share much with the more traditional concepts of ideal type analysis, or of modal personality types in anthropology. That is to say, the generalizations seek to capture the essential spirit of the politics, the underlying norms that govern group behavior, the shared fantasies about the potentialities and limitations of power and authority. The purpose is to highlight attitudes and latent values that shape the political process and help to illuminate political behavior.

This means that at times we will be compelled to employ what I have called "as if" hypotheses.[27] For example, we may say that the Chinese political system at certain times has operated "as if" nationalism were a dominant force. Indeed, the key to much of our search for understanding of contemporary China has to take the form of thinking through what must have been the compelling values and considerations that caused the Chinese system to do the things it did. Although consistency is not necessarily important in the development of political culture hypotheses, there is little to commend studies of Chinese politics that must be totally revised, if not rejected, every time there is a change in China's zigzagging political evolution. We certainly must be getting closer to the realities of Chinese political development when we have more enduring generalizations that can survive such short run changes. This does not mean that China's political culture is a constant, but rather that change at the fundamental level is certain to lag far behind the temporary shifts of policies and personnel.

There are three fundamental bases for constructing an "as if" hypothesis. First, the hypothesis must have value in explaining or predicting developments in the particular political system. Even though direct "testing" is impossible, the hypothesis must meet the test of utility. That is, it must provide an enriched, reliable understanding of political developments in the particular setting. Second, the hypothesis must be rooted in accepted general theories about the workings of culture and the nature of personality. These theories should reflect the best insights about personality and society. Therefore they should exploit all available knowledge about the patterns of cause and effect in the development of individual psychology and the shaping of cultures. Third, the hypothesis must be grounded in knowledge about all manner of social, cultural, and intellectual habits and practices of the particular people. What is known about the primary institutional patterns of the society, from family life to more general social behavior, and what can be derived from the people's world of imagination and fantasy as expressed in its art and literature, should be utilized to gain the insights necessary for arriving at an "as if" hypothesis. In short, the political culture hypothesis should be consistent with what is known about the general proclivities of the culture.

Needless to say, we can hope that as we learn more about any particular culture our "as if" hypotheses can be more directly "tested" and thereby become normal hypotheses. At this stage in the evolution of science it is, however, not clear whether theories have to be literally true or only convenient fictions that produce accurate predictions. There is no reason to believe that political scientists will be able to answer this question, which pertains to the philosophy of science, before the physicists have. Therefore, we should be able to remain as open-minded as they are.

In comparing political cultures, what is important is the totality of configurations that makes up the distinctive character of each particular culture, and not the distinctiveness of any particular hypothesis about an aspect of the cultures. Sometimes critics are under the illusion that they have demolished a culturally oriented interpretation of, say, Chinese political behavior by pointing out that Americans, for example, share one or more of the particular qualities ascribed to the Chinese in the analysis. This, of course, is foolishness, because nobody pretends that Chinese and Americans are different in all respects and that they do not share many qualities. What are different are the totalities that comprise the two political cultures. Specific similarities will take on somewhat different degrees of importance, depending upon the place they occupy in the larger context of the different political cultures. Thus the fact that certain populations will share certain specific characteristics does not mean that those characteristics cannot play important roles in producing two quite different political cultures. This is a point that people who are adamantly opposed to social science generalizations have a hard time absorbing.

The Singular Importance of Political Culture in Chinese Politics

Many of the problems that arise in defending political culture in general terms evaporate when the subject becomes Chinese politics, for it is simply impossible to deny the importance of attitudes, sentiments, and subjective considerations in the changing society that is China. Indeed, cultural factors dominate public life in China more than in just about any other country. There are several reasons why this is so.

First, the strangely potent mixture of Confucianism and Leninism seems to agitate passions and arouse visions. This is to be seen not only in the explosive history of the People's Republic of China but also in North Korea and Vietnam. The purposeful dedication to controlling history inherent in Marxism-Leninism, when applied to the great Sinic civilization with its enormous travails of change, has produced something more profound than Mao Zedong Thought. To the extent that Chinese politics has been a politics of awakening, it has been driven by strong contending sentiments and endless clashes of ideas—clashes, however, that have had to be muted, because the traditions of Confucianism and Marxism-Leninism have sought to keep a straitjacket on dissent. People have to hold in private their real views as they practice the traditional Chinese art of feigned compliance. The subjective realm consequently has consistently been repressed, only to explode periodically, thereby playing a decisive role in shaping Chinese public life. Politically conscious Chinese can hardly avoid questions about where their country has come from and where it should be heading. Consequently, much of politics is played out in the domain of visions and promises, of manifest hopes and fears, of prophecies and moral hectoring. The world of symbols and the world of ambitions are more real than the world of China's limited, actual accomplishments.

Other traditional cultures have, of course, also sought to modernize under the banner of Marxism-Leninism, but there remains something distinctive in the blend that is Confucianist Leninism. The Chinese, like the North Koreans and Vietnamese, did not abandon the essence of their Confucian legacies before adopting Communism. As a consequence the three societies share many characteristics, and they are distinctive among all the other Leninist systems. The marriage of Confucian habits and Leninist imperatives is not entirely natural, for even apparent similarities have produced tensions, but out of the interactions of the two has come a highlighting of psycho-cultural factors. We can see this first of all in the critical importance that both traditions attach to socialization practices. More than with almost any other people, the Chinese believe that children must be taught to do right and not just allowed to grow up. Thus today Confucianist Leninism builds upon a past tradition that held that the future of every family depended upon its children learning how to behave correctly. All the Communists needed to add was a new vision of how the product of unrelenting socialization pressures should look. Moreover, today the pressures of molding are not relaxed after the first efforts at character formation. Every major institution in the land takes upon itself the duty to see that nobody is in doubt as to what constitutes correct conduct and what is totally unacceptable.

It is clear, given the pervasive influence of the ideal of conformity in China, that one must appreciate this feature of China's political culture to understand its politics. Conformity and rebellion are the breath of Chinese politics. The imperative of conformity fosters a make-believe world of politics, where words are not what they seem and code words and slogans take on complex implicit meanings, and where there is a great deal of shadow play and pretense. The problem is even more complex because the emotional importance attached to maintaining "face" produces a style of human relationships in which feigned compliancy is often the norm. People pretend to go along, supporting conformity, so as not to "lose face."

A second reason for the exceptionally dominant role of cultural factors in Chinese political life is that Confucianist Leninism places supreme value not just on ideology, but on highly moralistic versions of ideology. In the traditional Confucian world view the principal causal force of history was the moral conduct of leaders.[28] The Maoist tradition has kept alive the Chinese belief that the collective good will be advanced if everyone acts morally and in accordance with the correct definition of his or her role. And, of course, disaster is to be expected if immorality takes over. Few cultures can compare with the Chinese in suppressing the id and extolling the superego—a fact that has obvious implications for the importance of political culture in China.

The stress on the moral behavior of individuals is, moreover, framed in the context of a collectivity that is always perceived to be precious, be it the family, the Party, the country. Most Chinese simply cannot believe that China is not superior to all other countries—in moral, if not in general, terms. Chinese diplomats take it for granted that in negotiations they have a rightful claim to holding the moral high ground, and it never seems to cross the mind of Chinese that they might seem to insult others when they suggest that China is being threatened with moral contamination from abroad.

The emphasis upon correct individual conduct in a social context in Confucianist Leninism also produces considerable conscious attention to the management of superior-subordinate relations. Displays of deference by subordinates and grace in asserting command by superiors are the hallmarks of Chinese political culture.

More importantly, there is in that culture a marked instinct for hierarchy. Indeed, the creation of bureaucracies has long been a part of the genius of the Chinese people. The Chinese in their search for order, especially after a period of confusion, are quick to array themselves in hierarchies. In their personal relationships there is always a clear understanding of what is properly involved in superior-subordinate relations, and by adhering to the appropriate rules the Chinese can automatically line themselves up in rank order with very little disciplining. Since relations among equals are seen as more troublesome, there is likely to be great difficulty in horizontal communications between the separate hierarchies. Outsiders are inclined to believe that these hierarchies are command structures, and therefore the top officials ought to be able easily to enforce their will. This is understandable, because superiors do like to pretend to be autocrats and they will issue frequent orders. The hierarchies, however, are not command structures but rather prestige alignments. The lower orders therefore will pretend to comply but in practice they will go on doing what they feel is in their best interests. The superiors know that there are limits to their capacity to command so they are usually quite prepared to play act their authoritarian roles and not press too hard for details about how their commands are being implemented. Since there is universal agreement that there is great virtue in both conformity and harmony, nobody, except a maverick, has an interest in exposing the ineffectualness of the arrangement. It is, of course, the burden of high rank to ritualistically scold subordinates for their failings; and conversely subordinates have the obligation to match the ritual, and to confess their inadequacies while praising to the sky the wisdom of their superiors, whose words they are ignoring as best they can.

This propensity toward hierarchy has, ironically, created problems for carrying out what the Chinese call "political reforms," by which they mean separating the Party bureaucracy and the government bureaucracy. This is a difficult task, because the Chinese instinctively think that all authority should be arranged in a single pecking order, and that the only way that authority can be properly divided is between acknowledged superiors and inferiors. If there are to be parallel hierarchies, they should be completely separated, each autonomous and with no communications with other agencies or departments. The idea of two parallel but somehow interrelated bureaucracies of Party and State, easily accepted in the European Communist countries with their traditions of Church and State, is hard for the Chinese, because they need to know who is above whom in every relationship. The fact that when the Chinese speak of "political reforms" to match Deng's economic reforms they are really referring only to administrative reforms is further evidence of their propensity toward orderly hierarchy and not toward dynamic processes.

Whereas in the West bureaucracies are presumed to exist in order to implement the collective will by carrying out public policies, this is not the full story in China. What is distinctive about the Chinese hierarchies is that while they may appear to be the same as public bureaucracies in the West, one of their main reasons for being is to give security to individuals, by allowing their members to gain esteem and advancement by displaying correct work styles. In some ways they are more like the bureaucracies that were introduced by Western colonial masters into Asian and African societies that had no traditions of public administration, and whose officials therefore also think more in terms of status than of performance. The proliferation of governmental bureaucracies in China, and for that matter North Korea and Vietnam, has less to do with implementing public policies and more with providing career opportunities for cadres. In Confucianist Leninism, the advancement of officials is based mainly on the impressions they make upon their superiors through their work styles.[29] The success or failure of the policies for which they are nominally responsible is of secondary importance. Indeed, at times there seems to be an inverse relationship between the success of policies and the speed of promotion, because often when little is being accomplished in terms of policy, individual officials can more easily attract attention and thus be seen as deserving of advancement. The reason the Chinese attach so much importance to the form of individual behavior and discount the substance of policy is that they tend to see conformity and harmony as opposite sides of the same coin, and for them the desirability of smooth, orderly relations is second to nothing. The classical Confucian assumption that all will be right with the world if everyone conscientiously performs his or her assigned role is still operative in Confucianist Leninism. The powerful urge for orderliness is driven by the intense Chinese fear of *luan*, disorder and confusion. For all the bold talk to the effect that "disorder is everywhere, the situation is excellent," the Chinese political leaders manifestly want disciplined behavior on the part of everyone. Proof of this lies in their deep distrust of any hints of pluralism.

Finally, and possibly most important of all, the study of political culture is important for understanding Chinese politics because of the unique relationship between the primary institutions that are so important in socializing the Chinese and the public institutions of national politics. Historically, Confucianism was a distinctive ideology in part because it fitted the ideals and needs of both the rulers in their political realms and the common people in their family and clan settings. Mandarin scholars and officials could teach the doctrines of the Sage as the basis of the legitimacy not only of the imperial system but also of the authority systems of the fathers and elders throughout the country. In modern times, however, and most especially with the arrival of Confucianist Leninism, there has been a distinct bifurcation into the two realms, but there remains an odd, and quite Chinese, way in which the two still reinforce each other so as to provide continuity in the socialization process but also flexibility in national policy orientations. This has been possible because the daily life of almost all Chinese is bound up in immediate, face-to-face relationships that carry heavy demands about correct behavior. The family, the work group, the neighborhood committees, the *danwei* see that the individual is still socialized with great intensity. This cellular structure of the basic society provides cultural continuity, both by insuring conformity in the learning process and by insulating individuals from disorienting external forces. It also teaches people respect for authority, an attitude that sets the stage for the rulers to have the freedom to carry out a great variety of policies. Thus the political domain can have its zigs and zags of policy changes while the people remain sheltered in their separate settings. Viewed nationally, China may seem to be going through constant changes. At the personal level, however, there is much continuity, of a kind that guarantees the leaders continued freedom to proclaim policies—but not necessarily to carry them out. (The execution of policy is another matter, to be treated later.)

We could list many more reasons why the concept of political culture is so important for understanding Chinese politics, but this will, we hope, become ever more apparent as we proceed with this study. We shall start by exploring how it is possible that Chinese political culture could have produced both Maoism and Dengism, two styles of ruling that seem to be polar opposites. The dramatic differences between the rule of Mao Zedong and that of Deng Xiaoping raise fundamental questions about possible tensions and ambivalences in China's basic political culture.

We will turn next to an examination of the distinctive characteristics of Chinese pragmatism. Just as Chinese cultural characteristics modified China's experiences with the ideology of Marxism-Leninism, so, it would seem, these characteristics will inform Chinese practices of pragmatism. The Chinese leaders seek, in their words, to "Build Socialism with Chinese characteristics," but are probably, in Roderick MacFarquhar's insightful words, "Building China with Socialist characteristics."

Our examination of Chinese pragmatism will be followed by a reexamination of the Cultural Revolution, that great watershed event of the People's Republic of China. Finally, we shall look at the mystique of leadership and legitimacy in Chinese culture, a topic of special importance because of the abiding Chinese belief that a rule of men is superior to the rule of law.

CHAPTER II

THE PSYCHOLOGICAL ROOTS OF CHINA'S
OPPOSING POLITICAL CULTURES

The world marvels at the changes Deng Xiaoping brought to China, in no small part because of the stark contrast between China under Deng and the China over which Mao Zedong ruled. The differences are like day and night, and they raise the puzzling question of how the same society, the same generation of people, could produce such opposite forms of public life. In executing the abrupt transition from Maoism to Dengism, the Chinese have performed one of the miracles of the modern world: abandoning the passionate politics of ideology and taking up a distinct version of pragmatism. The rapid passage from one political pole to the other by the world's most immense population has been accomplished with apparent effortlessness, and with so few signs of trauma or tension that it seems to have been as simple as putting away winter clothes and taking out summer ones.

It is true that there has been much pushing and hauling, power struggles and policy contention, factional battles and purges. It is also true that much remains in place: the system is still in the control of a single party that, as the Chinese like to say in other contexts, "will brook" no opposition. Yet, given the distance that has been traveled from the days when Mao demanded ideological enthusiasm for the dogma of his Thoughts to today, and the technocratic spirit of economic development that prevails under Deng, the changes are impressive. Equally impressive, the Chinese have carried them out without the travail that usually accompanies a revolution of such proportions. It is still an authoritarian regime in which the paramount leader calls the tune, but the tune is totally different and the people seem to have learned the new words instantly.

Both the speed and the ease of China's dramatic changes suggest that there must somehow be "two Chinas," or maybe it is "one China, and two political cultures." The China, or the political culture, of Maoism once seemed to be the very essence of the "Chinese revolution" and to capture what was most distinctive about China's drive to find a place in the modern world. Yet Deng Xiaoping's China, or political culture, also seems quintessentially Chinese, even though it is totally different from the first.

These observations raise two fundamental questions. First, how was it possible for China to go so easily and rapidly from one extreme to what would seem to be its polar opposite? Second, why should there be just these two particular extremes? Could there be even a third or a fourth "China" unrelated to the Mao-Deng continuum? Or is there something distinctive about the general characteristics of Maoism and Dengism that make them the natural extremes that bound the range of Chinese political change?

We shall be addressing these questions in reverse order. In the next chapter we will look into the nature of Chinese pragmatism and analyze the ease of political change in China. We need here only note a few characteristics of Chinese culture in order to get our feet on the ground for tackling the second question, "Why these two particular cultures?"

First, it is necessary to keep in mind that, though China is immense, Chinese society is operationally organized around small, intimate, face-to-face groups, the family and the *danwei*. When change is required, individual Chinese are not forced to reorient themselves with respect to large and impersonal social forces. Rather they can take their personal cues for behavior from well-established, familiar relationships, knowing that they thereby also act in step with the demands of the national authorities, though these are demands they may not fully understand.

Second, Chinese leaders do not have to pretend, as American leaders do, that they are always consistent in their words and deeds. Both leaders and followers have less trouble with cognitive dissonance because they accept as rational the idea that with any change in circumstances there can and should be a change in attitudes and behavior.

Finally, in Chinese culture there is a profound appreciation of the need to respond to the logic of the situation, to be guided by a sense of realism that may at times seem to take on the characteristic of conformity.

We will expand on these elements in our discussion of the distinctive character of Chinese pragmatism when we explore in greater depth why the Chinese find it easy to make certain kinds of changes—there are, of course, others that are very hard for them to bring about. But first we must take up the second fundamental question, "Why the particular dualism of Maoism and Dengism in Chinese political culture?"

China's Two Cultures

As a general proposition, most major political cultures have contradictory tendencies that make certain swings in style and emphasis seem historically "natural." The poles of political "right" and "left," have, of course, provided the most popular continuum for generalizing about Western politics. Indeed, the battles between Marxists and anti-Marxists have fueled political passions enough to make "right" and "left," and all the clusters of attitudes and values associated with each, seem the most natural of political dichotomies. Moreover, all national political cultures have in addition their unique, subtle polarities. In American political culture, for example, James David Barber has identified a "pulse of politics," a twelve-year cycle of, first, politics as conflict, then politics as conscience, and finally politics as conciliation before starting over again.[1]

The dichotomy of "left" and "right" has to be grotesquely strained to fit Chinese political realities. The awkwardness of foreign observers in trying to label Maoists and Dengists as "left" or "right" is only exceeded by the absurdity of the Chinese themselves when they attack each as other as "Leftists" or "Rightists."[2] For years Hua Guofeng and his followers made fools of themselves by denouncing the Gang of Four as "ultra-Rightists" after their arrest. Today, Western observers who are calling Deng's opponents "conservatives" are hardly better off, for it is certainly a violation of political language to classify those who oppose a greater role for the market, favor greater central planning, and call for greater commitment to Marxism people of the "right."

For China, the shorthand designation of the two poles has generally been that of ideology versus pragmatism, but in reality a continuum exists that is more complex. The rhythm of Chinese politics has not consisted of pendular swings between left and right, but an up-and-down motion. The polarity involves, at one extreme, an emphasis on conformity, repressive centralized controls, and orthodox beliefs and discipline. At the other extreme are a greater tolerance for private initiatives, a relaxation of controls, decentralization, and a liberation from orthodoxy. This has been true not only of politics in the People's Republic of China but also in traditional China, where the basic tension was between the central imperial authorities at the capital and local authorities. Traditionally, Chinese politics has not customarily been organized according to competing interests, the essentials for a "left" versus "right" system; rather, Chinese politics has been predominantly that of tensions within institutionalized hierarchies, and hence conflicts between centralization and decentralization, between orthodoxy and heterodoxy.

In this context it has been customary to note several polarities within the dominant Confucian tradition that might themselves comprise the basis for different political cultures. Benjamin Schwartz has written about such polarities in Confucianism as tensions between self-cultivation and the ordering of society, between the inner and outer realms of reality, and between knowledge and action.[3] Frederick W. Mote has researched in depth the Confucian traditions of eremitism, which provided a basis for the acceptance of an extraordinary range of individual behavior between the extremes of engagement and withdrawal, on the part of the involved official and the withdrawn hermit, whether isolated scholar or protesting official.[4] Indeed, within Confucianism there were many schools that could have provided the foundations for different patterns of political behavior.

Yet the fundamental polarity of China's traditional cultures was between the orthodoxy of Confucianism and a heterodox blend of Taoism, Buddhism, and more localized belief systems. The traditional Chinese contrast was thus between an elitist high Confucian culture that glorified the established authority of the better educated and rationalized their claims of superiority on the basis of possessing specialized wisdom, and a passionate, populist heterodox culture that glorified the rebel and trusted magical formulas to transform economic and social reality. The culture of Confucian orthodoxy was defended and upheld by the mandarin class and its rationalistic traditions of scholarship and of governance by reasonable men. This was the political culture that venerated education, distrusted mysticism, wanted an orderly structuring of society based on a hierarchy of merit and reason. The other culture was the populist blend of Taoist-Buddhist mysticism used in mobilizing peasant rebellions and in the bonding of secret societies.[5] It idealized more egalitarian values, despised formal education and the pretensions of those who thought themselves to be the moral and intellectual betters of the common man, and placed great faith in elixirs and in magical slogans as formulas for political success. The contrast was thus between the restrained rule by example' of the certifiably wise and the mysticism of the propagandists of willpower.[6]

These dual poles of China's traditional political cultures are well-documented in the historical literature. The earliest records of Chinese history seem to reflect an appreciation of the existence of these contrasting elite and mass cultures. The *Shih-ching* or *Book of Poetry* has a verse " . . . that sounds like Shang *versus* Chou, in the form of peasant protest of 'men of the East' against aristocratic luxuriants, 'men of the West.' "[7] From the early rebellions during the Han period, such as those of the Yellow Turbans or "The Way of Great Peace" and "The Way of Five Pecks of Rice," to the Taiping Rebellion of the nineteenth century, the Chinese countryside supported a tradition of counter-Confucian mores.[8] The same anti-Confucian ideals were central themes of such popular novels as the *Shui-hu-chuan, Yüeh-chuan,* and *Fen-shen-chuan.*

Historically, tension between the two cultures was checked by the tendency of each to incorporate some elements of the other, often in a sly, almost devious manner. There was, for example, the great paradox of the persistent contradiction between ideology and behavior: the mandarin elite proclaimed the Confucian creed of purposefulness in action while practicing the Taoist ideal of effortlessness, of leisurely non-effort; the masses believed in the Taoist creed of *wu-wei*, non-effort, but behaved in the spirit of diligent purposefulness demanded by Confucianism.[9] Some Confucian scholars were attracted to utopian themes of the popular culture, even when these contradicted basic tenets of Confucianism. Kang Youwei, for example, in outlining his idealized *Datung* or Universal Commonwealth, dismissed the most sacred of Confucian institutions, the family, and proposed that men and women cohabitate for a year and then change mates, that nurseries take over the care of babies, and that there be public dormitories and dining halls for everyone. The escape from orthodoxy, in traditional China as well as under Mao, usually took the form of utopian socialism that approximated the nurturing protection idealized in the popular culture. There was thus a modest degree of syncretism in the relationship between the two cultures.

In spite of their fundamental antithesis, the two cultures shared two important qualities, which helps to explain why they endured over the centuries and why neither succeeded in destroying the other. First, they both accepted the idea that the ultimate ruler, whether the emperor or the *wang*, had a divine or mystical dimension. As Levenson and Schurman have observed, in the Shang dynasy " . . . the *wang* was not only a chief, but the supreme shaman, who carried out sacrifices and performed rites of divination. He was thus the holder of magical powers. . . . It is not impossible that some of the magical-religious awe with which the people of the Shang era viewed their shamans may later have been transmitted to the scholar-bureaucrat class. In fact, contemporary descriptions of nineteenth-century China refer to the local magistrate as a kind of shaman who performed magical rituals for the population under his control."[10] Yet, needless to say, the Confucianists were repelled by the mysticism of the rebel religions, calling them *yao-tsei* or "magic bandits" who " . . . were stirring up the dark world of magic, the terrible forces of superstition, which Confucian rationality sought to tame in man."[11] Of course, the performance of religious rituals and sacrifices was precisely what the Son of Heaven was expected to do for all within the empire.

Though both Taoism and Confucianism had mystical elements, the adherents of the two differed in the intensity of their beliefs in other-worldly matters. The rebel culture, like Maoism, had a passion for faith, while the Confucianists, like the Dengists, were more restrained in their ideological protestations. Historically, Chinese generally understood that fanatical, magico-religious belief was the force inspiring the rebel movements, just as contemporary Chinese came to see ideological passions as a similar force for the Maoist culture. Just as the Confucianists, who were not atheists, knew the dangers of unchecked religious passions and superstition, so the Dengists, who are not without their Marxism-Leninism faith, are in constant fear that ideological stirrings will get out of hand.

The two cultures were also alike in that they both idealized harmony as a supreme value, no doubt because of an intuitive awareness of the potential for disharmony in the culture. The concept of harmony made both cultures stress the importance of the group over the individual. However, the elitism of Confucianism, with its emphasis upon self-cultivation, allowed some room for individual development, and indeed, came close at times to recognizing that the individual is associated with civilization and mass behavior with barbarism. The popular culture was mass oriented and consequently had no sense of the dangers of barbarism. In Confucianism harmony was, of course, related primarily to social relationships, while in Taoism the ultimate objective was the uniting of the subjective and objective worlds in order to become in tune with the One, or the Way. Although Taoism, and the bastardized version of it incorporated by the rebel ideologies, could extol the glories of limited government, if not anarchy, the Taoists were as concerned as the Confucianists were with the dangers of disorder, *luan*. Their form of anarchy, or nongovernment, was essentially pacific; hence ultimately they idealized a spirit of harmonious community.

The two Chinese Communist cultures have not been as explicit in praising harmony. Indeed, Mao lauded contradictions and conflict. But in fact, his ultimate ideal was that of a harmonious community, not unlike the expressed goals of the traditional anti-orthodox political cultures. The Dengists are like the Confucianists in wanting conformity and singlemindedness on the part of everyone in pursuing the regime's priorities.

Though the two cultures had these two similarities, what is more historically significant is that they remained essentially separate and distinctive. Confucianism, with its doctrines of "authoritarian social responsibility," and the "self-oriented anarchism of Taoism" preserved their quite different identities.[12] The conflicts were at times intense, even bloody, but neither culture could exterminate the other, nor was there any search for a common denominator, even with the emergence of neo-Confucianism. When dynasties fell and the country was in a state of presumed chaos the differences still remained, for, as Wang Guangwu has convincingly shown in a careful study of the Five Dynasties era, the hierarchical power structure that upheld the higher Chinese tradition remained solidly in place in local settings even during that time of decline and disorder.[13] This Chinese cultural ability to reestablish hierarchical power arrangements almost instantaneously after periods of revolutionary disorder was once again demonstrated with the ending of the Cultural Revolution, the "ten bad years," and the restoration of centrally guided policies when Deng replaced the Gang of Four.

The clash of the two political cultures evident throughout Chinese history has lasted, under different labels, into the Communist era. It lies at the base of the two contrasting Communist cultures of Maoist revolutionary passions and Dengist compulsive pragmatism.

It would be much too simplistic, however, to suggest that Maoism is merely a continuation of the traditional popular rebel culture in modern garb, and that Deng's pragmatism is just a revival of the common sense tradition of China's historic high political culture. In a complicated way there are some distinctive elements of continuity from the traditional pair to the more contemporary one, yet there are some striking reversals of lineage. What is definite is that certain enduring dichotomies have persisted and that these are, for the Chinese, natural sources of lasting tensions.

Key Psychological Ambivalences Shape the Two Cultures

Rather than trace the elements of continuity and change in the two political cultures in further detail, we will proceed down a different road and identify a series of polar opposites that continue to characterize Chinese culture because of certain key psychological ambivalences that are basic to the Chinese psychic life. These contradictions seem to define the main boundaries of the two contemporary cultures and to give them their distinct dynamic vitality. The strength and character of the two cultures are, we shall argue, delineated and reinforced by profound sentiments, though these sentiments are not entirely antagonistic nor truly divorced from each other. It is of profound importance that the differences between the two cultures are not just random or idiosyncratic; rather, the cultures are interrelated at a deeper level by the powerful feelings of attraction and repulsion inherent in all fundamental cultural ambivalences. That is to say, the intensity of the clashes between the two cultures is a function less of the degree to which they differ and more of the fact that representatives of each culture can recognize the attractions of the other in themselves and thus feel the need to resist the other aggressively. At the same time, the core ambivalences help to explain why the same individual could at one time be an enthusiastic participant in the Maoist culture and then feel equally at home as a Dengist.

I am suggesting that vacillation in response to a series of key ambivalences governs the essential dimensions of the two current political cultures. The paired alternative values have their roots in the traditional Chinese political cultures, but they are sustained by central contradictions generated by the Chinese socialization processes. Since the adherents of each of the cultures recognize that the values of the other culture have some validity in terms of the larger traditions of Chinese culture, they tend to have strongly ambivalent feelings about those values—they can neither entirely reject them nor legitimate them.

Our argument will be that the result of their general socialization process is to cause most Chinese to share certain contradictory sentiments that can be readily translated into strikingly different policy approaches. Many Western analysts have tended to assume that Chinese politics involves groups of leaders with quite different policy approaches.

We are suggesting that, while differences do emerge out of the interplay of power and policy, all of the participants intuitively understand the sentiments behind the thrust of their competitors' positions because such sentiments are in part their own. That is why Deng Xiaoping could at one time sincerely support the essence of Maoism, and why Mao in his turn was not insensitive to the values behind what we now call Dengism. Deng and Chen Yun must certainly understand each other at a level deeper than just that of reasoned calculations. Differences do, of course, get concretized into rigid positions as the result of public posturing and the need to be loyal to particular groups active in the dynamics of policy choices. Yet these differences tend to fit into the mold established and sustained by specific ambivalences.

In turning now to a detailed examination of each of these pairs, we will also be identifying the underlying ambivalences that rigidly maintain these contradictions.

Egalitarian Brotherhood versus Formal Respectability

The first polarity is that between the idea of egalitarian brotherhood, which lay at the heart of the traditional heterodoxy, and the principle of respectability and propriety based on correct conduct, which was the very essence of Chinese orthodoxy. Egalitarianism was, of course, also at the core of Maoism, while in Dengism there has been a revival of emphasis on dignity, respectability, and deference toward superiors.

The Chinese generally share an understanding of the craving for brotherhood that inspires the spirit of the rebel and that dominates popular novels depicting bands of blood brothers united in defiance of any kind of hierarchy. They readily appreciate the tradition of hostility toward bureaucracies and hierarchies and the popular worship of egalitarianism. Yet, equally, all Chinese seem to believe that respectability, dignity, and a degree of aloofness in relations are necessary if there is to be an orderly society. They understand that there is security in having a hierarchy and in arranging things in an orderly fashion with everyone in his rank order. Formality produces correctness, and correctness guarantees individual security and public order.

In Chinese life there is a profound ambivalence between a craving for a sense of belonging and unrelieved togetherness, on the one hand, and, on the other, a belief than one can only find ultimate personal security by maintaining that essential degree of social distance that inherently results from upholding propriety. In Maoism, brotherhood became comradeship; with Deng's pragmatic reformism has come a restoration of concern over gaining respect by acting correctly according to international standards. Indeed, a guideline for pragmatic political policies has been the principle of acting with dignity in the pursuit of modernization, of wanting only the "best" from the outside world, and seeking ties with the most established and elite foreign enterprises. Today Chinese officials seem embarrassed about their former claims that "China has friends everywhere," and downright sheepish about their once-popular athletic slogan, "Friendship first, competition second."

The traditional idealization of brotherhood was premised on an awareness that loyalty was a rare but highly valued sentiment in Chinese society, especially in relations that extended beyond the bonds of family and clan ties. From the Robin Hood novels through the ideology of the Taipings, the idea of *chung-i*, of loyalty and brotherhood, was a very moving sentiment, not only for the practitioners of the populist political culture but for most ordinary Chinese.[14] The practices of elaborate rituals of initiation, solemn oaths of fealty, and even tests of self-mutilation all testify to the exceptionalness of true brotherhood.[15*] In contrast, the Confucian high culture distrusted close intimacy among power holders. From the examination system's ideals of impersonalness and impartiality and the practice of not posting officials to their home districts, to the abstract ideals of benevolence, propriety, and correctness, the high culture stressed the notion that personal friendships could cause trouble in a system supposedly based on virtue and self-discipline.

In traditional China and today, the two poles of egalitarian brotherhood and formal respectability involve, however, far more than just the contrast between informal and formal modes of behavior. Each pole has its psychic attractiveness for Chinese, yet each can, under certain conditions, also seem repulsive. To some degree the contrast reflects class characteristics, with the spirit of brotherhood more a part of the style of peasant culture and formal respectability a part of the elite society. Yet the attractions and repulsions run deeper and clearly cross class lines. The educated elites could and do idealize brotherhood, and the peasants have for their part been wary of egalitarian rhetoric, suspicious of those overly anxious to befriend them, and capable of appreciating the security to be found in the arm's length protection of formalized relationships. For neither class are there unambiguous social cues as to whether brotherhood or formalism should be the preferred posture in various situations. Thus, to a limited extent the uncertainty as to which of the two extreme ways of structuring relationships is likely to provide the greatest security can make a choice between the two an ambivalent one.

Yet it seems clear that this polarity provokes deeper tensions than would arise if the problem were only one of how to choose wisely in a situation requiring rationality. I suspect that the polarity of brotherhood and formal respectability is emotionally magnified by the fundamental problem the Chinese seem to have with intimacy. For a culture that has always extolled the supreme importance of human relationships, Chinese culture is striking for its ambivalences about intimate personal associations. The culture provides few opportunities for establishing truly intimate relationships. Historically, marriages were arranged; in contemporary times courting is done largely on the sly, almost as though signs of affection were evidence of promiscuity. The relationships of father and son and brother with brother have been idealized as being based on strong, binding ties, yet in practice they are not close relationships. In Chinese literature, scenes involving the sharing of secrets are seen as exciting, but characters rarely are depicted as exchanging their deepest thoughts. Introspection is rare, but even rarer is the verbal exchange of deep personal sentiments.

The objective physical conditions of social life for most Chinese set limits on the possibilities for privacy. Much of Chinese life has to be played out in a group setting. Throughout most of China entire families sleep in the same bed or *kang*. No one has his or her own room. People have to find isolation by withdrawal even while living in a group setting. One has to live with the knowledge that everyone else is aware of one's private affairs, such as one's income, one's job prospects, one's family status, and how one is getting along with one's superiors. Therefore there is the need to develop the distinctive Chinese art of finding aloofness in a collective setting.

Yet this is not the only reason for the scarcity of intimacy in Chinese life. The Chinese are uncertain about the value of privacy, for they associate it with secrecy, which they in turn often identify with illicit activities. Hence anyone who seems unduly interested in having privacy is usually suspected of being up to no good. It is not just servants who barge in without knocking on closed doors. In Chinese hotels people routinely leave their room doors open. The foreigner is often startled by the blunt questions Chinese will ask about matters that people in other cultures tend to see as invasions of privacy, if not offenses to modesty.

Yet the desire for intimacy persists. While most of life must be played out in a group context, the Chinese crave the bonds of particularistic friendships. In modern times, strong attachments are not uncommon, and the nuclear Chinese family of today can be an exceptionally warm one. In contrast to the traditional Chinese family, in which relations tended to be both aloof and formal, in recent years there has been more privatization of life and a searching for personal ties that idealize intimacy. Still there remains the astonishing Chinese tolerance for prolonged separations of husbands and wives, as though intimacy need not be the norm. And when the long separated pair do meet again there is no compulsion to have spontaneous physical contact, to kiss or to make other displays of emotion, but rather they are more likely to go off for a family feast.

Since in Chinese culture intimacy turns out to be an unobtainable and, more importantly, a somewhat suspect ideal, there is a need to block out the craving for it by denial. The result of supressing such a strong desire seems to have produced an almost classic type of reaction formation. What has been suppressed has to surface in reaction, and it takes the form of the socially acceptable but totally opposite sentiment of admiring propriety, correctness, and formal respectability in personal relations. Correctness can, of course, take the form of the dignity of aloofness and self-absorption.

This Chinese longing for the unattainable ideal of intimacy can be seen in the fact that no culture makes more over the abstract ideal of friendship. The rhetoric of Chinese social relations abounds with profuse expressions of friendship. In China people can become instant "old friends," a status that is supposed to represent the ultimate of shared intimacies. Truly intimate friendships are much rarer, and hence much of the talk about "friendship" becomes not a sign of brotherhood but a reference to the opposite pole of formal respectability. The building of emotionally intimate friendships is usually difficult after adolescence, partly because people seldom feel comfortable exchanging their inner thoughts or exposing their deeper feelings. Instead the alternative to the security of intimate friendship is sought in correct conduct, in respectability, which insures protection from most forms of criticism. Friendship itself becomes a matter for skillful management as the individual seeks to constantly expand his networks of personal ties. The result is the accumulation of a host of "friendships," but very few that are emotionally close. The low intensity level of the relationships often insures that they can be quite long-lasting. Yet there is a longing for the lost opportunities for the intimacies of true friendship. Hence the vacillations between the ideals of brotherhood and those of respectability.

The tension in Chinese culture about intimacy can also be seen in the peculiar emphasis Chinese give to the idea of distance. In poetry it is the friend far away, the friend who is missed, who is the true friend. Typical in this spirit is Qu Yuan's "Encountering Sorrow":[16]

> Traveling on, on and on again—
> Parted from you while still alive;
> Gone from here a myriad miles or more,
> Each at different borders of the sky.
> The road is both difficult and long—
> How to know when we shall meet again?

In Chinese art the viewer is expected to be able to empathize easily with the lonely figure in a distant landscape. In Chinese painting emptiness is valued; in literature what is left unsaid is readily appreciated. In spite of having a group-oriented culture, Chinese have an extraordinary ability to withdraw from others, to passively work alone, and to endure long periods of isolation. This capacity can be seen at all levels of the society: from the lonely scholar, especially those now studying abroad, to the worker far from home saving his earnings for eventual return to his family. Distance and loneliness capture the longings for intimacy while also suggesting the values of dignity and formalism.

The ambivalence between brotherhood and formal respectability is also found in the vacillations in Chinese diplomacy, which at times proclaims "We have friends all over the world" and welcomes every guest as being exceptional, yet at other times takes the opposite posture of boasting of having an "independent" foreign policy, of claiming Chinese "correctness" in conduct while demanding that the other party rectify its faults. The Chinese seem to be equally comfortable professing friendship or basking in their self-proclaimed propriety. Moreover, Chinese will frequently try to square the circle by claiming friendship and correctness simultaneously (that is, by asserting that they are acting in the spirit of friendship by correcting the faults of the other party, thereby claiming their superior respectability). This same tendency can be seen in the current Chinese belief that under Deng's policies Beijing has "opened up" to the whole world in a spirit of friendship even while its "correct" foreign policy of "independence" means that it has no close alliance ties with any particular country. No major power in world politics is as isolated as is China today. When Chinese specialists on international relations are asked to what country they feel China is closest in world politics, they have a hard time answering and usually have to end up mentioning North Korea—a country with which China certainly does not have the kind of relations other countries would consider close.

The same fundamental issue of intimacy makes the Chinese believe that it is possible to grade the degree of closeness or distance in any political or international relationship. This belief translates into the penchant of the Chinese for making much over what they judge to be "progress" or "retrogression" in each of China's relationships with other states. The Chinese like to believe that other governments have a compelling desire for closer relations with them even though they, the Chinese, feel it unnecessary to abandon their own rectitude to create warmer ties.

Precisely because of the dynamics of their ambivalence about intimacy the Chinese tend to have contradictory feelings about their personal and particularistic relationships, which they call *guanxi*. They cannot deny that *guanxi* is a quietly welcomed reality in many spheres of social and political life, yet at the same time they are almost universally ashamed to even mention the idea of *guanxi*. The Chinese take an instrumental view about the bonds of *guanxi*, and they do not infuse the relationship with the subjective dimensions of a truly intimate association. Two people are assumed to have *guanxi* because objectively they share some particularistic relationship; for example, they came from the same place, studied at the same school, served in the same unit, are thought by others to be related in some way or other. But they may not necessarily (indeed it would be rare if they did) have the strong emotional feelings for each other that Westerners associate with the sentiments of affection, even love, that are inherent in their concepts of friendship. Chinese treat *guanxi* much as Puritans treated sex, as a necessary fact of life but not something to be acknowledged as honorable, or appropriate, or even quite right.

The sum effect of the Chinese problem with intimacy is to produce powerful cultural sentiments that resonate to the ideological appeals of either brotherhood or formal respectability. It also helps to explain how a people, who at one time can be swept away in oceanic feelings of egalitarian comradeship—as during the Cultural Revolution—can in another mood become self-centered within their own feelings of righteousness. In short, a dialectical tension in the psyches of individual Chinese centered on questions about intimacy gives resonant support to two quite different ideological approaches in the political realm.

Loyalty versus Effectiveness

A second pair of opposites in Chinese culture that is key to the contradictory attractions of Maoism and Dengism comprises the conflicting values of loyalty and of effectiveness in commitment and performance. At one extreme there is the ideal of the purity in beliefs, the intensity of the passions of commitment to either a cause or a symbol. At the other pole there is the valuing of masterly performance, of skill and elegance in action.

Loyalty as an extension of the ideal of brotherhood was integral to the values of the rebel political culture, both traditional and Maoist. For the Maoists, dedication, commitment, and self-sacrifice constituted the essentials of loyalty, which is a key value in all of politics. Such loyalty involved both blind obedience and constructive initiatives, but not necessarily effectiveness or efficiency. The contrasting ideal was that of performance measured against abstract standards of excellence. The Confucian belief in the perfectability of man through education and training supported the principle that the distinctiveness, and indeed the superiority, of rulers rested upon their mastery of difficult skills. In modern times the polarity has taken the form of the Maoist's demands for total loyalty to the Party and the revolution as against the Dengist's belief that public figures should be educated technocrats and not mere ideologues.

The contrast is captured in the dilemma of "red and expert." What has not been well recognized is the reason why the Chinese have such psychological problems with matters that in other cultures would not seem necessarily to involve conflicting values. For the Chinese, it apparently seems natural that technical skills and commitments based on loyalty are contradictory. What is it in Chinese culture that makes it seem self-evident that people who are skilled are unlikely to have strong attachments, but also that it is inappropriate to raise questions about the technical competence of intensely dedicated and loyal people?

I suspect that the answer has to do with the complexity of Chinese feelings about a concept that is basic to Chinese culture, the concept of sincerity.

The Chinese attach tremendous importance to sincerity. One of the highest compliments they can pay is to say that someone is truly sincere. Yet, the more a Chinese person values the notion of sincerity, the harder it is for him to determine its existence in any particular relationship. The Chinese almost universally reject the notion that sincerity might be, as in the West, associated with spontaneity, for any such outbursts of feelings would seem too instantaneous, hence possibly fleeting, to be manifestations of what Chinese take to be the weightiness of genuine sincerity. Whereas in other cultures the bubbling enthusiasm that may overwhelm formalities can be taken as proof of sincere feelings, such spontaneity is not possible in Chinese culture, where sincerity must be artfully expressed. Sincerity for the Chinese is usually associated with a willingness to take great care, to make the effort to act in precisely correct ways. Sincerity and formal etiquette are complementary and not contradictory ideas for Chinese.

If we probe a little deeper we find that sincerity is problematic for the Chinese in part because they generally believe that it is difficult to know what other people are really thinking. The social education of Chinese involves learning early to control one's emotions, to mask one's inner thoughts, and to make one's manifest behavior accord with what is expected and not with what one feels. Consequently people are aware that others are not necessarily revealing their true personal sentiments, and thus there can be considerable uncertainty about whether someone else is acting with genuine sincerity. This tradition of Confucianism has been reinforced in recent decades by the harsh application of thought control, which has made it prudent to conform in words and deeds, in private as well as public settings.

This behavior results in the widespread practice of feigned compliance, about which we will have much more to say in later chapters. Briefly, the Chinese have developed to a high art form the practice of pretending to agree with the commands of superiors or the consensus of the group, thereby masking their private feelings and beliefs. Sometimes the compliance consists of acting in line with the commands of superiors; at other times people merely proclaim obedience while carrying on according to their own thoughts. Senior officials can never be sure whether the reports they are receiving are accurate or only attempts to tell them what it is assumed that they want to hear. They are puzzled as to whether they will get better reporting by demanding greater loyalty or greater skill. In the meantime everyone knows that there is a great gap between surface pretensions and inner feelings.

To compound matters, the Chinese seem to be equally convinced that people as a rule are highly partisan, have hidden agendas, and will in the end, in forthright or devious ways, always act in accordance with their biases or preferences. In short, there is little expectation that social discourse will be based on objective analysis or neutral statements of opinion. The legitimacy, or even desirability, of objectivity is discounted as everyone strains to figure out what the hidden purpose is behind pretenses at analytical explanations or interpretations. Western visitors frequently find that Chinese are uncomfortable hearing objective descriptions or analyses unless they can be assured that the speaker is a "friend" and hence has the right motivations. Once that has been ascertained, the speaker's words no longer can be interpreted as threatening criticism. Indeed, the Chinese's sense of relief may be so great that they dismiss the analysis entirely.

It is imperative to know where others stand, where loyalties lie, in a culture in which most people have learned that it is safest to be guarded about one's true sentiments. The very essence of Maoism is a profound distrust both of people's true feelings and of the durability of correct emotions. Mao himself believed strongly that the Chinese people needed to unmask their collective passions, break away from their tradition of guarded sentiments, and articulate fully their feelings—which he believed could become the locomotive force for revolution. Lenin, of course, saw the problem in Russian culture as being precisely the opposite. His concern was that Russians could all too easily dissipate their feelings, going from enthusiasm to apathy in a matter of moments, and hence the imperative of Bolshevism became the counter-Russian rule of controlling emotions, of never letting sentiments creep into decisions and actions.

The problem of sincerity in Chinese culture is also related, in my judgment, to a profound questioning in modern China as to what can and should be the basis of social morality. With the decline of Confucianism and the erosion of religious sensibilities, the Chinese have been left without an unquestioned source of moral imperatives. Why should anyone expect another person to behave in a morally upright fashion? The absence of an unchallengeable code of ethics or a widely-held belief in otherworldly retribution sets the stage for a purely opportunistic calculus of behavior. The problem has been intensified with the decline in ideological faith in Communism and the consequent weakening of the concept of "socialist morality."

In a fundamental sense modern Chinese society has been moving into a condition not too dissimilar from that of Victorian England as described by Gertrude Himmelfarb, in which a decline in religious faith produced the need for a new, and unquestioned, imperative for morality.[17] The gentleman's code that some things "just aren't done" was thus elevated by the English into an absolute standard to replace the decline of the inhibiting imperatives of religion. In contemporary

China the rules of conduct for the "good Communist" have in a sense been the functional equivalent of Victorian morality, and hence it is not odd at all that people observe a strong streak of puritanism in today's China. Fear of "spiritual pollution" is not the monopoly of a few "conservative" old leaders; it resonates in the hearts of the majority of the people, who worry about what would happen if ethical norms were to be truly foresaken and people were left without protection from evil-doers. Yet such a secular basis for morality opens the door wide to pretensions of correct behavior as a mask for devious actions. For the Victorians the response was widespread hypocrisy, which, as the compliment vice pays to virtue, became the Anglo-Saxon way of forcing people to behave better than they might wish to do.

In Chinese culture the still strong concept of "face" has been the functional equivalent of Anglo-Saxon hypocrisy. Sensitivity about gaining and losing "face" has compelled the Chinese to be as sanctimonious as the Victorians. A general awareness that people are constantly striving to gain face means that social game-playing is endemic. The result is a heightened concern about sincerity throughout Chinese society. Are the other person's actions genuine, or are they mere pretensions? What is sham and what is real? It is good that people's concern about "face" makes them act uprightly, but there is also the danger that "face" may be only a veil for dark and devious plotting by an immoral character.

The almost constant search for reliability in human relationships encourages not only the importance attached to "face" and to protestations of friendship, but also a tremendous sense of relief and comfort in associating with people of similar backgrounds who seem to share one's outlook and ways of thinking. Security comes from being in tune with the surrounding community and from knowing that one is dealing with people who have similar values. This need for security, in turn, tends to become a powerful force that spontaneously drives people toward conformity. Conformity is the rule in Chinese culture not only because of social pressures and fears of being out of step, but also because people believe that they can better judge the inner qualities and likely moral behavior of people who are just like themselves. In this way the Chinese, following a somewhat different route than Westerners, have arrived at a situation in which their earlier tradition of being "inner directed" people, with internalized and strict moral norms, has given way to "other directed" practices reflecting great sensitivity to the views of others and "consumer oriented" behavior, to use the terminology of David Riesman.

Turning all of this back to the implications for Chinese political behavior, we can deduce that in Chinese politics there is a fundamental problem of people doubting that they can accurately judge where others stand, or what their intentions may be. The years of turmoil and confusion have made everyone cautious about revealing his or her true sentiments. The responses of the political class have been ambivalent; it has either tried to compel subordinates to make manifest their commitments by protestations of loyalty (the Maoist response) or tested people by demanding more effective performance (the Dengist response). In the Maoist political culture the means for overcoming the problem of sincerity was to extract ever more fervid protestations of faith in doctrinal beliefs; in the Dengist culture, not only must the use of words stand up to performance tests, but actions are supposed to be judged as effective in supporting the orthodoxies of modernization and nationalism. Both cultures are profoundly concerned about cynicism, and desire people to be *both* "red *and* expert." In practice, however, Chinese know that people will instinctively favor either one quality or the other as they try to resolve the problem of sincerity.

Protesting Mistreatment versus Stoic Fatalism

A third polarity that helps to define the two Chinese political cultures and makes the advocates of each sensitive to the pull of the other is the profound Chinese contradiction between an acceptance of the legitimacy of venting emotions over any form of mistreatment by authority and a sense of the propriety and wisdom of controlling feelings and accepting one's situation fatalistically. On some occasions and in some situations, it is acceptable for Chinese to rage in public, to cry out in anguish at having been mistreated. Yet in Chinese culture it is deemed equally honorable to endure one's sufferings stoically, to hold in one's anger, and to accept the sovereignty of fate.

The Maoists, in keeping with the traditional rebel culture, built their politics upon the idea that resentment of mistreatment is one of the most powerful motivating forces in human life. Moreover, this tradition of the rebel culture has held that any evidence of mistreatment ought to trigger impassioned outbursts. Action is best inspired by suffering. Or better still, by hearing others tell their tales of bitter woes.

The Confucian tradition shared with the rebel culture a general understanding that protest might be legitimate. Not only were officials expected to tolerate the complaining of the mistreated and to be brought back to the paths of righteousness by them, but officials themselves were expected to protest if they believed the policies of the emperor to be unjust.[18] This understanding, however, constituted an exception; the Confucian tradition was in general more reserved, calling for discipline and the controlling of emotions. Life will have its ups and downs, but the superior man can maintain his equanimity; this view, when carried to extremes, becomes a form of fatalism. Under Confucian orthodoxy, as in Deng's "Reforms," the people are expected to manifest patience as a sign of their trust in the benevolent wisdom of their superiors.

Chinese political culture has traditionally recognized the necessity of tolerating petitioning about complaints as a safety valve, even to the extent of permitting public demonstrations by individuals. The figure of the distraught person wailing before the *yamen's* doors, the magistrate's office, was ubiquitous throughout the imperial and early republican periods. The Maoists exploited that tradition by calling upon older people to share with the younger ones stories of their mistreatment "before Liberation." Such behavior, called "eating bitterness," might seem to products of other cultures to border on self-pity, but for most Chinese the activity is both legitimate and moving. The same psychodynamics is at work today, as Chinese publicly bewail the hard times they had during the Cultural Revolution without asking any penetrating questions as to why their system of government made them suffer. The cathartic effects of making public their misfortunes seem to be enough to stifle the urge to find fault with the politics.

Yet traditional Chinese culture upholds equally the ideal that enduring suffering without complaining is honorable. To shout against one's fate can be seen as laughable, the mark of a fool who cannot adapt to reality. The current regime seems to find it normal to encourage the writing of the "wounded literature"—that is, tales of the suffering of people sent to the countryside during the Cultural Revolution—while at the same time extolling model heroes who suffered great hardships without complaint. Fatalism also has a negative dimension, as the Chinese masses have learned from long experience that their capacity to influence politics is close to nil. Having so little sense of political efficacy, they feel that the better part of wisdom is to leave the affairs of government to their political superiors.

This particular dichotomy between fatalism and public bewailing of mistreatment is especially acute because the two stances address the same subject, the actions of authority. Fatalism is associated with the impossibility of questioning the ways of authority; at best it is pointless to challenge the whims of the powerful, at worst it is dangerous to attract the attention of amoral authorities. By contrast, the articulated anger at being mistreated stems from frustration at injustice; it is associated with the expectation that authority should be fair and that the proper response for the virtuous person damaged by an unjust superior is to try to shame the superior back into being properly benevolent.

What is it then in Chinese culture that encourages the development of two such contradictory views about authority? The answer lies in the Chinese socialization process. Chinese socialization dramatizes the idea that authority figures are supposed to be revered as models of benevolence and morality. The child is not allowed to give expression to any feelings of hostility toward parental authority. Children are expected to accept the authority of their parents in the spirit of unquestioning filial piety, and above all not show the slightest aggression against their fathers, regardless of their private feelings. The cultural demands of filial piety require that from earliest childhood Chinese learn that they have to accept without complaint the dictates of their supposedly benevolent fathers. The natural inclinations to rebel in the early years are therefore firmly repressed, only to surface in later life when some other form of supposedly benevolent authority mistreats them. Unable to express aggression in childhood, the Chinese youth outside of the disciplining confines of the home welcomes the possibilities to rebel and to publicize mistreatment by authority figures. Yet the child has also learned that it is prudent to accept his fate without complaining. Years of quiet obedience to paternal authority teach that it is usually best to display no emotions, accept fatalistically what is called for, and suppress one's anger.

Furthermore, there is a contradiction at the very core of the Chinese socialization process. On the one hand, children are taught to recognize distinctions and gradations, to accept discrimination, and to assume that no two people are likely to be treated in the same fashion. Girls are treated differently from boys. Elder sons get some favors but have their obligations, while younger sons are subordinates with their special duties. Parents are open in saying which of their children are their favorites, and their preferences can change with whatever mood they may be in that day. Yet, at the same time, children are also taught there are the enduring Confucian values that uphold the ideals of benevolence, propriety, and correct conduct, all of which suggest the existence of some norms of justice—norms that should apply to authority figures in particular.

The combination of discrimination in practice and the verbalizations of lofty virtues seems to produce powerful feelings of envy towards those perceived as being better off, and intense desires to have the best for one's self and one's country. Envy is thus a constant reality at all levels of the culture. Those who are better off are sure that others are jealous of them; most people know the feeling of wondering why they are less fortunate than someone else. When peasants get rich under Deng's policies, the urban workers feel mistreated; when the workers get bonuses, the intellectuals wonder if they are not falling behind. Everyone feels that it is only right that he should know how much money everyone else is getting. Yet at the same time everyone has been taught that discrimination is a natural condition of life, and therefore it is foolish not to accept one's lot and hope that in time good fortune will, in its random way, come around and bless one's life. Thus envy and resignation are two sides of the same coin that was minted in the socialization process.

The result is a distinct tension between passivity and aggressive articulation of mistreatment. Psychologically, the two extremes of public complaining and stoic fatalism are equally consistent with the Chinese modal character. Both Maoism and Dengism contain elements of the two polarities; Maoism gives greater legitimacy to rebelling and to publicizing previous mistreatment, while Dengism calls for greater patience in waiting for better conditions. Those who have not as yet benefited from Deng's "reform" are expected not to complain but to accept their lot with dignity, for in time their turn will come. Yet the problem of suppressed aggression against authority figures means that there is an unstable balance between stoicism and rebellious complaining, a basic cultural ambiguity that is one of the pillars of the two Chinese political cultures. Patient suffering can explode into raging anger, a feature of the Chinese character that rightly worries Deng's Reformers. The easy bursting forth of hate, displayed during the Cultural Revolution and later against the Gang of Four, is a reminder to the Dengists that tolerance can suddenly turn into destructiveness if Chinese feel mistreated by the authorities.

The delicate balance is made even more tenuous by the extraordinary importance of shaming as a Chinese socialization method, a practice we shall have the occasion to take note of repeatedly. One of the dynamics of shaming that no doubt makes it attractive to the Chinese is the expectation that from a small effort profound changes of behavior can follow. Although used mainly by authority figures to guide the conduct of misbehaving children or inferiors, the practice could be reversed: the weak could seek to influence the behavior of the strong. Indeed, it is in a sense an ideal tactic for the weak. Consequently, demonstrative complaining and stoic acceptance of one's fate can have the common purpose of trying to shame authority into correcting its behavior. Furthermore, although seemingly polar opposites, the two reflect the same sense of what will motivate right conduct. The hope is that the powers of shame, whether triggered by loud protesting or silent but heroic suffering, will alter the behavior of the authorities for the better.

Self-Sacrifice versus Self-Aggrandizement

A fourth conflict that connects the two poles of China's dichotomous political cultures is the tension between the ideal of self-sacrifice and that of self-advancement; between the obligation of being ready to suffer for a larger group and the need to work for the aggrandizement of a more limited group, or even of one's self. In the popular, rebel, culture, particularly as it was magnified in the Maoist visions of the heroic revolutionary, there was always a strong romantic streak: acts of personal sacrifice were expected to evoke unalloyed awe.[19*] With Maoism the element of theater is, of course, heightened by dramatizing "supreme sacrifices"; a tragic end—such as Lei Feng's death from a toppled telephone pole or Chang Zhiwen's drowning in a pit of night-soil—is a prerequisite for entry into the pantheon of revolutionary heroes in the People's Republic of China.

Opposed against this idealizing of sacrifice is the equally respected vision of the prospering notable who has combined good luck, quick wits, and hard work to advance himself. The very success in economic development of the Confucian cultures of Japan, South Korea, Taiwan, Hong Kong, and Singapore suggests that there has to be something in those cultures that encourages personal achievement. In the political realm the instinct for self-aggrandizement can also take the form of the perennial Chinese problem with corruption among officials. From the scandals of entrepreneurial officials on Hainan Island to the press reports made in the winter of 1988 that more than $48 million allocated to poverty programs had been embezzled or misappropriated by local officials, the Chinese public is constantly being reminded that it is a short step from having power to looking after one's private interests.

In the Confucian high culture, individuals had an obligation to care for their families and ancestors and therefore were expected to reduce risks to their physical well-being and to seek rewards for their efforts—needless to say, the benefits they sought supposedly stopped short of conspicuous corruption, but the lines between propriety and greed were tricky and often crossed. The Confucian ethic recognized the principle that people should work hard for proper achievements, which did not necessarily exclude material gain. Thus the followers of traditional Confucianism were, and its present-day heirs are, basically group-oriented people, ready to sacrifice for the collectivity, but they were and are prone to think about material advantages for themselves.

This tension between the ideals of sacrifice and the benefits of personal reward is central to Chinese culture in large measure because for the Chinese, the self is essentially defined by the individual's sense of belonging to some larger group or community—in particular the family or clan, but by extension the Chinese race and nation. The individual's sense of self arises almost totally from his group identity. More precisely, the Chinese sense of identity comes from the notion of a greater self, or *da-wuo*, and from the necessity of "sacrificing the smaller self to fulfill the greater self."[20] Sensitivity to the importance of the *da-wuo* reinforces tendencies toward conformity and debases the value of individualism. Although yielding to the demands of a collectivity is the norm in Chinese society, the very obligation always to do so seems to stimulate the two logical counter-norms of either idealizing self-sacrifice or rationalizing greed.

Trained to think of the "larger self" as the core identity, the Chinese end up with a blurred sense of the boundaries between Self and Other. Immediate "others" have to be considered parts of the self. The result seems to be an exceptionally vivid sense of gradations among the "others." The need to identify so closely with some "others" seems to legitimize the classifying of more distant others as potentially dangerous foes. The result is a strong sense of clannishness and a ready distrust of foreigners, of the *gwailo*. Note how, even in governmental decision-making, the Chinese definitely prefer to deal with ethnic Chinese of other countries, even with people who were once strongly anti-Communist, rather than with those they consider to be real foreigners.

The Chinese approach of basing the individual's identity primarily on the larger self or group identity and secondarily on the smaller self is, of course, the opposite of the Western tendency to base individual identity on the ideal of self-realization and then broaden to take into account the secondary dimension of group identity. For the Chinese there is fuzziness as to how much legitimacy the smaller self can claim if it is not essentially defined by the collectivity. Hence it is natural to see individualism in a negative light, and as the source of corruption and selfishness. Westerners, in contrast, have a more vivid and positive view of self-realization and a less distinct sense of being defined in terms of the group. The individual should contribute to the group, for team spirit is valued, but it is also assumed that such a contribution can best be made by improving one's own skills and status.

The traditional rebel culture, and its modern Maoist version, sought to give a heroic dimension to the hard work and sacrifices that have been the routine necessities of rural life throughout Chinese history. The glorification of sacrifice became an acknowledgment that individuals deserved to be rewarded for the sacrifices they have to make for their group, rather than having their sufferings treated as everyday matters. Conversely, it also makes it possible for everyone to find in himself a bit of the heroic, for each can see in the model heroes elements of his own life, blown large.

Working for personal rewards has a similar heroic rationale: one should seek the betterment of one's "greater self" and, conversely, in advancing the interests of one's family or clan one deserves some personal recompense. Helping one's smaller self can easily be rationalized as helping the greater self; in many cases, this means that corruption is easily justified as necessary to meet one's larger responsibilities.

The themes of self-sacrifice and reward create tensions between the two Chinese political cultures precisely because there is such ambivalence in Chinese society about the questions of for whom one should be working and who deserves the credit for the achievements of the individual. The Maoist tradition gives emphasis to self-sacrifice and the greater glory of the collective identity, while the Dengist approach allows for greater scope in seeking personal rewards and advantages. The denial of the legitimacy of individualism in Chinese culture establishes the basis for an essentially insolvable problem. It is others, rather than one's self, who have the right to determine how much one is expected to sacrifice for others and how much one should be personally rewarded for one's accomplishments. The individual can only hope that according to one or the other of the two his conduct will be seen as deserving.

The playing out of this tension can be seen in the endlessly repeated story of individual Chinese who worked and saved for the betterment of their families throughout most of their lives but who in old age became self-indulgent and dissipated the family fortune. The fear that such a thing might happen has been the recurring worry of wives and sons in Chinese novels. This tension has also been acknowledged by the Communist leaders in today's campaigns against corruption. For example, the Central Discipline Inspection Commission issued a circular in early 1986 entitled "Cherish Revolutionary Honor and Uphold Revolutionary Integrity in One's Later Years," in which the whole Party is exhorted to draw a lesson from the case of the retired cadre Zhang Yi, who had been expelled. According to the Commission, Zhang Yi had joined the Party in 1941 during the war against Japan, when he had " . . . withstood the test of life and death amid the flames of war filled with the smoke of gunpowder and the hail of bullets" but in time "he slackened his efforts at study, gradually lost the spirit of sacrificing oneself for revolution . . . and turned his back on serving the people wholeheartedly. Consequently, he was defeated by the 'money bullet' and fell captive to money."[21]

Pride versus Humility

The ambivalences of the Chinese about the boundaries of individual identity also seem to contribute to another fundamental polarity of the two political cultures, that of a sense of grandeur that may spill over into the boastful extolling of achievements, on the one hand, and self-deprecating modesty and humility on the other. When the individual's fantasies of self coincide with the *da-wuo*, pride can easily take over; when the self is inflated to its maximum dimension the result is the well-known phenomenon of Han chauvinism. At the other extreme is the individual who shrinks into the "lonely self," for whom status and security are best achieved by exaggerated postures of humbleness.

The ideal leader of the traditional rebel culture was one with superhuman powers and a tactical cleverness that set him apart from ordinary mortals. In contrast, the ideal leader of the elite culture was a statesman whose greatness was masked behind a protective shield of modesty and humility. The rebel leader, of course, was not above speaking to the needs of the common folk, but his legitimacy ultimately rested upon more than a hint of exceptional greatness, so it would not be folly to follow his lead in risky and bold adventures. Similarly, the Confucian concept of power was not without its grandeur—witness the expanses of imperial palaces—but the mandarin style was essentially one of seeking dignity in aloofness, which could be taken as a proper degree of humility. Mao Zedong, of course, combined the rebel's style of personal greatness with the grandeur of mass demonstrations in

Tienanmen Square, while Deng Xiaoping has gone to the other extreme of commanding supreme power while modestly holding no post except the chairmanship of the Military Affairs Commission. Although Mao was capable of expressing the two extremes—claiming greatness at one moment and adopting a stance of modesty at the next—his basic inclinations were in the direction of triumphant boasting. He jubilantly claimed that China would catch up with Great Britain in fifteen years, and that China, at the time of the Great Leap, had moved ahead of the Soviet Union in reaching the promised land of true Communism. In contrast, the Deng leadership proclaimed on the eve of the Thirteenth Party Congress that China was at the stage of "immature and imperfect socialism"—a unique category unheard of in the entire tradition of Marxian socialism, yet a designation so modest as to be dangerously close to laughable.

While in all forms of politics people project an ego larger than the private self, in Chinese political culture the actors gravitate toward the pole of grandeur and self-proclaimed greatness. True humility is difficult in any form of politics, and it is especially awkward in the context of an awakened nationalism. Mao's boasts that the Chinese people had "stood up" and that the Chinese "revolution" was an appropriate model for all the developing world were typical grand articulations of Chinese nationalism. Deng's call for a less flamboyant style has overtones of the tradition of humility, but it is not devoid of an ultimate appeal to Chinese cravings for greatness. Indeed, his slogan of striving for "socialism with Chinese characteristics" nicely blended modesty and a claim of uniqueness, while leaving vague precisely what the goal was.

The striving to gain and maintain "face" further tilts behavior in the direction of proclaiming greatness whenever possible and of taking offense at any perceived slights. The desire to bring honor to collectivity, to the "larger self," also inspires expressions of uncritical optimism about national development and boastfulness about public accomplishments. If questioned, the Chinese are likely to respond with prickly pride (leaning toward the pole of greatness), or a retreat into modesty (a move toward the pole of humility).

Although the nature of politics may cause a tilting toward the pole of proclaiming greatness, it is significant that humbleness carries the most attraction for those who are the most secure and knowledgeable about what constitutes greatness according to world standards. The rural peasant rebel of earlier days and the parochial Maoist revolutionary were the most spontaneous exponents of their own sense of being earth-shaking, while Deng's elite technocrats, in their greater cosmopolitanism, have more room for humility. Yet one of the greatest potential sources of destabilization for Deng's reforms is an inherent Chinese vulnerability to pretensions of greatness that can undermine efficiency and effectiveness.

The posturing of overstatement and of understatement equally obscure the importance of reality as the basis of political discourse. The tendency in Chinese politics has been toward overstatement of what has been accomplished and of inflated prognosis of what lies ahead, or exaggerated protestations of modesty that are recognizably fake. These disconcerting tendencies feed into the next dichotomy shaping the particularities of China's two political cultures.

The Power of Symbolism versus the Constraints of Realism

Chinese political history is filled with testimony to the contradictory tendency to treat the manipulation of mere symbols, such as the incantation of slogans, with solemnity and respect in some contexts, and in other contexts to act in a down-to-earth, realistic fashion that focuses only on physical realities.

In the rebel and Maoist traditions there was faith in what often could only be called magic. For the believers reality could be transformed by the mouthing of formulas or slogans. Even Dengism shows some tendency in that direction, as, for example, in the simplistic extolling of the idea of the "Four Modernizations" or in the belief that through enthusiastic repetition of the slogan "one country, two systems," Taiwan can be won over to reunification. The traditional Chinese popular political culture was permeated with magical possibilities; disbelief was easily suspended in favor of the expectation that the implausible could happen. For a rural people accustomed to speculating on the feats of ghosts and spirits, it was natural to be unconstrained by this-worldly causality when they turned their thoughts to what might be realized through energetic political action. In the ideologies of most secret societies and rebel bands, enemies might be conquered and victories won by denying the gulf between reality and magic. If combat was called for there were usually enough amulets to go around. The Chinese fascination with the idea of becoming invisible and of suddenly having superhuman physical strength—common in cultures in which the socialization process dramatizes the differences in power between children and adults—was readily transformed in the counter-political culture into the belief that even the most hopeless rebellion might suddenly triumph, especially if led by a shaman or pseudo-shaman. Needless to say, this propensity for wishful thinking was captured by the Maoist tradition of asserting that everything would be possible if willpower were concentrated by blind faith.

In contrast, the elite culture scorned the introduction into politics of talismans and otherworldly considerations and held up the ideals of reason and realism, much as the Dengists insist they are now doing in the wake of the superstitious follies of the previous era of leftist sorcery. The boundaries of the traditional elite culture were supposedly set by the realities of social relations and concrete institutional concerns. In their rhetoric the Maoists followed the rebel tradition of characterizing their enemies as "demons" and "freaks," while the Dengists stepped into the shoes of the traditional Confucianists, castigating the "Gang of Four" and the forces unleashed by the Cultural Revolution as revivals of superstition and black magic.

Among historians there is some disagreement as to the reasons for the elite culture's distrust of the sorcery found in the popular culture. For Levenson and Schurman the clash was between superstition and enlightenment, between mysticism and rationality. They argue that the early peasant revolts dating from 137 A.D. usually had Taoist overtones, that the participants were called *yao-tsei* or "magic bandits," and as we quoted earlier, that "to the Confucian historians and officials of the time and of later generations, these bandits were stirring up the dark world of magic, the terrible forces of superstition, which Confucian rationality sought to tame in man."[22] Against this view, Philip Kuhn, in a careful study of Ming and Qing legal practices intended to control sorcery, argues that the Chinese officials abhorred such practices, but accepted as plausible the sorcerer's acts of magic because they recognized that their own legitimacy rested also on a form of magic.[23] The fact that the government found such activities abominable is documented in the legal codes, which decreed extremely severe penalties for acts of sorcery—one hundred strokes with the heavy bamboo for deception, death by slow strangulation for public performances, and death by a thousand slicings for agitating the masses. Kuhn suggests that the severity of the punishments reflected the awareness of officials that sorcery challenged the authority of the state and thus had to be treated as second only to treason. The clash was thus not just one between superstition and reason. Sorcery was an intolerable practice precisely because it threatened the legitimacy of the state, which was based on a mandate that came from a supernatural source, Heaven.

The power of the rebels stemmed from a belief in the magical powers of symbols—but so also did the power of the mandarins. A belief in the power of form over substance was behind the idea that officials merely by their example of correct behavior could control the behavior of the population. Clearly, this called for faith in the efficacy of nonmaterial, intangible forces. The rituals performed by the emperor purportedly had, if correctly carried out, a potency that could no better be explained in terms of rational cause and effect than could the magic of sorcerers. Both endowed symbols with supernatural powers.

Although professing belief in the supernatural is no longer an established feature of Chinese culture, there continues to be a strong propensity for wishful thinking and the hope that it should be possible to discover formulas that can yield astonishing success with minimal effort. Leaders keep declaring that they are about to transform the implausible into the likely. Consequently, the political slogans of the day are treated as though they have the potency of magic.

The counterpart to this faith in the magic of symbols is the equally powerful Chinese tradition of realism, in which it is accepted that nothing can come easily, and that any accomplishment demands total concentration, laborious effort, and sacrifice. Behavior should always be guided by a factual appraisal of one's immediate circumstances. Anyone unable to perceive his situation clearly is certain to make a fool of himself by helplessly blundering about. One cannot wish away realities; one can only act purposefully and steadfastly.

The polarity of symbolism and realism produces the peculiar Chinese combination of wishful thinking and cold practicality. The two poles seem to be held firmly juxtaposed by another fundamental ambivalence in Chinese culture. This is a stark contradiction inherent in the Chinese view of where the locus of control lies in human affairs. It is common for Chinese to believe that events are dominated by impersonal forces largely beyond the control of man—forces such as fate, luck, nature, time, the stars, the Tao—but simultaneously to believe that individual efforts can be efficacious. Furthermore, Chinese are not insensitive to a third possibility: that their destinies are controlled by people who might just possibly be at the outer limits of their personal influence. Both in the range of forces to which they attribute the control of events and in their tolerance for holding to logically contradictory beliefs on the matter, the Chinese differ from Westerners. American psychologists have found that they can divide American populations rather tidily into only two categories: those who believe that they personally control their fate and those who believe control is external to them. For Americans it is largely an either/or matter with respect to these two alternatives; the Chinese think it wiser to assume that all three alternatives noted above are possible. This complex attitude is instilled from earliest childhood. First the child is assured that he is the center of the world, in total and happy control of his environment by merely asserting his will. But then later the child is made to feel vulnerable, aware of his total dependence upon the family and the forces of his ancestor's spirits. But he is also given the contradictory signal that if he acts correctly and avoids errors, he can hope to affect his fate. Thus he learns that affairs may be governed by the invisible forces of luck and fate, but that it is also important to apply willpower and to singlemindedly pursue his goals.

For Chinese there is considerable uncertainty as to precisely where the locus of control is in their lives. There is not a clear demarcation as to what matters lie with fate and what is under their personal control. The boundary line between where self-reliance should end and help from others begin is far from stable. This means that Chinese can behave in quite contradictory ways. Sometimes they will be totally passive, apparently leaving developments to the play of impersonal forces; at other moments they act as though their personal effort is all that counts. In fact, however, the passive posture may reflect not fatalism, but the intent to wait for the propitious moment to spring into action. Indeed, precisely because the Chinese see the range of forces controlling events as more extensive, they often display a more elaborate vision of the nature of power than is common in the West. Specifically, they tend to assume that much of the power that shapes human affairs lies outside the domain of control of any of the participants. In contrast to the Western belief that power is divided in its entirety among the participants in the political process, in Chinese political thinking there is a substantial amount of power that is not directly possessed by any participant. Hence, strategy must always take into account timing and the unexpected changes in circumstances.

As I have noted elsewhere, "These attitudes produce a unique Chinese blend of single-mindedness and wishful thinking. In China people work tirelessly while always suspecting that their fate is in the hands of others. One can therefore hope for, or more correctly gamble on, luck—hence the ambivalence about effort and willpower in Chinese political culture. Sometimes Chinese leaders are keenly sensitive to the dangers of dissipating their energies and seem anxious to find strategies that will bring success with a minimum of effort or risk—another example of the value of deception and surprise. At other times they call for a maximum expenditure of effort by demanding that the masses display willpower and determination."[24]

This basic ambivalence underlies the two contradictory attitudes of awe for the power of symbols and respect for cold reality, attitudes basic to the two major alternative Chinese political orientations. It is this distinctive combination of attitudes that makes it possible for Chinese in one frame of mind to believe with naive enthusiasm that miracles are possible (and therefore a politics of chanting formulas is reasonable) but in another frame of mind to embrace skepticism. With Mao much of politics was reduced to faith in symbols and a tolerance for obvious lies because the impossible was treated as entirely plausible. Under Deng the danger has become the opposite likelihood that realism will produce disbelief and cynicism. Chinese politics can thus easily swing between simplistic solutions based on symbols and a hardheaded realism that leads to cynicism or a fearless confronting of all obstacles to desired ends.[25*]

Paradox and Contradiction versus Firmness and Continuity

Another, closely related, polarity consists of the Chinese tendency under certain circumstances to see the world as being in constant flux, filled with contradictions and the unexpected, and under other conditions to assume that reality is quite fixed, that there exists a clear hierarchy in values that calls for firmness and steadfastness in actions.

The first set of assumptions is basic to the popularistic notions of the yin and the yang and the Maoist doctrines of the unity of opposites, all of which suggest that much is illusion, that things can turn into their opposites, and that appearances are deceptive. The Maoist political culture rejoices in the prospect of the unexpected, the exhilaration of quick adjustments and dramatic changes. Mao himself delighted in contradictions, in finding, for example, the bourgeoisie in the Party, "capitalist roaders" in the most unlikely places, and things going wrong just when they seemed to be working out well—all of which is a part of the Chinese tendency to value cleverness and to delight in conundrums.

At the other pole is the view that the world is essentially stable, that yesterday's single-mindedness will pay off. Since reality is constant, steadfastness is appropriate in most pursuits. Perfection by repetition becomes reasonable because the development of particular skills will be of lasting value. Moreover, it is useful to think in terms of what is the "best," because quality is a constant. Above all, any problem will have a single, "best" solution. Indeed, practical wisdom consists of finding the correct single answer to each problem. Just as the child is taught that there is only one way to write each character, and that a single mistake can produce total failure, so there is a tendency to look for, and be satisfied with, monocausal explanations. Once a problem has been defined and its appropriate correct solution identified, all that is required is persistence and the application of blind determination. Hence the tradition of perseverance and patience in carrying out enduring commitments.

This paradoxical polarity of tolerance for contradictions and belief in the existence of only one correct solution of any problem is not easily explained. I suspect, however, that a partial answer is to be found in the complicated attitudes Chinese have about the impersonal forces that they believe govern so much of life, which constitute a variation on the locus of control problem we have just noted. We must recognize the important place of divination, from the prehistoric time of the Oracle Bones to today's respect for geomancy (*feng-shui*). Richard J. Smith has written about the importance Chinese traditionally attached to "knowing fate" (*chi-ming*), and about the variety of ways of foretelling the workings of superhuman forces.[26] The orthodox means of divination was to consult the *I-ching*, but there were popular forms of "spirit-writing" (*fu-chi*), dreams (*meng-chan*), the interpretation of omens (*chi-hsiung chih chao*) and, above all, geomancy (*feng-shui*). The complexities of "calculating fate" (*suan-ming, shu-ming*), involved a variety of cosmic variables: the *yin* and the *yang*, the four seasons, the five elements (*wu-kua*), the eight characters (*pa-tzu*), the nine mansions (*chiu-kung*) the ten heavenly stems and twelve earthly branches (*t'ien-pan, ti chih*), the twenty-four solar periods (*erh-shih-ssu ch'i*), the twenty-eight constellations (*erh-shih-pa-hsiu*), the sixty-four hexagrams (*liu-shih-ssu kua*), and over two hundred auspicious and inauspicious "stars" (*hsing*).

The intensity of the Chinese's concern with divinations reveals their vacillation between faith in superhuman forces and anxiety about their predestined fates. Their belief in fate fuels their eternal hope that magic is possible, and the politically impossible can happen; yet it also suggests the possibility, if not the probability, that disaster may be in the offing. The desire to know what is already determined is driven by the thought that with "knowing fate" (*chih-ming*) something might still be done to mitigate the worst or to exploit the good news.

In some respects these attitudes are reminiscent of Max Weber's interpretation of the paradox of why Calvinists, who believed in predestination, were a driven people, always seeking worldly accomplishments even while they worried about the ultimate otherworldly outcome. The analogy is far from perfect, for the Calvinists were worried about their souls in a hereafter of eternal duration, while the Chinese focus is upon immediate this-worldly benefits. But like the Calvinists, the Chinese tend to recognize the dominant role of external forces in arranging a predestined future, and like the Calvinists they respond to their anxieties by trying to prove themselves to be masters of their fates. Unlike the Calvinists, the Chinese respond to the prospect of a happy fate with a gambler's spirit of wishful thinking. Comparable to the Calvinists, the Chinese respond to the thought of a negative fate with the belief that there still may be an antidote, a correct answer that could save the day if pursued with determination.

The Chinese respond to the dilemma by sharpening the distinction, not between this world and the other world, as the Calvinists did, but between the symbolic and the mundane. To the symbolic they have ascribed many of the properties of magic, which encourages their joy in wishful thinking; on the mundane they concentrate their determined efforts and their expectation that singlemindedness can pay off.

It might seem that the Chinese should be troubled by the contradiction, and driven, as the Calvinists were, to find a coherent solution. Yet for the Chinese the tension is tolerable because they believe there is nothing to be logically resolved. Indeed, we should note that it has been well established by many researchers that the Chinese seem to be tolerant of cognitive dissonance; they do not feel obligated to resolve logical contradictions. Logical consistency is not an imperative, and eclecticism is more the norm than the exception. Witness, for example, their easy simultaneous acceptance of different religious beliefs: in China an individual can comfortably subscribe to several religious doctrines.

Yet when it comes to particular actions the pragmatic Chinese long to be able to calibrate their conduct to reality; hence they yearn for a predictable social world in which they can anticipate the payoffs and the pitfalls of their own actions. They crave a world in which conformity is possible and rewarding. Contradictions can prevail in the realm of ideas and beliefs, but in human relations the ideal is reliability, by which the Chinese mean not just loyalty but also predictability. Where others may see complex tradeoffs among preferences, the Chinese assume that there can be a clear and enduring hierarchy of values. For example, in the marketplace the Chinese hold that there is a "best" of any product, and they remain remarkably loyal to their particularly esteemed products.

One way in which Chinese minimize tensions over their cognitive dissonance about the orderliness of the world they live in is to deny the need for an answer by optimistically looking to the future. In the political realm this takes the form of trying to minimize the problems and confusion of the day by holding out the promise of great and glorious tomorrows. The idea of a "New China," filled with greatness, has been the universally shared dream of the politically conscious for decades. Even the pessimists rarely talk of the possible prospects of disasters, but rather usually strive only to break the excessive enthusiasm of the optimists. Whereas in American political culture it is conventional for politicians to compete to see who can outdo the other in identifying problems, proclaiming impending disasters, and warning about the certainty of crises, in China the political rhetoric of leaders and the press is almost entirely upbeat. Given the fact that the history of modern Chinese is the story of one tragedy after another that must have constituted an unbroken series of shattered dreams for most Chinese, there must be in the culture powerful psychological needs for the defense mechanism of denial so as to sustain the conventions of optimism at a level that might seem almost Pollyannaish.

The Significance of the Two Patterns

Our analysis has become rather complex, and it is no doubt hard to keep in mind the series of polarities and their underlying psycho-cultural bases. It may seem that the polarities have been randomly picked and that in some cases the psychological ambivalences may overlap. The selection, however, was not random, but it is true that the polarities and their underlying sentiments impinge on each other. This is so because they all share a common origin at an even deeper psychological level. That is, they all relate to a core problem of Chinese culture: the problem of self identity in a culture that gives ambiguous instructions about the relationship of the self to others. Behind each of the ambivalences—whether it is the one that arises from problems with intimacy, or with sincerity, or with "face," or any of the others—there is the more fundamental problem of how strong and willful the self can and should be in a context in which the collectivity—be it the family, the group, the party, or the nation—has paramount claims in dictating behavior.[27*] Whether it is the problem of self-esteem associated with the gaining or losing of "face" or that of where the locus of control lies in human affairs, there is profound uncertainty as to where the boundary between self and other should be drawn. The central notion of "face," whether as *lien* or *mienze*, provides undisputable testimony of the extent to which the self is not only defined by others in Chinese culture, but is excruciatingly vulnerable, and needs to be on guard and actively defensive, if not assertive. The self exists only along a continuum from the individual to the other. The self is thus always a part of a relationship. For, as Confucius taught the Chinese, it is paired relationships that provide the dimensions of the most important realities in human affairs.

There is thus in Chinese culture no distinct concept of the self except in terms of the other, which is generally a collectivity. Yet there is no strong bonding, no easy outpouring of feelings to the very people who give one one's identity. One is always part of a group, but there may be little sense of team spirit. This is because emotions have to be controlled. One is thus often alone, almost isolated, even while being a part of a dominating collectivity. Yet for the individual there is little sense of having a distinctive psyche or soul, and there is certainly no legitimacy for introspection. The result is the paradox of widespread egotism by people with fragile egos.

Assertiveness and submissiveness are equally honored and despised. Consequently there is profound ambivalence as to whether one's behavior can best be guided by an inner "gyroscope" or by following "radar" signals that record the opinions of others. The need to conform is great, but so is the desire to be outstanding. The Chinese may thus easily accept labelling of the self by society—as when Mao established his "good" and "bad" categories of people based on the past roles of fathers and even grandfathers—for as Donald Munro has tellingly noted, there is no place for a "private self" because the self is defined by society and government.[28] But the Chinese are also capable of profound frustration and anger at finding the result can be the making of a caste society.[29]*

The source of this profound tension over the relationship of Self and Other is to be found in the Chinese socialization process. More particularly it seems to arise from the sharp contrast between the highly indulgent and nurturing treatment common in the first years and the demanding discipline and outside controls imposed in subsequent years. The supportive and warm first period encourages willfulness, a narcissistic belief in the preciousness and goodness of the self, a faith in the possibilities of magical control over others, and a general enjoyment of oceanic feelings of togetherness, of blissful harmony, of being in total and effortless command. Then comes the cold shock that reality requires yielding to the will of others, that one's destiny is decisively determined by others, and that security is best found by going along with the tide, by conforming to the wishes of others. The ecstasy of willfulness clashes with the rewards for obedient submissiveness. The self may gain strength from identifying with the other, but it also seeks autonomy. Whereas in some cultures self-realization is emphasized, and in others the stress is on bending to discipline, in the Chinese socialization process both extremes are highlighted, but at different times and under different circumstances.

The problem of the interrelationship of the self and the other in Chinese culture is made even more complex because the norms of socialization tend to be exceedingly strict, in particular with respect to repressing feelings of both aggression and sexuality. In the traditional culture the emphasis was mainly on repressing aggression and only suppressing sexual drives. The imperative for correct conduct demanded the repression of any overt manifestations of anger or hostility, especially in relations with authority figures. Indeed, the child was taught that it was a serious crime to display any of his normal feelings of aggression against his parents because of the imperatives of filial piety. Although rules of propriety did surround sexual behavior, it was an activity that was taken as natural. Consequently, in Chinese society there was a great deal of indirect surfacing of aggression—talking behind people's backs, damaging reputations by gossip, and above all reporting to superiors about the failings of peers—whereas there was far less of the diffuse and indirect surfacing of sexual themes such as occurred in the West (where sex has been the most severely repressed human instinct). More recently, however, the Communist culture has championed puritanical norms that dictate the repression of sex in thought or deed.

There are probably few cultures in the world that make greater demands in seeking to repress these two basic human emotions. The intensity of the repression helps to explain the resistance to introspection in Chinese culture. To look inward is to risk the dangers of confronting in one's secret thoughts severely tabooed sentiments. Moreover, since the ego faces this heavy demand in repressing two such strong natural tendencies, it tends to be highly vulnerable, indeed fragile, and thus easily threatened by the opinions of others. Just as the individual knows that beneath the surface he has to contain a host of "bad" thoughts and feelings, so for society as a whole there is a keen awareness that lurking beneath the conventions that give order to the community there are powerful forces of anarchy. A vicious circle is thus established with respect to both the individual and society in which the awareness of the dangers of repressed "evils" requires ever sterner norms, which only repress the drives further and make them more threatening. The leaders are left hypersensitive to the dangers of disorder, which leads to the periodic demands for tightening controls.

This is not the place for a detailed examination of Chinese socialization practices.[30*] We are obligated only to point to their importance, not because of any exaggerated faith in Freudian formulations, but because, as we suggested, there is a need to make clear that the continuities in Chinese culture do not stem from any innate or racial considerations but from the social processes by which each generation learns to become Chinese. Like all people, the Chinese become as they are by how they are brought up, and by how they react to that experience. Continuities come from nurturance, not nature, from social and not genetic factors. Moreover, we have surely reached a stage of enlightenment in the social sciences at which it should be unacceptable to suggest that any continuities in Chinese culture can be explained by the mysterious workings of an invisible hand called History.

All of this is to say that the polarities that we have identified as basic to China's two main political cultures are not just random tendencies or quaint propensities. They spring from some of the most basic emotions that shape the human character, for there is little that can be more fundamental than the self-other relationship.[31*] It is these sets of polarities that establish both of the two seemingly contradictory political cultures of Maoism and Dengism as being, in fundamental respects, acceptable for the Chinese. People who have responded instinctively to one can also find merit and integrity in the other. The patterns of Maoism and Dengism are thus not random developments, thrown up by the turmoil of modern Chinese politics. Each is as much a part of the Chinese cultural tradition as were the historical alternatives of the elite Confucian and the populist rebel cultures of ancient China.

The ongoing existence of the two different but related cultures characterized by the above polarities helps explain the transformation of Mao's China into Deng's China. Although individual Chinese will have to live with the consequences of what they did while Mao's rule prevailed, and thus could have difficulty being accepted under the Dengist alternative, such people can certainly understand the norms of the current system. It is not as though the Chinese were suddenly required to adapt to a totally foreign cultural system.

All of this does not mean, however, that if Deng should "fail" the inevitable result would be the automatic revival of Maoism. We are not suggesting that Chinese history is a revolving door between cultural equivalents of Maoism and Dengism. Maoism was not a replication of the traditional rebel culture, nor is Dengism a revival of the historic elite culture. Maoism and Dengism each contain elements of both of the earlier traditions. They also have their unique qualities, for there have also been innovations.

This suggests that change will not necessarily take the form of a total reversal; it may consist of a modification involving new combinations of the polarities. Dengism can adopt numerous elements of what might seem to be its Maoist opposite but continue to be seen in Chinese eyes as adhering to its central tradition. To the Western mind, with its more vivid sense of the dichotomy of truth and falsehood, the prospect of the modification of one of the cultures is the promise that the other is about to emerge—just as the abandonment of some features of central planning leads many Westerners believe that capitalism is about to surface in today's China. Or that any slowing down of the reforms means to some that a return to total central planning, and even Maoism, is in the offing.

Before speculating about whether Dengism will be modified in the future we should try to get a clearer picture of the distinctive dimensions of that system, by turning next to a cultural analysis of Chinese pragmatism.

CHAPTER III

ON CHINESE PRAGMATISM

The orthodoxy of the day is that Chinese politics is now pragmatic. The China that was once the ultimate in ideological politics in both the intensity of its passions and the lunacy of its principles has vanished as by the wave of a conjurer's hand. The primacy of ideology, the hallmark of Chinese communism under Chairman Mao Zedong, has been replaced by the no-nonsense philosophy of Deng Xiaoping, who does not care about the "color of the cat" so long as it catches "the mice." With near unanimity scholars of contemporary China welcome the change. It promises not only liberation for the Chinese people from the heavy hand of doctrinal politics but also the prospect that analysis of Chinese developments can emerge from the realm of murky esoteric interpretation into the fresh air of reasoned policy evaluation.

A consensus seems to be building that the triumph of pragmatism means that the Chinese are shedding mystification and joining the community of enlightened and rational people.[1] In a sense, pragmatism has become a code word that signals an end not only of ideology but also of all that seemed to make China culturally unique. Pragmatic policies, like pragmatic behavior, are assumed to be nothing more than what intelligent people the world around would do in China's situation. Therefore, the argument goes, to understand China now requires not specialized knowledge, but just clear-headed reasoning.

This sort of reasoning is a result of our tendency to suppose, in our short-hand way of talking and writing, that somehow pragmatism is simply a pure form of rationality, untainted by cultural biases. Yet in truth there is no such thing as value-neutral, culture-free pragmatism.

Any version of pragmatism, especially a version that can command the adherence of both a ruling circle and a national population, inescapably reflects a set of basic predispositions, a kind of latent, unarticulated ideology, in Clifford Geertz's sense of culture as ideology.[2] Pragmatic politics can no more achieve a pure state of objectivity than can any other human activity, including the practice of the social sciences. And of course, in the real world of politics there is far less value attached to achieving objectivity than there is in the world of scholarship.[3*]

China scholars have understandably desired to believe that common sense should be the same the world around. We cling to the idea that rationality is universal, the same for all people. Yet, of course, pure rationality is rare and should not be confused with what is called pragmatism in any country. What is self-evident for some people is not so for others. Chinese pragmatism has its own distinctive characteristics and is unlike pragmatism, in, say, British or American public life. In Britain "pragmatic" means essentially the opposite of "ideological," much as in the Chinese case. For many Americans the term has the pejorative overtone of "being unprincipled"; it is almost a euphemism for opportunistic, as Walter Mondale discovered to his sorrow in 1984, when he was perceived by many as trying to be all things to all people.[4*]

Therefore a challenging task for current scholarship should be to analyze what is distinctive in the Chinese brand of pragmatism. In what respects will Chinese pragmatism be decisively influenced by the characteristics and predispositions of Chinese culture? In the 1950s and 1960s, when China was proceeding down the ideological path, scholars debated the extent to which the rigid doctrines of Marxism-Leninism would be altered by Chinese cultural predispositions. They argued, for example, about the consequences of Mao Zedong's having to rely upon peasant armies rather than industrial workers for his revolution. Unfortunately, the debate at the time did not become so penetrating as to analyze basic Chinese cultural attitudes and thereby explain why Mao's policies were destined to favor industry over agriculture. Similarly, even before the explosive violence of the Cultural Revolution made it apparent for all the world to see, the study of Chinese political culture should have suggested that Mao's ideological style of ruling would probably tap the suppressed aggression that Chinese socialization practices can produce and ignite demands for a nobler, purer form of authority to match the cultural ideals of what authority figures should be.[5*]

Now that pragmatism has taken over, is it not likely that cultural factors will become even more important for predicting Chinese developments than when the constraining influences of Marxism-Leninism were dominant?

When Western analysts say that Chinese politics is now pragmatic, the implication is that Chinese politics has become less ideological and more practical, and therefore public policies will emphasize economic rationality and the advancement of most of what the world associates with secular modernization. For some analysts the ascendance of pragmatism in China means little more than a decline in the importance of ideology, for others it means only that China is in flux, but for most it means a stress on economic development and technological modernization. Yet even such apparently neutral conceptions of pragmatism cannot get away from the fact that Chinese politics has to be based on some shared assumptions that stem from a combination of cultural norms and unarticulated ideological perspectives, such as those of an operational code.[6] It is precisely this mix of Chinese cultural predispositions and the biases inherent in the current Chinese Communist approach of "seeking truth from facts" that must be analyzed if we are to forecast likely Chinese developments. In doing so we must keep in mind that in politics, respecting "facts" is not the same as being "practical," for as Henry Adams admonished us, "Practical politics consists in ignoring facts"—as is certainly the case in American politics.

The questions that must be answered go beyond the level of policy analysis and judgments about the probable successes and failures of economic programs. What is called for is the study of the more fundamental characteristics of Chinese pragmatism and the identification of the positive potentialities and the limiting constraints inherent in how the Chinese elite are prone to manage public affairs. We need to try to foresee the directions in which the Chinese political system is likely to move under a regime of "pragmatic" rule. The task does not call for an evaluation of the distribution of political attitudes throughout the Chinese population, for the goal is only to determine those attitudes and inclinations that are likely to be the most decisive in shaping Chinese political development. General cultural patterns, however, can be helpful in suggesting probable elite dispositions, since the Chinese elite political culture does have to resonate to some degree with the Chinese mass political culture.

Our approach in the pages that follow will be, first, to try to identify those features of Chinese culture that may explain the extraordinary flexibility of Chinese pragmatism, which has permitted breathtaking turns of policy that have astounded the world. The marvel of Deng's China is not just its amazing reversals of Mao's ideological politics but the rapidity with which new policies have been introduced and the alacrity with which the Chinese public has adapted to the new ground rules. For the leaders, of course, their policies are never implemented fast enough, and hence they constantly complain of too much inertia, too many people dragging their feet, too many tensions holding back progress. Yet they tend to have their way, and the changes are extraordinary by the standards with which experienced people usually measure the customarily tortoise-like pace of political change. Therefore, we need to explain why Chinese pragmatism leaves both leaders and followers free to accept all manner of changes as though in fact there were no such things as inertia, friction, or tension.

Our analysis will then look at the cultural constraints on this otherwise remarkably adaptable pragmatism. What are some of the limits that the culture sets on the future pattern of political development? More specifically, what features of Chinese political culture might set limits for realizing the three main advantages of pragmatism: achieving desired practical results, maximizing efficiency, and learning from experience?

What Is "Socialism with Chinese Characteristics"?

Before we turn to an analysis of the character of Chinese pragmatism, three qualifications are in order. First of all, we must recognize that while outsiders may have reached near unanimity in concluding that China is becoming pragmatic and is even beginning to experiment with capitalistic ways, the Chinese leaders themselves hold that they are still loyal to Marxism-Leninism-Mao Zedong Thought. The Chinese deny that they are abandoning socialism and giving up the guiding powers of Marxist ideology. They assert that they are building a "commodity economy" as a necessary prelude to achieving socialism and, eventually, Communism. Not all Chinese seem to be clear as to what exactly is meant by the term "commodity economy." Those who do understand take seriously Marx's argument, as expressed in *Das Kapital*, that after the earlier stage of a natural or barter economy, capitalism began with the development of a world market in which commodities were exchanged for money and money for commodities. It was then that profits accrued and capitalism emerged through the workings of the law of surplus value. In the view of the Chinese theorists, the previous attempts under Mao Zedong to move China directly to socialism, and even beyond, must now be seen as gross examples of "leftism" that ignored the laws of Marxism, which require a preliminary state of capitalism. "Socialism with Chinese characteristics" thus means, for the ideologically oriented, that China must develop a "commodity economy" under the leadership of the Party before attempting the jump to socialism.[7]

In the "rectification" campaign of the mid-1980s and in the "anti-bourgeois liberalization" campaign, cadres explained to Party members and others that China is not abandoning the goal of socialism, or eventual Communism, and that the introduction of many features of capitalism is entirely proper. The Chinese are told that amassing profits and welcoming foreign investments are necessary prerequisites for achieving "socialism with Chinese characteristics." Thus, while foreign observers may speak of China's turn to pragmatism, and thereby suggest an abandonment of Marxist-Leninist ideology, the Chinese themselves are insisting that they are steadfast in their commitment to socialism. The "struggle" against "bourgeois liberalism," which Deng has said may last fifty years, should be a reminder to all that China's "Reformers" are not publicly renouncing their Marxist-Leninist persuasions.

At the Thirteenth Party Congress of October, 1987, the leadership came up with a new definition of "socialism with Chinese characteristics." They decreed that China is in the "primary stage of socialism" (*shehui zhuyi chuji jieduan*), and that this stage could last 100 years from the time of the establishment of the People's Republic.[8] Thus, in contrast to Mao Zedong, who at the time of the Great Leap held that China was ahead of all countries in getting to the Promised Land of Communism, the Deng leadership now places China well behind those countries that call themselves "socialist."

All of this is only to say that while many Westerners may think that China has abandoned ideology, many important Chinese still take ideology seriously, and would not agree that the country has pragmatic politics. It might be well to remember how in the 1940s many people misjudged the Chinese Communists and thought of them as only "peasant reformers" because they proclaimed that China was not ready for "communism" (since, according to the laws of Marxism, China had to pass through the phase of a "bourgeois-democratic revolution" before it would be ready for "socialism").

Pragmatism with Lofty Principles

A second qualification we must note is that the Chinese generally insist that they are acting in accordance with "high principles" when others might think that they are being pragmatic. At the very moments when the Chinese are apparently acting quite pragmatically in, say, defending China's interests, they will passionately proclaim that they are on the contrary steadfastly holding to lofty "principles." This practice suggests a Chinese abhorrence of even the idea of pragmatism.

This behavior is seen often in foreign affairs, for example, when the Chinese announce that their demands are based on "principled reasoning" and do not reflect selfish considerations of national interest. The implication is that because their position is "principled" it cannot be changed, while the other party, having only self-interest in mind, can and should defer to the Chinese need to uphold their high principles. If their actual conduct should deviate from their announced principles, Chinese officials will generally close their eyes or look the other way, pretending that it is not happening. If challenged about the gap between practice and principle, they will usually dogmatically reassert their principles and take umbrage that anyone would suggest that they were not acting, as they like to say, "in a principled way."

In other societies, and particularly in the United States, it is customarily believed that having to adhere to high principles works against one's material interests. The assumption is that principled conduct usually inhibits options and makes pragmatic moves more difficult. A moral foreign policy is thus one that places constraints on one's ability to be self-serving. However, when the Chinese refer to "high principles," it is almost always in support of their negotiating position; therefore they expect the other party to give in to their demands. Thus, the Chinese practice of claiming that their policies are "principled" ones, and not self-serving, has the effect of being oddly pragmatic. It would indeed be hard to find examples of the Chinese not seeking pragmatic advantages out of their claims of having "principled" policies.

Symbolism over Substance Makes Feigned Compliance the Norm

A final qualification that one should keep in mind when thinking about Chinese pragmatism is that in Chinese politics there is often quite a gap between words and reality, and therefore it is often difficult to determine whether policies have in fact been carried out or not. The Chinese have a propensity to ascribe reality to symbols; words and slogans often pass in their minds for established facts or accomplishments. The result is that there is often a very large make-believe dimension to Chinese politics. Everyone may agree that a new day has arrived, and that new policies have been successfully carried out, but little may actually have changed. Change, in other words, may often be greater in its description than in its practice.

Lower level officials will report upward what they know their superiors want to hear. Indeed, proclaimed change is often greatest at the most unlikely moment—instantly after a new policy has been announced—for it is then that the lower ranks seek to display alacrity in making the wishes of their leaders a pleasing reality. The consequence is that while the leaders may go along with the shadow play, they also are inclined towards suspicion, and the result is complaints about inertia, tensions, opposition, and calls for ever greater efforts to make sure that the policy is in fact implemented. In time leaders and followers come to accept the pleasant fiction that great things have been accomplished. It is easier to live with shared falsehoods.

Thus the very essence of Chinese pragmatism is at times the acceptance of fictions as reality. The ability to make instant myths is a hallmark of Chinese pragmatism. The realm of words, especially printed words, becomes more real than what otherwise strikes the eye. Western analysts, limited as they all too often are to the printed word about Chinese developments, can only hope that the gap between words and reality is not too great in the areas of their interests. Unfortunately, economists have to rely on the printed word in the very areas where the pressures on subordinates are the greatest to report "facts" that will gratify their superiors.

The Cultural Sources of Exceptional Flexibility

In the previous chapter, in noting the ease with which the Chinese made the transition from Maoism to Dengism, we were pointing to what perhaps is the most distinctive feature of Chinese pragmatism: the remarkable capacity of the Chinese political culture, more than other political cultures, to be flexible and adaptable, to allow leaders to proclaim policy reversals without apologies, and to insure the equanimity of the public in accepting such reversals and new departures. The history of Chinese politics is one of sudden zigs and zags in announced policies. It is not just that new leaders bring new policies, but the individual leaders have no strong obligations to be consistent. Chinese leaders will routinely introduce new policies that totally reverse previous commitments, and everyone goes along with them, not because they say that the national interest calls for particular changes, but because they now claim that the new policy is "correct."

Such exceptional changes in direction are acceptable to the Chinese public above all because they have the stamp of the leader's sincerity—and as we have seen, the Chinese stand in awe of sincerity. The mystique of sincerity is such that Chinese leaders can do much as they please if it is done in the spirit of what might be called sequential convictions, that is, one earnest proclamation of what is correct after another, with no logical connections. Moreover, it is not just the Chinese public that easily accepts such sudden changes in policies and justifies them in principled terms. A surprising proportion of professional China-watchers have been just as prepared to play along and insist on the meritoriousness of every new policy direction of the Chinese, forgetting that they welcomed in the same spirit the quite different previous policies. For some of these observers, no shift in Chinese policies is so swift that they cannot accept the new principles that justify what the Chinese say they are about to do.

The obvious starting point in thinking about this feature of Chinese pragmatism's capacity for justifying reversals is the broadly shared view that Chinese are supreme realists who have a vivid sense of the here and now, and who are quick to adjust their behavior in order to exploit the logic of whatever the situtation is in which they find themselves. Furthermore, in defining their situation, the Chinese tend to treat human relationships in very concrete terms, thus making them a part of substantive reality. Indeed, Chinese generally sense social and political reality so vividly that they believe their perceptions must be shared by everyone except the hopelessly foolish. The demands of realism help to create expectations of conformity and thus reinforce the potency of authority. Indeed, it would be quite wrong to assume that the roots of conformity lie only in fear of state and party sanctions and to ignore the role of social and peer group pressures. The passive spirit of the public reflects a combination of realism and fatalism, a fatalism that tells the public that it can do little to affect politics. The power of Chinese leaders verges on the omnipotent because the masses have so little sense of political efficacy.

Much of the world's astonishment over Chinese behavior during the reign of ideology under Chairman Mao came from the shocking thought that the Chinese might have become romantics and might no longer be the realists they were thought to be. Now, however, the ease with which they have been able to reorient themselves and abandon their Maoist rhetoric is evidence that Chinese have not lost the ability to act according to the circumstances of the moment. It was prudent under Mao to profess ideological convictions, and it is prudent today to march to a different baton.

Many social scientists, starting with Francis L. K. Hsu, have noted that, with regard to social behavior, Chinese believe that it is eminently reasonable for people to conduct themselves according to what makes sense for them in particular circumstances.[9] Therefore, when conditions change, it is only natural that people's behavior and attitudes also change. The conventional explanation for this capacity for adaptability is that Chinese cultural norms tend to be highly particularistic, and therefore people learn early that with different relationships and with changing contexts behavior ought also to change. To a significant degree Chinese culture is spared the tensions (and their potentially psychologically debilitating effects) common in cultures that have more universalistic norms and that require behavior in different situations to be made to appear consistent with absolute principles.

Because of the vividness with which Chinese see the realities of the immediate situation, these realities will often so absorb their attention as to make them insensitive to how much their views may have changed from what they were under different circumstances. Visitors making annual trips to China report that in talking with the same friends they find not only that those friends have changed their positions on many matters, but also that they seem honestly to have forgotten where they stood the previous year. Since there is no virtue in being consistent in Chinese culture and since the imperative task is to understand present realities, a Chinese person's concentration understandably fixes on the immediate situation and he feels free to put out of mind past positions. Nor is there any virtue in being flexible—so nobody will admit to having changed his views.

In terms of economic behavior this characteristic manifests itself in keen sensitivity to market fluctuations. Few peasants in the world would have been able to respond as quickly as the Chinese did to the opportunities offered by the introduction of the responsibility system. The rapidity of the growth of a consumer society in recent years is further testimony to this ability of Chinese to seek their own advantage realistically. The only conspicuous constraints on an almost pure market mentality are, first, pervasive suspicion about being cheated and, second, a propensity to assume that there is stability in the ranking of value of things.

The Chinese's ability to grasp the immediate situation and their keen market mentality sometimes leave the impression that Chinese behavior is largely unaffected by more complex human sensibilities. There seems to be little room for sentimentality, or great anguish over change—as long as it comes about smoothly. People who were devoted worshipers of Mao accept the total abandonment of his policies without rancor and join in praising what is current public policy. It is enough for Chinese to explain the behavior of others in terms of concrete, essentially surface appearances, and they generally feel no need to engage in complex speculations about their own psychological state. Within the political class there is almost no awareness of the rich potential of the human spirit in the realms of aesthetics and religious sensibilities. They dismiss religion as superstition. The this-worldliness of Chinese culture runs far deeper than just the doctrinal materialism of today's cadres.

Scholars, including Max Weber, have, for example, long noted the this-worldly orientation of Chinese religions and their relatively low interest in metaphysical speculation.[10] One should not say, however, that Chinese culture is essentially secular and without religious sensibilities. The Chinese have traditionally been interested in other-worldly matters, especially the activities of ghosts and spirits, and their practicality has often made them wonder about how these invisible forces might help them with the problems of this world. The orientation of popular Chinese religions has been toward asking for help with immediate, concrete problems, such as gaining good luck or fertility.[11] Therefore, neither the Chinese's religious traditions nor their views of human motivations have operated as significant curbs on the Chinese imperative of realism and their market mentality approach.

With respect to political behavior, these characteristics of Chinese culture make sudden changes possible with surprisingly little tension over loyalties to past commitments. Dramatic zigs and zags of policies have been easy to execute in part because the Chinese public takes it as reasonable that with any change in circumstances there should be changes in behavior.[12*] In modern Chinese politics, sudden departures can thus be the norm, not the exception, as leaders and followers have generally been ready to treat any authoritative declaration as establishing the new political realities to which they should respond.

The extreme shifts in Chinese foreign policy, which always represent fine calculations of China's national interests, stand as testimony to the Chinese's sense of reality, unaffected by sentimentality, and to their keen understanding of the current play of power in world affairs. When Chinese analysts describe the state of world politics, the picture they give is extraordinarily mechanistic and reflects the belief that geopolitical reality can be measured with exact scientific precision—this superpower is now on the "offensive," that superpower is on the "defensive," these forces are on the "ascendency," those forces are in a "disadvantaged position." From all this the implicit conclusions for Chinese policies are assumed to be vividly self-evident; the perception of a slight change in the power ratio of the United States and the Soviet Union legitimizes a need for modifications in China's foreign relations.[13]

In domestic politics a few clues as to what is new are usually enough to define an unambiguous reality. Small changes at the top can produce dramatic changes among the rank and file. The political "reality" that Chinese perceive is at times only a symbol or a slogan. Indeed, the Chinese press is capable of making "realism" as much of an abstract symbol as the "utopianism" it denounces.[14*] It is taken for granted by the Chinese leadership that the Chinese public will respond as desired when they are told which key words are positive and which ones negative. There is no need to elaborate the meaning of "seeking truth from facts," but only to repeat the importance of the idea. The use by top leaders of a few code words, such as "spiritual pollution" and "bourgeois liberalism," is enough to send all the necessary signals about reality to Chinese intellectuals. Campaigns can be stopped as abruptly as they were started.

Chinese leaders do not have to cope, for example, with the restraint American politicians have of needing always to appear to be consistent in their views. In American political culture, behavior is supposed to be guided by binding principles, so there is little tolerance for politicians who change their stated positions merely because conditions have changed. Chinese officials often do not understand why others cannot be as flexible as they are in reacting to changing circumstances. For example, over the past few years they have had difficulty comprehending Washington's problems about Taiwan. To Americans the new relations with the People's Republic are welcome, but there are still obligations to old friends. In Beijing's view the logic of the world situation has changed, and thus Washington should make the appropriate adjustments, with only minimal concessions to what Beijing dismisses as some "legacies of history." Chinese officials find Washington's problems incomprehensible because, as pragmatists, they have had no difficulty shifting from being allies of Vietnam, as close as "lips to teeth," to becoming that country's hated foes; they have easily changed from being friends to being enemies of the Soviet Union, and similarly of India; to say nothing of making the dramatic change in their relations with their once arch foe, the United States.

In the same vein, Chinese officials seem surprised that others should be perturbed when Chinese policies are changed in response to new circumstances. Officials professed to be astonished that foreign businessmen's confidence might be shaken by the call for the renegotiation of contracts in mid-1985 because Beijing found it only prudent to tighten the use of foreign exchange after a six-month decline in reserves.

Particularistic Loyalties and the Management of Sentiments

Why is it that old loyalties and the natural inertia of established sentiments do not act as a stronger brake on Chinese pragmatism? Of course, they do cause friction and tensions, but to a surprisingly limited extent.

One explanation for this phenomenon may be found in the distinctive character of *guanxi*, one of the strongest ties of personal relationships in Chinese culture. *Guanxi* seems to be based on the idea that there can be enduring human associations that will survive changing circumstances. The logic of *guanxi* is that people are expected to seek out personal connections precisely when they find themselves in difficulty because of changes in their situation. How are we to reconcile this with the Chinese propensity to follow the logic of the situation to the point of tolerating dramatic changes of loyalties?

The answer to this apparent contradiction lies, first of all, in the fact that *guanxi* is governed largely by objective, rather than subjective, considerations.[15] It is not primarily an emotional bonding of individuals, and it is expected to operate even among relatives who have not known each other and have no warm personal feelings. *Guanxi* does have an affective dimension called *ganqing*; this, however, is not to be confused with deep personal involvement or affection. Rather, it is the affective element that can develop out of the objectively structured *guanxi* relationship.

Guanxi is entirely consistent with an approach that emphasizes the logic of the situation because most *guanxi* ties stem from shared particularistic relationships that have an objective situational context. People who come from the same localities (*tongxiang*), or were classmates (*tongxue*), or served in the same unit (*tongshi*), are expected to have *guanxi*, even though as individuals they may be near strangers. Chinese are usually reluctant to talk about the workings of *guanxi* because they see it as a cultural embarrassment, a feudal remnant, but when they do it turns out to be a surprisingly straightforward, indeed a pragmatic, concept. In any situation everyone should be able to know who has *guanxi* with whom because *guanxi* is less a private relationship than the performing of a role expected of one because of one's past or present situation.[16]

In this sense the Chinese concept of *guanxi* is quite different from either the otherwise analogous Japanese notions of *on* and *giri*, or the Southeast Asian systems of patron-client ties. In the Japanese case, powerful emotional dimensions infuse particularistic relationships with binding feelings of obligation and, indeed, of guilt if the proper response is not made. Similarly, in Southeast Asia, patron-client relationships have strong subjective aspects, and are more private than public matters. The career backgrounds of people would not necessarily provide any hint as to who has ties with whom in, say, Indonesia, Thailand, or the Philippines. But such information will suggest basic relationships in Chinese politics.[17]

The implicit logic of *guanxi* is that the parties to the relationship shared something in the past; it is mere coincidence that one is now in a favored position and the other the dependent. If objective conditions were the other way around, the roles of benefactor and recipient would naturally be reversed. Of course, it usually works out that the benefactor and the dependent remain the same, but the pretense is that there need not be continuity.

Above all, *guanxi* is not based upon a narrow calculus of quid pro quo, as are the Japanese *on-giri* relationship and the Southeast Asian systems of patron-client ties. Obligations are supposed to be reciprocal to some degree. Yet in the Chinese case it is possible for the presently dependent party to ask for repeated favors and to feel that previous acts of benevolence on the part of the more fortunate party will justify a continuing pattern of granting favors even though little has been done in return. He who gives the benefits gains "face," and will be acknowledged by others as behaving respectfully toward the other. Yet he tends also to be the prisoner of his circumstances. Once a relationship has been acknowledged, one can repeatedly employ it by, as the Chinese say, "pulling" *guanxi, la guanxi.*[18] Americans, who operate in the spirit of quid pro quos, are constantly frustrated by the failures of the Chinese, in such areas as cultural exchanges or trade benefits, to reciprocate. The Chinese seem unembarassed to ask for repeated favors without making concessions in return.

In sum, *guanxi* does not inhibit the flexibility of Chinese pragmatism, in part because both accept the logic of the situation and the paramountcy of objective reality.

A second significant reason why the flexibility of Chinese pragmatism is not encumbered by the drag of feelings is that the Chinese can live easily with cognitive dissonance. There is again substantial social science research suggesting that Chinese are relatively unperturbed at having to uphold positions that logic would indicate are mutually inconsistent, and may not experience great inner tensions when belief and fact do not readily coincide. Chinese pragmatism is almost by definition syncretic, based on a readiness to tolerate and accept what others might feel to be irreconcilable doctrines or beliefs.[19]

Tolerance for cognitive dissonance reinforces a third source of the flexibility of Chinese pragmatism: the Chinese ability to simultaneously hold emotions that in other cultures would be taken as incompatible. The Chinese find it relatively easy to maintain simultaneously contradictory sentiments, like the *yin* and the *yang,* or the sweet and the sour, without a blending or a diminution in the intensity of the separate feelings. Nathan Leites identifies several pairs of such apparently contradictory sentiments that Chinese can compartmentalize without allowing either feeling to neutralize or prevail over the other. Let me quote the examples he notes of how Chinese can take as unexceptional the combining of sadness and rage, two sentiments that generally seem to Westerners to be poles apart. " 'Can it be said,' exclaimed somebody imagined by Teng T'o, (one of those who covertly criticized the regime in the early 1960s) 'that God would seal my *resentful* lips and forbid me to utter one or two *sighs.*' 'I am overwhelmed,' observes the fifth century Pao Chao, 'in *sad, resentful* thoughts.' The young man about to commit suicide in *A Peacock Flew* (written between the third and fifth century) is drawn to do so by 'the *grief* that surges in his *boiling* breast,' by 'anger and sorrow mingled,' in a poet's word."[20] One is also reminded of the Chinese expression: "I am so angry I can laugh!"[21]

In Chinese politics this assumption that opposite emotions can endure without a diminishment in the intensity of the feelings or a blending of sentiments facilitates a tolerance for contradictions that often seem to

Westerners to border on the ludicrous. Stuart Schram recently had occasion to cite once again Mao's formulation of July 1957: "We must bring about a political climate which has both centralism and democracy, discipline and freedom, unity of purpose and ease of mind for the individual, which is lively and vigorous."[22]*

Given this feature of Chinese pragmatism, we can expect that the Chinese will make seemingly contradictory pronouncements and will routinely follow policies that others might judge to be irreconcilable. As long as others do not make an issue of it, Beijing seems quite content to display such contradictions as denouncing Israel while seeking out Israeli technical assistance; calling for a "third united front" with the KMT while holding to the right to use force against Taiwan; or, in domestic politics, demanding both more ideological rigidity and greater openness in economic policies. This characteristic, which gives such remarkable flexibility to Chinese pragmatism, could, however, lead to unfortunate misunderstandings. For example, it seems to me quite possible, indeed I would say probable, that Beijing will in the years ahead seek to establish closer relations with both Washington and Moscow, while being relatively insensitive to the dangers of offending the standards of acceptable behavior in two cultures in which there are far narrower limits to tolerance for contradiction. As long as the Chinese feel that they can benefit from more extensive relations with both the United States and the Soviet Union, they will easily convince themselves that it is reasonable and proper to carry on separate but friendly activities with both. Other governments may feel that they have neither permanent friends nor permanent enemies, but only permanent interests. The Chinese government does not seem to have even permanent interests, because so much can change with circumstances; therefore it is not surprising that no nation today is confident it can have comfortable and enduring relations with Beijing.

This tolerance for contradiction in Chinese pragmatism may also produce in China a previously unimagined combination of socialistic and capitalistic practices. Indeed, as Benjamin Schwartz has observed, the Chinese see little reason to become emotional about the relative importance of the public and private sectors of the economy, and therefore they do not share the Westerner's instincts for the partisan struggle over the extent of governmental involvement in economic matters.[23] Chinese pragmatism embraces much that others would see as incongruous and inappropriate.

Plunge In and Then Cope, but Be Cautious

Up to this point our analysis has concentrated on some of the reasons why Chinese pragmatism has such exceptional flexibility. Now we need to turn to the question, what are some of the constraints that may bias Chinese pragmatism and affect the Chinese capacity to be practiced and efficient, and to learn through experience. We can begin by noting a distinctive feature in the relationship between thought and action in Chinese political culture. Whenever the road seems clear there seems to be almost no thought before action, but when there is uncertainty there can be paralysis in action, if not in thought. At times, when the top leader feels free to make decisions, there is an instantaneous response as the whole country plunges in to carry out the leader's wishes. The most extreme examples of this were when Mao plunged ahead with the Great Leap and the Cultural Revolution and when Deng initiated his "reforms." At other times when the leadership seems undecided or divided there can be interminable delays, endless pulling and hauling, and when the decision does come there is likely to be a dragging response. Examples of this are the occasions when the whole leadership gathers for a summer at Lushan or Beidaihe.

It was not just under Mao that China would plunge in one direction and then another. Note the spirited way in which the Chinese opened the doors to let students out of the country to study in the United States, proclaiming that with their new knowledge of science and technology China would soon be making great progress, but then not knowing what to do with the students when they returned to China. Somehow the initiation of the policy was going to solve all problems, and less thought was given to the complex questions as to how the Chinese system could most effectively utilize the people who had been allowed to study abroad. The pragmatic policy of sending students to the West was not a fully thought-through policy, as returning students discovered when they got back to China and there were no detailed plans as to how they could fit back into Chinese society and help the country to benefit from their experiences abroad.

Or, as another example, programs were set up in China with considerable fanfare to provide training in management, but once the degree courses were completed the graduates found that there were no plans for their employment. And in the area of industrial development the examples are too numerous to mention of enterprises plunging into new areas only to discover later that actions had run ahead of plans for either access to resources or the finding of markets.

The general pattern is that when the signal from above is clear subordinates will respond instantly to the perceived wishes of their leaders and thus reflective thought often comes only after compulsive actions. If the leaders seem to want something, that is enough for people to spring into action. Initially the stress is on getting ahead with the job, with only routine but unspecific cautions about not making mistakes. Action is extolled, and it should come first, and only afterward comes the counseling that thought and reflection may be necessary. Initiatives are often triggered with little preparation. The impression is one of plunging in and then coping. The results are prolonged periods of reform and revision, during which there are exhortations for prudence and patience. On these occasions there seems to be little inertia in the system and few problems with procrastination in responding to the initiatives of the top leaders.[24] A central theme of Chinese pragmatism is indeed action. Actions that come from the orders of superiors generally are not sequences of calibrated moves but result, rather, in large swings and sudden reversals in direction.

After mistakes have been made, fear rises among the subordinates. The bureaucracy can become paralyzed. Hesitation characterizes the implementation of the grand plans. But when the leadership sends down new signals, the rank and file is off and going again. It is true that leaders frequently counsel against recklessness, but when their messages are passed downward, the translation invariably stresses action over reflection. Thus, for example, when a commentator in the *Guanming Ribao* sought to explain Premier Zhao Ziyang's admonition in his government work report that people should "take one step and look around before taking another," the moral he came up with was that everyone should first focus on "taking the step, because the sacred duty of Communists is to push forward the wheel of history."[25]

This stress on action, and on the connection between action and thought, was of course central to the concept of pragmatism as expounded by Charles Sanders Peirce, William James, and John Dewey. Traditional Western pragmatism called for learning through action and distrusted the practice of prolonged rumination and speculative deductions before acting. The New England pragmatists were, however, responding to quite a different problem from the one that seems to exist in the current Chinese political culture. Peirce was reacting against what he saw as the paralysis of excessively refined ratiocinations that inhibited decisive actions. Thus he called for more systematic learning through action and by experimentation.[26] In contemporary Chinese political culture, the inherent problem is almost the direct opposite, in that the responses to calls for action come so easily.

Moreover, in the Chinese case it is hard to judge whether they are actually engaging in experimentation. Does the thrusting first in one direction and then in another constitute experimenting, or is it more a frantic search for a way out? It was conventional during the Maoist era to say that the Chinese were "experimenting" as one shift in policy followed another. In retrospect it is hard to say what, if anything, was learned at the time. Even today it is difficult to judge whether the reversals that come with reforms are merely desperate responses to failure or whether they are accompanied by enough reflective analysis to explain what initially went wrong. Deng Xiaoping has on occasion said that his reforms were "experiments," but he has also insisted that China will not "change directions." In June, 1985, he told an Algerian delegation that Shenzhen was "an experiment that might fail" and that "if it fails we can draw lessons from it"; but in July he told the visiting prime minister of Trinidad and Tobago that while his open-door policy had encountered twists and turns and even mistakes, it was a test, and "We must pass the test" without changing directions.[27*]

Unfortunately, the continued secretiveness of the Chinese political system makes it difficult to determine whether, when the leadership seems indecisive and appears to be engaged in "debates," they are actually examining results of policies in an empirical fashion, or merely searching frantically for a solution. Most often they seem to be absorbed with appearances: How will the actions look in terms of the stated ideology? How will outsiders read the proposed actions? How will the cadres interpret any particular decision? Who will be seen as winning and who as losing?

The Imperative of Optimism Places Boundaries on Memory

In Chinese political culture the imperative to be optimistic about the future discourages reflections on the past. Ritualized enthusiasm inhibits pragmatic learning through experience. Few people live as much in the future as people do in China, where most individuals are absorbed in the promises of tomorrow and where modest improvements of the day seem to herald unlimited prospects. This propensity eases the tasks of Chinese leadership; whether due to Mao's ideological promises of what fervent faith could bring or Deng's vision of successful reforms, the result has been the tapping of the wellsprings of Chinese optimism. The imperative to be optimistic reinforces a long-standing tendency in Chinese political culture to avoid critical evaluations of the present by accentuating the horrors of a past that no longer has defenders, and by glorifying a future that all can welcome. Moreover, this perspective on time maximizes the possibilities for ensuring consensus and stifling criticism. The political culture thereby uses hope to turn the pains of the immediate past into balm for legitimizing present conditions, which thus become harbingers of a better future.

The need always to be optimistic prevents Chinese leaders from being as down to earth about the future as pragmatic leaders are expected to be in other cultures. In the West it is an obligation for leaders, as both candidates and office holders, to identify potential troubles ahead and propose possible solutions to avoid disaster. In Chinese political culture any hint by leaders that difficulties may lie ahead is likely to be interpreted by the others as being aggressive criticisms and not objective analysis. Thus Chinese pragmatism must operate largely without the benefit of constructive criticisms about current policies or detailed analyses of past mistakes.

The past is, of course, not forgotten; rather, boundaries are drawn on its memory. The past becomes slogans to be used by the leadership to champion today's issues. As long as the current authorities can confidently control the outer limits of the criticism of the previous era, of the "ten bad years," all the anger at what went on then can only help to legitimize the present leaders.[28*] The fact that Deng suffered during the Cultural Revolution makes the outcries of those who suffered even more a trumpeting of his legitimacy. The disillusioned and the alienated are thus made into defenders of current policies through the uncommon power of Chinese optimism.

More astonishingly, the power of that optimism can trivialize the abominations of the past and legitimize their replication, as when the ritualized denouncing of the imperialist encroachments of the Treaty Port system goes hand in hand with today's establishment of special economic zones, special cities, special stores, and even a special currency for foreigners who clearly have special rights. All such concessions can be justified because the future is supposedly so promising.

This tendency to use optimism to put current problems out of mind and to buoy up with future prospects is a quality that Lu Hsun saw as central to the Chinese national character in his recounting of the simpleminded wishful thinking Ah Q displayed even as he faced execution. This quality is present in Hu Yaobang's February 8, 1985 speech, "On the Party's Journalism Work," in which he says, "If a writer writes something that shows no hopeful future for our society and our people, how can we say that his works conform with the actual course of historical development and that the writer himself has faithfully performed his social duties? . . . We should reflect both the bright and dark sides of things, but the purpose of exposing the dark side is only to educate the people to eliminate it. We have the confidence to eliminate the dark sides in our society, so we should not show gloomy feelings even when writing about the dark side."[29]

The intensity of the up-beat optimism of Chinese political culture is somewhat puzzling in the light of Chinese socialization practices. Chinese children are generally brought up to be extremely sensitive to risks in life and to feel instinctively that the slightest mistake can bring calamity. True, they are also taught that perfection will yield rewards, but the balance is usually more toward avoiding dangers than toward expecting benefits. Children are taught that the margins for error are very narrow indeed, whether they are learning to write Chinese characters or to behave correctly so as not to "lose face."[30]

Possibly, therefore, the hyper-optimism of the Chinese reflects both a need to reassure and a need to repress anxieties about potential failures. It is significant that the Chinese have not reacted strongly to early failures of Party promises, but rather have stressed the physical sufferings associated with the Party's disastrous policies. People's disappointment over national progress has been less important than the personal misfortunes they suffered as a result of those policies. Some grief is expressed over the loss of "ten years" in national modernization, but compared to the outpourings of sympathy for personal suffering there has been a miniscule critical analysis of the continuously faulty performance of the Chinese political and economic systems.

It seems that possibly there has been little real learning about what was actually involved in the failures of recent years. The extraordinarily painful experiences of the past decades are usually summed in the vow "Never again." If one is to believe the horror stories of those who suffered during the Cultural Revolution, a "pragmatic" approach would seem to call for the current leaders to denounce the ideological inspiration of that awful movement. Chinese pragmatism, however, operates according to a contrary set of rules: the leaders manifest a defense of Marxism-Leninism-Mao Zedong Thought and the Four Great Principles while surreptitiously subverting those ideologies. Mere hints that they are doing so is enough to stimulate Chinese optimism that all will soon fall into place for those who are bitter about the price of Mao's ideological demands.

The easy escape route provided by the strand of optimism in Chinese political culture has made it possible for the elite to avoid confronting the obviously troublesome question of what caused all the past failures. Could it really be only the personal failings of a few people? Or was it more fundamental? Something in Chinese culture? Or in Chinese Marxism? The Chinese power holders have not demonstrated that they have engaged in the kind of systematic, critical examination of the past that would be necessary for true learning.

One wonders whether there may not have been more soul-searching about the past than is apparent in Chinese utterances—a fundamental question that needs answering if we are to be able to judge the prospects of Chinese pragmatism. All of the traditional Confucian societies have had problems mastering modernization, in part because of a fundamental sense of cultural superiority over the West. For those that have succeeded it took the trauma of unambiguous defeat and profound national humiliation to clear the way for effective modernization. For Japan it was the catastrophic defeat in the Second World War and the reality of the Occupation that obliterated the warrior tradition, or turned it to other purposes; for the Kuomintang it was the profound humiliation of defeat at the hands of a despised peasant army that compelled them to think through what had been the unthinkable. As with the Germans after their awakening from the dark night of Nazism, the response of these Confucian cultures was to seek spiritual self-reaffirmation through the materialism of economic success.

Has the Cultural Revolution, the "ten bad years," been the equivalent in trauma of what the other Confucian societies experienced from war? One does sense a profound change in mood in China, which hints that this may be so. In the 1970s visitors to Chinese enterprises and institutions were ritualistically asked for criticism: "We want to learn from others." If the foreigner did respond, the Chinese usually became defensive. Today, there seems to be a somewhat more genuine search for advice and suggestions. Any persisting postures of arrogance may be no more than a grasping for respectability.

Behind the continued shield of optimism the Chinese may be less culturally defensive. Yet the evidence is mixed, in no small measure because Chinese culture has never made acceptable the baring of one's soul. The Chinese, as David Shipler has said of the Russians, have " . . . a profound aversion to the Western habit of turning the darkest defects of society into the sunlight for ruthless scrutiny. Our delight in self-criticism, and our guilt when we fail to dissect ourselves with sufficient honesty, bring to [them] something close to visceral revulsion."[31] Chinese do not easily articulate their deeply held sentiments. Chinese cultural norms are anchored in the presumed security of objective group relationships and not in the subjective realm of the individual. As of now, the Chinese literature on the Cultural Revolution lacks the soul-searching, introspective dimension necessary to capture the full tragedy of a people passing through purgatory with all its spiritual and psychological dimensions. Rather, the literature tends to deal with the misfortunes of luckless individuals who have suffered greatly and deserve sympathy. Just because the culture lacks the forms for articulating the shock of profound cultural change, however, does not mean that change has not taken place.

Complaining Rather than Critical Analysis

Another obstacle that makes it difficult for the Chinese to gain the benefits of learning from past mistakes (supposedly a virtue of pragmatism) is the fact that Chinese culture, as we saw in the previous chapter, easily legitimizes complaints about mistreatment by authority while placing strong taboos on any generalized, abstract analysis of the behavior of authority. Chinese political culture makes a sharp distinction between complaining, which is generally permissible, and criticizing, which is not. Harold Isaacs's account of his "reencounters" with Chinese writers and intellectuals who had suffered grievously ever since the Anti-Rightist Campaign of 1957 provides striking testimony to this characteristic of Chinese political culture. In interview after interview with old acquaintances from his early Shanghai days, Isaacs heard such writers as Ding Ling, Mao Dun, and Lin Zunji tell of their personal sufferings, but try as he did, he could not get any one of them to analyze in general terms what went wrong politically and thereby engage in what Westerners would consider to be normal political analysis.[32]

Again we must be careful not to assume that silence means the absence of deeper reflection. Yet if China's leading writers seem unable to engage in even a modest degree of critical analysis with an old friend, it suggests that the outpouring of personalized complaints provides for the Chinese a catharsis that alleviates pent-up demands for deeper criticisms of the significance of their experiences. It should also be acknowledged that some writers are trying to go beyond the limited, surface accounts common to the recent school of the "literature of the wounded" or "scar literature" and to raise more profound issues—as, for example, Ba Jin seems prepared to do in his latest writings.

In Chinese culture, when one rises above complaining one may feel it right to forego criticizing authority. When the Chinese-American journalist and editor Lu Keng, who had been incarcerated in a Chinese Communist prison for twenty-two years, met General Secretary Hu Yaobang in Zhongnanhai, he waved off any sympathy for his suffering by helping out Hu with a Mencius quotation and then dismissing Hu's suggestion that he had "suffered quite a lot," by saying, "Never mind, never mind. That was a great era. During a period of historical change, inevitably some people will suffer some bitterness under certain circumstances."[33] If people who were unjustly jailed for two decades will not criticize what was done to them, why should the authorities worry about injustices in the future?

Monocausal Explanations

Beyond the obligation of optimism and the suspicion that a questioning attitude masks an antagonistic spirit, there are other features of Chinese pragmatism that limit the extent to which the Chinese can learn from experience. There is, for example, the tendency in Chinese pragmatism to settle for single explanations for the complex causes of events. The pragmatic Chinese mind seems to come quickly to rest when presented with monocausal explanations—or at least people do not generally ask for further, more varied interpretations once they have been presented with one that is plausible and authoritative.

For some time after the Cultural Revolution, it was enough to blame all the difficulties on the "Gang of Four" and the "evildoers" who had "infiltrated" the Party and government. The standard explanation for more recent problems has been the appearance of "unhealthy" trends and practices. Morality remains for the Chinese a prime factor in determining policy successes, a point to which we shall have to return when examining the relationship of pragmatism to ethics.

The Chinese practice of settling for single explanations reflects in part a pronounced preference for an orderly scheme of things, for a clear hierarchy of values, and a desire that human relationships be unambiguous so that where people stand on issues can be clearly understood. Multiple explanations suggest confusion and raise anxieties. To open the door to alternative explanations is to tolerate unbecoming controversy. The disinclination to seek ever more complex explanations of events is a way of preserving social harmony and realizing consensus, values that are important in Chinese political culture. To probe for further causes can raise troublesome thoughts and speculation. Because to the Chinese it is not pragmatic to stir up confusion, awkward questions that do not seem relevant to the immediate tasks that need doing are suppressed. However, we should be aware that while people may seem to be satisfied with such simple answers, they may be asking themselves more profound questions. Therefore they may be primed to reject with ease the current version of events and readily accept the new consensus view when it is presented to them.

The Need for Models

Closely related to the Chinese acceptance of monocausal explanations is the surprising persistence of the Confucian belief that people are prone to emulate the good and the successful; if proper models are held up to the public, it is believed, there will be widespread imitation. Chinese pragmatism inclines its adherents toward concentrating on positive examples rather than on problem areas or lagging sectors. The models need not be individual heroes, but can also be successfully developing enterprises or regions. This belief in the merit of models has made it easier to shift from the Maoist stress on equality to the idea that it is permissible for some people and some places to get rich sooner than others. Examples of success can fill the need for proper models.

The exposure of Dazhai, the ideologues' model commune, as having been a fraud did not deter the pragmatists from believing that such special economic zones as that at Shenzhen can provide inspiration for other regions of China, even though Shenzhen, like the now discredited Dazhai, has received more infusions of state resources than any of its potential emulators can hope to get. The Lei Feng of the ideologues has been replicated by the pragmatists Zhang Hua and Zhang Haidi. Realism thus must be supplemented by the appeals of hero worship.

This continuing belief in the power of models suggests that in Chinese pragmatism there is still the traditional Chinese blend of respecting the inherent goodness of the public while insisting that the public needs guidance and direction. Furthermore, the belief in the merit of models implies that the goals of policy can be readily defined in very concrete terms. The desired objectives are thus assumed to be already known by the leadership and there can be little scope for spontaneous developments. The need for leaders to be living models for the people means that they must constantly act as though they have the necessary and correct answers to all problems, and that they are therefore more obliged to "teach" the people than to represent their views. Chinese pragmatism thus becomes more than just a concern for means or procedures; it also includes assumptions about goals and values that go beyond the practical objectives of achieving economic development and national power.

Pride and Pragmatism

This brings us to another dimension of Chinese pragmatism, namely the limits placed on it by the demands of national, if not racial, pride. The goal of Chinese pragmatism is not just to be practical and realize immediate objectives by whatever means are available. What is to be done must satisfy the requirements of collective pride; it must make others respect and admire China. Consequently, Chinese pragmatism sets standards for being "the best," not just practical.

At present, among those who are considered to be the most pragmatic are many who want China to gain the most advanced technologies and move to the forefront of electronics and biotechnology. Key Politbureau and Central Committee members have read Alvin Toffler's *The Third Wave*, and they believe that while China missed out on the first two great technological revolutions described by Toffler, the country can skip over them and move to the top in the current information revolution.[34] Paradoxically, some members of the Chinese Academy of the Social Sciences who concur still insist that China needs to build a "commodity economy" because it is impossible to leapfrog Marx's stages of development.

In this same vein Deng Xiaoping for a long time repeatedly protested that Washington was holding back on transferring to China the most advanced technologies. Similarly, we have numerous examples of the Chinese complaining about joint ventures that have not brought to them the most advanced technologies, even though the lesser technologies might have generated more employment than the "best" would have done.

One might have thought that in China's situation pragmatism would have called for labor intensive rather than capital intensive technologies, but the opposite has been the case. This discounting of the trade-offs between labor and capital because of considerations of prestige raises some questions about Mark Elvin's eminently reasonable theory that China failed to develop technological skills because her early growth in population made it more rational to rely upon manpower than to invent more efficient machines.[35] Could it have been that cultural pride historically also placed limits on pragmatism, making the Chinese prematurely self-satisfied with their technology, just as such pride now demands the most "advanced" rather than the most practical?

The limits to pragmatism set by this concern for the "best" are quite firm because they stem from Chinese sensitivity about "losing face." Historically, as Joseph Levenson and others have pointed out, the Chinese tried to cushion their acceptance of foreign ways by insisting that they could preserve their superior values while adopting only techniques from the West.[36] This *ti-yong* formula is still apparent today when the Chinese speak of keeping out the "bad features," the "spiritual pollution," of Western societies—as though China never had its own bawdy tradition. (Maybe the guardians of Chinese morals are befuddled because for so long they have used the euphemism of "earthy" to describe the vocabulary of their sainted Chairman.)

There are, however, problems for the Chinese pragmatists in still using the *ti-yong* rationalization. The basic values they would now protect are no longer pure Chinese ones; instead they are part of a foreign import, socialism in its Marxist-Leninist form. True, the Chinese have modified the import, but what remains is hardly something to be protected from foreign contamination. Indeed, the very goal of Chinese pragmatism has become confused as leaders speak of building "socialism with Chinese characteristics" without specifying what they now consider to be either "socialism" or "Chinese characteristics." The target is for China to catch up with the advanced industrial countries some time in the next century, but there is almost total silence as to what will still be distinctively "Chinese" about that desired state. Thus, in a peculiar historical reversal the Chinese now find that their pragmatism makes it easier for them to describe which foreign practices they wish to emulate than to spell out the Chinese values that they still claim are precious to them.

There is a second, more awkward reason why it is psychologically more difficult for the Chinese pragmatists of today to use the old Chinese formula of taking the techniques of despised foreigners while preserving the higher values of a superior Chinese civilization. In the nineteenth century the challenge came only from the West, the unambiguous source of a higher technological civilization; today, however, Chinese pragmatists looking for "the best" must take into account Asian neighbors whom the Chinese have always looked down upon. It is no longer possible for knowledgeable Chinese to ignore the fact that it is not just Japan but also Korea, Singapore, Taiwan, and even Thailand and Malaysia that have moved ahead of them in pursuit of the modernization that is the main goal of Chinese pragmatism.

Thus there is a fundamental ambivalence in Chinese pragmatism. In "seeking truth from facts," the Chinese should be ready to learn from their more immediate neighbors, but it would be humiliating to admit to doing so. The successes of South Korea, Thailand, and Malaysia are more relevant than those of the city states of Hong Kong and Singapore, but the latter are "Chinese" and hence fit the ideal of Chinese superiority. Taiwan presents an awkward problem because, while it is manifestly the most "Chinese" of them all, it has been ruled by what Beijing has long called the worst rulers in all of history. Therefore Beijing must act surreptitiously, and at the same time try to take ever greater shortcuts to an even higher domain of technology. Pretending to ignore the experience of their neighbors, they look optimistically to the day in the next century when they will be the equals of the most advanced industrial societies. They believe the goal to be realistic because they tend to place great store in what can be accomplished by human effort, when inspired by exhortation and moral persuasion. Although Chinese pragmatists recognize the need for some material incentives, they still have more than a bit of the ideologues' belief in the powers of moral persuasion and nationalist appeals for sacrifice.

Single-Mindedness

Although Chinese have a high tolerance for cognitive dissonance with respect to beliefs and theories, when it comes to action they prefer situations in which they can pursue unambiguous goals and act according to clearly set priorities. The culture highly values single-mindedness. When situations develop in which it is no longer appropriate to act single-mindedly the result can be a level of anxiety that compromises effective pragmatic behavior. At times this can create the expectation that when one state of affairs breaks down it is likely to be replaced by its extreme opposite. The "crisis of faith" of the late 1970s and early 1980s was in part stimulated by this cultural view that the alternative to pervasive political passions has to be political apathy, and that concern for private interests and professional development has to conflict with ideological orientations. Stanley Rosen has vividly described the dilemmas and tensions both Chinese youth and leadership of the

Communist Youth League faced in the post-Cultural Revolutionary atmosphere because they all assumed that only one of the two opposites could exist.[37]

Although the Chinese have consistently admired the generalist with multiple skills, whether it be the Confucian mandarin or the Communist cadre, they also seem to believe that success in almost any endeavor calls for total concentration and a focusing of all energies on the task at hand. It is taken for granted that anyone who has achieved greatness in any activity, such as in science or engineering, will not have many other interests. In more pluralistic cultures it is accepted that a person can be a successful scientist and have other dimensions to his life, including political and religious identifications. In Western cultures there was once great tension between science and religion because of intolerance for cognitive dissonance, but once the issue was worked out (or maybe more correctly, worked to death) it became possible for the individual scientist to follow his religious preferences without being questioned by others. In China the problem has not been one of having to resolve deep inconsistencies or contradictions; rather, the notion that excellence can only come with single-mindedness has resulted in a tendency to categorize people—so that, for example, they are seen as either "red" or "expert."

The belief that individual excellence calls for single-mindedness does get translated into the idea that the whole nation should focus its energies into limited channels. This means that Chinese pragmatism is severely limited in the diversity of policies or approaches it can follow at any time. It is assumed that all attention should be focused on only a limited range of public matters. Any attempt to expand the boundaries of concern can be easily treated as not just diluting policy priorities but actually subverting the national effort, for to compromise single-mindedness is essentially an immoral, irresponsible act. The fear of the introduction into China of the "bad features" of Western culture is heightened by this sense that anything that reduces single-mindedness and causes diversions of attention is an abomination.

Singlemindedness involves concentrating on present realities and not on transcendental principles. Mao's parable of "The Foolish Old Man and the Mountain" was an attempt to make Chinese change their propensity to shift the focus of their single-mindedness with every change in circumstances. The failure of Mao's teaching has left the Chinese with their distinctive blend of rigidities and flexibilities that often makes change easy but places severe limitations on their version of pragmatism.

The Uneasy Relationships with Ethics

This brings us to another restraint on Chinese pragmatism, the traditional Chinese imperative that power should always be cloaked in moral or ethical rationalizations. The denial of moral constraints on getting the job done is, of course, the hallmark of pragmatism in all cultures, for the unspoken rule of pragmatism is that the end will somehow justify all that was required to realize it. Current Chinese pragmatism would seem to be within the tradition as it discards the ideological and moralistic tenets of Maoism. Indeed, the ideal of equality is sneered at, and there is near boasting that some people and some places will get richer sooner than others.

Yet in Chinese political culture there has always been the pretense, if not the reality, that legitimacy is based on a claim to moral superiority. Chinese pragmatists would like to shed such ideological concerns and direct political attention to what needs to be accomplished. Yet the risks for legitimacy are too great. As a simple, practical matter it is easier for rulers to justify their authority by claiming moral or ideological superiority over the people than by actually delivering successful policies. Even for a nation of gamblers, the risks of abandoning the pretense of a virtuocracy in favor of legitimacy based on successful policies is too great. Thus, a need for compromise. The promises of pragmatism are not adequate for a very practical task.

But what are, or will be, the terms of such a compromise? There are no absolutes, no minimum requirements, no popular norms that would set even minimal limits on the scope of effective pragmatism. For Chinese pragmatism, the need to yield to ethical-normative considerations comes largely from a sense that pragmatic solutions may falter and that it is therefore prudent to reinforce legitimacy by asserting the moral superiority of a Marxist-Leninist form of socialism. Thus, right from the start constraints are placed on pragmatism, and lip service, at least, must be paid to a nonpragmatic basis of legitimacy.

This means that Chinese pragmatism will be constantly vulnerable to the intrusion of ideological constraints, not just from its political opponents but even more from its own need to insure that legitimacy will not depend solely upon practical accomplishments. The suppression of the "democracy movement," the checks on writers and journalists, and the opposition to the development of political science and other liberal arts disciplines in the universities should not be read as signs of the persisting power of "leftist" Maoists.[38] The most pragmatic of the pragmatists knows that authority in China continues to need the support of a substantial dose of ideological faith, and hence severe limits must be placed on skepticism about Marxism-Leninism-Mao Zedong Thought. Thus the institutional framework of Leninism is likely to endure with less alteration than might be expected of a system that otherwise has so much pragmatic flexibility. This basic need to hold on to the structural characteristics of a Leninist system will in turn produce constraints on the development of Chinese pragmatism.

The relationship between Leninism and flexibility is paradoxical. As the guide to the "operational weapon" for gaining power, Leninism is unsurpassed, because it is a doctrine that allows for great tactical flexibility. Anything that can provide the means to the end of power is acceptable in Leninism. Yet once in power, Leninism, with its stress on the absolute need for correctness, becomes a rigid doctrine, and hence puts an end to pragmatism.

The Iron Grip of Patriotism

Possibly the most severe constraint on the flexibility of the Chinese's pragmatism is their passion of patriotism, which is especially strong among Chinese intellectuals. Ever since the May Fourth Movement, members of the Chinese educated classes have operated in an atmosphere of pervasive nationalism. Their belief in the need to make sacrifices for the country is translated in practice into repressing open criticism and conforming to the political consensus of the day. Patriotism becomes the championing of national unity, which in turn often becomes support for orthodoxy.

Thus the introduction of pragmatically conceived policies can easily produce a spirit of passive acceptance by those who are qualified to appraise what is being proposed. The very people who might be expected to suggest improvements or alternatives to official policies feel inhibited because of the fear of not appearing to be properly patriotic. Patriotism thus reinforces a dependency upon authority among the people trained supposedly to assert autonomy.[39] Chinese intellectuals both in the past and today would reject, without understanding its meaning, George Bernard Shaw's point that, "Patriotism is a pernicious, psychopathic form of idiocy," although their behavior gives Shaw's aphorism more than the ordinary gloss of truth. Even as apparently wise a man as Liu Binyan, when sent down to a poverty-stricken village from 1958 to 1960, had to struggle in his inner thoughts with the possibility that the "higher authorities" might not have the "truth" when they tried to make his villagers, who hardly ate meat all year, build a zoo for lions and tigers, and construct a huge fountain in a place with no water except what the rain brought. His sense of patriotism and loyalty to the Party made it impossible for him to recognize manifest idiocy when it confronted him and his fellow villagers for nearly two years. His "struggle" was only resolved when the Party Central issued in 1960 its "Twelve Points on Rural Policy," which said it was right to "uphold the interests of peasants."[40]

Chinese intellectuals are not only powerless in criticizing policies; they also seem unable to engage in the usual intellectual activity of pointing up weaknesses and flaws in their society and culture. This is especially surprising since one would have thought that many aspiring intellectuals would have realized that the handful of China's most distinguished intellectuals achieved their prominence precisely because they excelled at bringing attention to blemishes in Chinese character. The fame of Kang Youwei and Liang Qichao, of Lu Xun, and of Bo Yang's The Ugly Chinaman today, stem from those individuals' clear-eyed and satirical criticisms of the Chinese national character. Yet the very fact that these are all seen as exceptional people tells a great deal about the inhibitions of the great majority of Chinese intellectuals.

Patriotism furthermore seems to gag the voices of Chinese intellectuals and leaves them mute because they are so easily overwhelmed with fear that anything they might write will bring discredit to China's international reputation. The faults that they can expose become only trivial ones, the failings of individuals. There can be no serious analysis of the failings of the system as a whole. It does not seem to cross the Chinese intellectuals' minds that by appearing to be blind to their failings they may be the cause of distress among knowledgeable "foreigners."

The leaders themselves are also prisoners of the conformity of this spirit of patriotism. That is, in advancing policies they have to make it appear as though what is being proposed is vital for the national interest. It would seem frivolous for them to suggest that their proposed policies reflect no more than hypotheses about what is appropriate and may be altered in response to experience. As a consequence, both the advocates and the best informed potential critics of policies feel inhibited by the demands of patriotism from treating public policy as a really pragmatic matter. Deng Xiaoping can pay lip service to the idea that his policies are merely experimental, and thus reduce his sense of responsibility, but everyone else must respond in a more gingerly way, treating policies as having the sacred dimensions Chinese associate with patriotism.

The Potentials and the Limits of Chinese Pragmatism

In conclusion let us repeat that Chinese pragmatism has great potential but that it is also circumscribed by severe constraints. Chinese pragmatism benefits from cultural predispositions that make behavior guided by the logic of the existing circumstances totally acceptable, and that allow for unsentimental abandonment of past commitments and outdated rationalizations. The culture fuels pragmatic motives by emphasizing the here and now. Optimism about future prospects is more respectable than the articulation of doubts and negativism. History can be used for present purposes but need not be a checkrein on current practices. Leaders do not need to fear being penalized for being inconsistent, for contradictions are easily tolerated.

The very flexibility of Chinese pragmatism can at times raise problems, particularly in foreign relations, as the agility of Chinese leaders can leave the more cautious and ponderous American (and Soviet) decision-making processes a step or two behind. The more sluggish superpowers, with their hard-to-change fixed ideas, are thus frequently left trying to gear their policies to outdated Chinese realities—as when American officials persisted in believing that Beijing was obsessed with the "polar bear" or when they repeatedly misjudged exactly how "open" China's "door" is at any moment. For China the result is a high degree of continued isolation in foreign affairs, whether desired or not.

However, there are boundaries that constrain Chinese pragmatism. Questions of pride, "face," and the continuing need for an ethical basis of legitimacy all conspire to limit Chinese pragmatism. Equally critical is the fact that the features of the culture that support aspects of pragmatism—such as a tolerance for cognitive dissonance and the avoidance of introspection—can stifle the realization of the full potential of pragmatism, particularly the possibility of learning through systematic experimentation. And, of course, there is our initial qualification that the Chinese have a distinctive capacity to create a world of make-believe, and to manipulate illusions rather than substance. Shifts in policy often take the form of abandoning one illusory world in favor of another. Skill at feigned compliance makes it possible for leaders and followers to go along with collective pretenses.

Yet it is possible to draw some general conclusions as to how the characteristics of Chinese pragmatism are likely to affect political developments in the years ahead. It is reasonable to expect that in practice Chinese policies can make substantial swings without creating anxieties about these policies' contradictions with stated programs. "Adjustments" and "reforms" can be routinely announced and accepted even though they may seem to the non-Chinese mind to be substantial changes. Great emotional investments in the relative priorities among public policies are not likely. In the spirit of Chinese pragmatism, government officials can announce that new circumstances call for new departures without fear of being criticized for inconsistency. Rigidity and flexibility will be governed above all by the criteria of "convenience" as seen by the authorities. A few examples of success, including government-subsidized "models," will be enough to herald the arrival of the new day.

The high priority given to the here and now in Chinese pragmatism means that immediate, and therefore somewhat narrow, calculations of national interest will prevail over the building of more enduring relations in foreign affairs. Although the distinction between friend and foe remains as vivid in Chinese pragmatism as it did in China's ideologically oriented politics, it will be easy to change the labels, particularly since the emotional commitments will not be as intense as when moralistic ideology prevailed. The Chinese are likely to be as wary in evaluating their cost-benefits in their relations with their "friends" as with anyone else. At the same time, Chinese pragmatism will continue to attach importance to symbolism, and therefore fine judgments will be made about how particular relationships are "improving" or "retrogressing," when little of substance has changed.

Key characteristics of Chinese pragmatism will make the problems of legitimacy increasingly difficult. Deng's successor will have even less chance than Mao's successor did of getting away with anointment from beyond the grave. His successor could not possibly hope to gain a meaningful mandate by claiming that Deng had said of him that, "With you in charge, I am at ease." If a blend of moderate policy successes and a compromised ideological tradition are not enough to ensure the successors' political security, the likely alternative will be increased institutional repression. While there is nothing in Chinese pragmatism that makes political liberalism a desired value, political tolerance is perfectly acceptable so long as it causes no "inconvenience" for the authorities.

The most critical question for the future is likely to be the relationship between Chinese national pride and Chinese pragmatism. Will Chinese nationalism prevent Chinese pragmatism from realizing its full potential, or will it be a motive force driving Chinese pragmatism to otherwise unattainable goals? Will pride impede or inspire what is practical? The answer, of course, lies in the conundrum that is the "Chinese revolution," which is nothing more than China's road to modernization, the subject that remains the central concern for all scholars concerned with contemporary China.

CHAPTER IV

REASSESSING THE CULTURAL REVOLUTION

Two decades after Mao Zedong ignited the Great Proletarian Revolution there is still no satisfactory accounting for the upheaval that Beijing now says caused millions of deaths and left some 100 million people scarred victims.[1] Ordinary imagination cannot grasp what took place during those "ten bad years of great disaster" (*shinian haojie*) as the Chinese now call them. Since so much at that time defied conventional theories of politics, outsiders quickly put the phenomenon out of mind once the turmoil ceased. For the Chinese, however, it has not been so simple. Those who personally suffered have tended to summarize the story according to their individual tragedies. Chinese seeking a larger perspective are caught between the inexplicableness of its causes and the incalculability of its consequences. Time has not made it easier to assess the Cultural Revolution. Partly because it was such a multidimensional event, touching people in so many different ways, no established form of analysis is capable of embracing its totality. According to the current Chinese version of the Cultural Revolution, there was no institution in the country, from the family and the school to the party and the government, that was not profoundly affected. Authorities today can attribute to those horrendous events the woes and failings of China, and they will suggest, whenever convenient, the frightful thought that without their leadership there could be another Cultural Revolution.

In looking back now and reassessing the Cultural Revolution, scholars must acknowledge that even as we have strived for historical objectivity, we have been decisively influenced, then and now, by what the Chinese have had to say about that event. Twenty years ago pictures of impassioned Red Guards marching across Tienanmen Square, waving their Little Red Books to the Chairman-author, were taken as proof that Mao's dream of an ideologically purer generation of revolutionaries might be in the making. Contradictory testimony of violence in offices, schools and workplaces, and evidence of the suffering of people sent to the countryside, were not entirely ignored, but they were frequently downplayed and treated, as the Chinese said they should be, as merely a part of the inevitable cost of revolutionary progress. Many scholars of China were not taken in by Beijing's claims of technological innovation by uneducated workers or of miraculous economic achievements, but there were not many either who publicly called such claims hogwash or pointed to the disaster that was Chinese society. Even more inexcusable was the number of supposedly sophisticated analysts who were as gullible as the naive Red Guards in believing that Mao's dictums in practice would actually work to favor peasants and reduce inequalities in Chinese society. Simon Leys, along with other critics, has reminded us of the foolish views of some foreign observers.[2] Intellectuals, whose obligation is to be doubters, should have seen through Mao's equalitarian rhetoric and recognized the inevitable consequences of his policies.

Therefore, in the light of what happened before, we should be cautious about going along with the official Chinese view that there are no redeeming features to that period. Any serious reassessment must try to get behind the political rhetoric of the day—even if it means having to be skeptical about one's own best wishes for China. This is particularly the case because the Chinese have failed to confront in an honest, self-critical way the psychological and sociological roots of the extraordinary mass behavior of that period. Few societies in history have acted as the Chinese did during the Cultural Revolution. In countless other countries governments have done abominable things to their subjects, but what was unique in the Cultural Revolution was that the Chinese government largely stood aside and applauded as its citizens went at each other, both verbally and physically, in an orgy of violence. The Chinese, however, are not as yet ready to examine critically their own conduct, and therefore it will for a time fall to foreigners to try to analyze the psychodynamics of such abnormal behavior. Moreover, the regime has imposed censorship upon the few intellectuals who are ready to ask troublesome questions about Chinese character and the Cultural Revolution.

The problem of assessing today the realities of the Cultural Revolution is made extremely difficult because of the Chinese practice, which we have already noted, of painting the past in the darkest possible terms so as to make the present more acceptable and the future more glowing. The regime of Deng Xiaoping has not only legitimized but actually encouraged complaining about personal suffering at the hands of the Red Guards and from the consequences of "leftist errors" of policy. Just as right after the Communists came to power people were called upon to tell pitiful stories about how awful life had been before "Liberation," so in the early 1980s people were urged to tell of their grievous mistreatment during the Cultural Revolution. Given all the wailing and lamentation it is hard to arrive at solid facts.

The problem is further complicated by an interesting twist in the official designation as to when the Cultural Revolution actually took place. Western observers have commonly assumed that the Cultural Revolution ran from 1966 to 1969, the year when Mao withdrew his blessings from the Red Guards and passed out his mangoes to those designated to bring stability to the country through the "revolutionary committees," and the Soviet threat came to a danger point with the border clashes. The Deng leadership, however, has stretched out the Cultural Revolution period so as to include the entire time from 1966 to the fall of the Gang of Four in 1976. Hence their designation of the "ten bad years of great disaster." What is of interest is that the Chinese stories of complaining show no indication of any difference in their suffering before and after 1969, the year that outsiders believed there was a change. Indeed, when the Chinese intellectuals get going on their sorrowful tales it is standard for them to take their accounts of mistreatment back to 1958 and the Anti-Rightist movement. The current leadership quite naturally wants to accentuate the differences between their China and that of the last days of Mao's rule. The readiness of so many Chinese to come forward with reports of being victimized leaves us with more than a casual suspicion that if it should ever become legitimate to decry the entire period of Mao's rule there would be plenty of Chinese who would cooperate with accounts of personal sufferings over the entire period. For whatever time period the authorities legitimize complaining, there will be Chinese to come forward with wailing lamentations.

However, looking at the other side of this problem, there must be in China today many people, indeed very many, who found the Cultural Revolution to their satisfaction but who dare not open their mouths today. It is not just that there must have been bullies who enjoyed victimizing the defenseless, but there must also have been untold numbers of opportunists who rejoiced at the chances to exploit near anarchy for their own personal benefit. Also there must have been some idealists who actually believed in the revolution. Maybe today they resent the ease with which they were manipulated, but in seeking self-respect they must still cling to the thought that there had to be some merit in their dreams of a better society.

Another problem that makes it hard to get an objective picture of the Cultural Revolution is that those who were most hurt by it are the most articulate elements of Chinese society—writers, intellectuals, party members—and they are also the people who for a time in the early 1980s were the most honored by the regime and hence the most free to speak out. Large segments of Chinese society were far less touched, and are now mute. The Cultural Revolution did not to any great extent disrupt life in the factories or in the rural areas. The peasants were far more seriously damaged during the Great Leap and the years of famine that followed. Indeed, we now know that the famine of 1960-62 caused the deaths of more Chinese than any famine in modern history, and it is probable that it will be proved to have been the worst in all of human history. Except for the fact that peasants had to welcome into their midst sent-down "Rightists" and rusticating youths, the Cultural Revolution did not greatly upset peasant society. Although Mao thought that the people sent down should "learn from the peasants," no peasant thought that he was being elevated to the rank of "teacher." Generally the peasants and the sent-down people kept their distance from each other. No doubt many peasants took considerable delight in the thought that so many intellectuals believed that they were enduring almost unbearable suffering by having to live the life of peasants. (Ding Ling publicly declared that she suffered more while living on a farm than during three years of solitary confinement, because in prison she was kept warm, had regular meals prepared for her, and could read all day the works of Chairman Mao.) We are not likely ever to recapture the views of the peasants on the Cultural Revolution, if for no other reason than that they are now far too busy rejoicing over their good fortunes with Deng's policies and they certainly must want to put out of mind all memories of how they fared under Mao's rule. As we have already noted, one of the strangest myths that has grown up in the telling of modern Chinese history is that Mao was a friend of China's peasants, understood them, and came to power through their help. His armies were, of course, "peasant armies," but then all armies in China were peasant armies, for in a population that is still 85 percent peasants, where else would soldiers come from except the countryside?

In short, it is still far too early for us to have heard the full story of the human dimensions of the Cultural Revolution.

With these qualifications in mind, let us turn to three subjects that belong at the center of any systematic reassessment of the Cultural Revolution. The first is the question of causes and origins. What have we learned that is new about how it all began? And at a deeper level of analysis, what can we now say in trying to explain how Chinese society could possibly have produced such a convolution?

Next we need to reassess how individuals experienced the Cultural Revolution. What do we no know about their personal crises that can help us reevaluate the Cultural Revolution? What has been the lasting state of mind and spirit of the survivors, both victims and victimizers? Finally, there is the summarizing question of the impact of the Cultural Revolution on the major institutions of Chinese society. What can we now say are the likely lasting effects of that period of turmoil on the key institutions that will determine the future shape of China's government, economy, and society?

High Marks on Immediate Causes, Low Ones on Fundamental Causes

From the perspective of twenty years after the events it seems that Western scholars analyzing the situation at the time, guided in no small measure by Chinese pronouncements and analyses, deserve high marks for understanding the immediate political and ideological causes of the Cultural Revolution, to the extent that these can be traced to the political elite. The meeting ground of journalists, government analysts, and academics was an almost collegial effort to examine the elite level of Chinese political action that encompasses mainly the motives and calculations of the day-to-day political interactions of the Chinese leaders. We seemed to be able quickly to penetrate the confusion and to sort out who was doing what to whom. Missing then, and still largely unexplored to this day, were examinations of the deeper cultural and societal forces that made possible such a unique phenomenon. To this day speculation about fundamental causes of the Cultural Revolution has not gone much beyond the rather superficial interpretations of the Chinese themselves.

Chinese officials have not been reticent about speaking out regarding the troubles they trace to the Cultural Revolution; indeed they generally lump together all the mistakes of Mao's rule and say they were a part of the terrible time when reckless attacks were mounted against the "capitalist roaders in the Party" who were supposed champions of "revisionism." There have, however, been very few official revelations about either the causes or the motivations behind these evil episodes. The most authoritative statement from Beijing was the resolution of the Sixth Plenum of the Eleventh Central Committee of June 27, 1981 entitled "On Questions of Party History." That resolution went far in pointing the finger at Mao, sacred figure though he was, saying that the Cultural Revolution was " . . . initiated and led by Comrade Mao Zedong." Moreover, the indictment held that "Comrade Mao Zedong's prestige reached a peak and he began to get arrogant. . . . He gradually divorced himself from practice and from the masses, acted more and more arbitrarily and subjectively, and increasingly put himself above the Central Committee of the Party." Mao's "Left errors" opened the way for "Lin Biao, Jiang Qing, Kang Sheng, Zhang Chunqiao and others . . . to exploit the situation" so that "The Ninth Congress of the Party legitimized the erroneous theories and practices of the 'cultural revolution.' "[3]

Although the resolution surprised the Chinese public for bluntly criticizing Mao, it also sought to protect his memory by saying that "Comrade Mao Zedong was a great proletarian revolutionary, strategist and theorist." In spite of the "gross mistakes" Mao made during the Cultural Revolution, "his contributions to the Chinese revolution far outweigh his mistakes. His merits are primary and his errors secondary." On the other hand, the official formula that the failings of the late Mao were more than offset by the accomplishments of the early Mao is not particularly convincing, because China today follows very few of the early Mao's policies. No explanations are given for why the government has abandoned everything associated with what it claims were the positive contributions of the early, or good, Mao and why it follows instead, at least in foreign affairs, policies introduced in the very last years of Mao's rule.

The Chinese have provided only a few revelations that will result in some adjustments in our earlier, conventional interpretations of the immediate political causes of the Cultural Revolution. No doubt, mysteries about certain details will be cleared up in time and we may get a better understanding of, say, Peng Zhen's and Kang Sheng's roles in the early group of five, or Lo Ruiqing's disappearance. We may learn the answer to such questions as whether Deng was "waving a red flag to oppose the red flag" when he made his militant pro-Mao speeches.

And, of course, there is still much to be learned about the Lin Biao affair. Of course, scholarly debates will continue over such questions as the relative importance of policy choices and Mao's personal arrogance, or the significance of this or that action, and precisely where different actors stood at different stages of the upheaval. Tidbits of information may clear up some points, but also produce new debates. Roderick MacFarquhar has, for example, argued in the second volume of his planned trilogy, *The Origins of the Cultural Revolution*, that the conventional view that Mao ignited the Cultural Revolution by urging Yao Wenyuan to criticize Wu Han's play, *Hai Ruil's Dismissal from Office*, is probably a "red herring"; MacFarquhar has unearthed evidence that Mao himself had just previously made an off-hand remark about Hai Jui's virtues.[4] So far most historians are staying with the conventional judgment. MacFarquhar seems to be on solid ground, however, in suspecting that the interpretation of the Cultural Revolution as essentially a struggle between "two lines" is probably incorrect, because at the beginning both Liu Shaoqi and Deng Xiaoping were still obedient followers of the Chairman. However, until MacFarquhar completes the third volume of his trilogy we are not likely to have explanations that go much beyond the shelf of books that came out soon after the event.

These works in varying degrees attributed the Cultural Revolution to such factors as Mao's personality, factional conflicts over policies, succession power struggles, the appeals of revolutionary utopianism, and the organizational problems inherent in governing a country of China's size and stage of development. Thus, for example, Lifton found motivations for the Cultural Revolution in Mao's personality, while Solomon singled out the tensions between Mao's motivations and Chinese traditional political culture.[5] Subsequent biographers who have had the advantages of greater access to Chinese sources—such as Bloodworth, Hollingworth, and Terrill—have been able to enrich their accounts with anecdotes and gossip, but they have added little that explains Mao's behavior.[6] Similarly, the early works of Bridgham, Karnow, and Rice clearly identified issues in the elite conflicts, while later works such as Liu's have added details, but not enough to alter the basic interpretations significantly.[7] Early works that stressed policy issues, such as those by Ahn, Chang, Dittmer, Domes, and Lee, have stood the test of time.[8]

Thus, China specialists deserve congratulations on their early interpretations of the immediate causes of the Cultural Revolution. Interestingly, the strength of that early research was its empirical substance and not its methodological sophistication. This is paradoxical, because in the confusion of the times solid facts were hard to come by, and loose speculation would have been easier. The intense effort at the time to get the story straight, in the tradition of sound journalism or government reporting, produced two interesting contradictions.

First, there was a tendency to take seriously all that was said and done by the leaders, with the result that rhetoric about goals or purposes was considered to represent the real motivations of the major actors. Presumed subjective differences automatically became objective differences in policy preferences. Thus any distinctions between the suspected wishes or preferences of various Chinese leaders became the unquestioned motives of their actions, and hence the "causes" of the Cultural Revolution. This was a striking reversal of the normal academic practice of giving priority to objective rather than subjective considerations in explaining historical events. The belief that we *knew* the motives and desires of Mao and all the others may have come from the fact that the Cultural Revolution was such a manifestly emotional event that subjective considerations seemed properly to deserve considerable legitimacy in explaining what was taking place. Yet at the same time most scholars shied away from explicit psychological interpretations of the presumed motives. Instead, they practiced a questionable methodological legerdemain: they transformed their speculations about motives into statements about policy preferences, which they then treated as having all the qualities of objective reality. What was subjective and psychological was thus dramatically reified and thereby transported to the more comfortable domain of presumed hard data, appropriate for objective analysis. Largely ignored was the basic truth that politics is a process infused with deception, especially about motives and preferences. Authors would casually write that "Mao believed . . . ," "Mao thought . . . ," "Mao was troubled that . . . ," and then presumably engage in some form of unspecified depth psychology that made it possible for them to come up with valid interpretations of motives. Shockingly, they would at best pin their judgments of motives on nothing more than something Mao had said. No Chinese leader would be so naive as to ignore that in politics words are cheap, and are used to disguise motives. As risky as this practice would seem to be methodologically, it did produce surprisingly solid works of scholarship.

The second striking characteristic of the literature on the causes of the Cultural Revolution is that it focused narrowly on immediate considerations and very little on more profound questions about social and political causation. Explanations largely remained at the level of trying to figure out the wishes and personal politics of the leaders and the passions of young people in particular. Few scholars asked deeper questions about why Chinese society as a whole reacted in such extreme ways to the initiatives of a small group of leaders. The operating assumption of most scholars seems to have been that the Chinese people are so politically sheep-like that they would docilely do whatever their leaders demand of them, and thus there is no need to ask deeper questions about Chinese mass behavior. The Chinese have not helped to explore deeper social and cultural considerations, for, as we have said, Chinese are not generally given to soul searching or introspection. When the Sixth Plenum Resolution went beyond blaming Mao and the Gang of Four, it suggested only that the Party lacked experience in applying "the scientific works of Marx, Engels, Lenin and Stalin" to the "swift advent of the newborn socialist society and for socialist construction on a national scale." Beyond that, the Resolution could only note that "feudalism in China has had a long history," and that "it remains difficult to eliminate the evil ideology and political influence of centuries of feudal autocracy"—as though parading around while waving little books or physically attacking teachers were long established Chinese practices. There have, however, been no deeper examinations of such purportedly traditional Chinese cultural traits—possibly because it would be awkward given the current goal of building "Socialism with *Chinese* characteristics," since it would force people to ask whether "Chineseness" constitutes good or bad traits in the minds of the leadership. Instead, the Beijing authorities prefer to assert over and over again their pledge, "Never again," a formula that has the dual advantage of increasing their popularity while also stifling criticism of their current policies. They have both implied and explicitly said that the most likely alternative to their current programs would be another Cultural Revolution. The nightmarish memories of that experience are enough to make most of the population thankful for the current reforms and disinclined to think about any further, and possibly more radical, alternatives. Needless to say, the Chinese leaders are following the conventional political practices of many ruling groups that enjoy caricaturing any opposition as being potentially disastrous for the country.

It indeed is puzzling that in analyzing causes Western scholars have not explored more profound social and cultural considerations. Western studies of, say, Nazism have universally made much over the character of German culture and the state of German society and have not stopped at just views about the motivations of Hitler and his associates. It almost seems as though there is a strange reversal in the index of respectability in the interpretation of history according to continents: in Europe it is seen as trivializing history to suggest that profound events were no more than the interplay of individual personalities, while in analyzing Chinese history it is considered offensive to suggest that fundamental cultural factors might have been decisive.

Yet clearly any ultimate explanation of the causes or origins of the Cultural Revolution must get at the question of how it was possible for so many Chinese to behave as they did. What was it in the nature of Chinese culture and society that not only permitted but encouraged the extremism of that period? Don't we need to learn more about the depth of frustration of the Chinese people who had sacrificed so much for so long in order to gain so little in their search for "wealth and power"? Given all that we know about Chinese psychology, weren't conditions right for the Chinese to explode with hatred toward the authorities they thought had failed them, even while still idealizing the pristine virtues of Mao Zedong? The Chinese themselves will probably not provide sophisticated guidance for understanding their propensity for the extreme behavior exhibited during the Cultural Revolution. The leaders have only their own simplistic explanations of the causes of the Cultural Revolution, and Chinese intellectuals have at best a weak tradition of critical introspection. They are prisoners of the idea that patriotism prohibits criticisms of the state for many reasons, not the least being, as Jerome Ch'en has pointed out, that in the Chinese language the same word, *guojia*, is used for both state and country, and therefore, "When one criticizes the state one is suspected of criticizing the country, hence treacherously [up] to no good."[9]

It is true that a few Chinese writers have tentatively asked questions about the relationship of Chinese society and the causes of the Cultural Revolution. Ba Jin, for example, has written: "It has taken me a long time but I am now able to admit to myself that the responsibility [for the Cultural Revolution] does not lie solely with Lin Biao and the Gang of Four. . . . They could not have done it, if we had not let ourselves be taken in."[10] Although a remarkable confession for a Chinese political activist intellectual, it is still not a very insightful explanation for what happened.

In searching for causes, future scholarship will have to focus on both elite behavior and mass actions. At the elite level the troublesome questions deal not with the content of the disagreements, or who said what to whom, or even who favored or opposed what policies. Elite politics in China has always been filled with disagreements over policies and struggles for power. Factional strife has always been the norm. The fundamental question is, why did such disagreements explode into violent hatreds at the time of the Cultural Revolution? If Mao felt a need to purify the Party and root out conspiracies, could he not have used more efficient means—even the brutal ones that Stalin used during the purges? How was it that the clashes among the elite got transmitted to the masses so as to turn them into such uncivilized animals? The comparison of the Cultural Revolution with the Holocaust is totally inappropriate for many reasons. One is that Hitler used the state apparatus and bureaucratic authority to carry out his unspeakable designs, while Mao ignited barbaric behavior among China's most educated people with only the most casual of commands.

The hard problem for understanding the Cultural Revolution is to explain the intensity of the mass violence. How was it that long-time friends and associates, from classmates to office workers, were so quickly brought to the state of attacking each other in life and death struggles? The removal of social constraints and the egging on of violence by the authorities seemed to have ignited astonishingly vicious passions in huge numbers of Chinese. People were caught up in trying to outdo each other in expressing rage. In *The Spirit of Chinese Politics* I gave my explanation of this phenomenon at the time it was taking place, when many Western scholars were reluctant to acknowledge the existence of such widespread violence. In retrospect it is even clearer that the repression of aggression in Chinese culture was much more severe than we realized at the time.

It now seems that the violent rage that carried forward the Cultural Revolution was also in part generated by a profound but still incomplete historic transformation of the psychological basis of the sensibilities of Chinese public morals. As we have noted earlier in discussing the ambivalences basic to China's political cultures, Chinese society in modern times has been experiencing profound uncertainties as to what can and should be the basis for moral imperatives. As in the West, the decline in religious authority as the basis for morality necessitated a more secular foundation for morality. The result in the West was the tradition of the Victorians and the rise of the values of bourgeois society—"among gentlemen and in proper society that just isn't done" became an absolute norm. In China, with its lack of capitalistic development, bourgeois standards of integrity never took strong root. Instead, with the Communists came the new but only partially absorbed standards of conduct associated with the ideals of being a "good

Communist." The basic thrust of the Cultural Revolution was thus an attack against those who were seen as having violated these new norms.

But why was there such rage? The explanation seems to lie in a second, and equally fundamental, transformation in the foundations of public morality. This transformation also occurred earlier and more completely in the West; it is only taking place with modernization in China, and is still only partially completed there. This is the transformation from the historical basis of morality—a concern of the individual as a person striving to be an upright man, a superior person—to the modern basis, which is a sense of moral indignation, shared by a community that demands punishment of all transgressors. Traditionally Confucian morality was driven by the ideal of self-cultivation, of striving for perfection as a superior person who should be respected by all, yet who felt comfortably self-assured in a cloak of modesty. Morality involved seeking virtue for its own sake. As for the behavior of others, one's duty was to act as an example so as to shame lesser people into the ways of propriety. Narcissism was the psychological force sustaining moral standards. Gradually in modern times, and more rapidly in the early years of Mao's rule, the Chinese people, particularly the young, began to see morality in a different light. They came increasingly to taste the passions of moral indignation, the indignation that upholds comprehensive criminal codes requiring the state to punish, with disinterested firmness, all crimes. Psychologically such indignation is driven by resentment and rage at the mere thought that someone else might be "getting away with something I am not allowed to do." The basic rationale is as follows: "If I have to suffer restraints and swallow my frustrations in being who I am, then it is only fair that everyone else should also suffer, and anyone who breaks the rules should be punished, not just in the name of fairness but also in response to the moral indignation of the righteous."

When a similar change occurred in the mode of thinking in the West, it was accompanied by a change in the psychodynamics of moral feelings. Morality became less a response to narcissistic feelings, in which a person wanted passionately to be seen by others as good and deserving of respect, and more a response to the feelings of aggression produced by the stern, uncompromising repressions of the superego. The distinguished Danish sociologist Svend Ranulf spent his professional life demonstrating that this historic transformation in the West was associated with the rage and resentments, the anger, envy, and jealousy, that were induced when stern and repressive socialization practices began to be practiced in Europe, especially among the Puritans and the rising middle class.[11]* He demonstrated by scholarship that went well beyond "the method of plausible guesses" that such repressive child training was not only associated with the formation of the middle classes in modern Europe, but also contributed to the demands for a comprehensive criminal code that came along with the rise of capitalism among the Calvinists as noted by Max Weber.

In the case of China, it does seem that a generation of young Chinese experienced enough of the repressive inhibitions of conformity in their socialization to have built up explosive frustrations and raging anger at anyone they thought might be getting away with not being equally disciplined and in control of themselves. Resentment was directed in particular against those in authority who were perceived to have violated the new society's repressive norms—for these were, of course, the very people who had imposed such strict ideals upon them and who were thereby the cause of their frustrations. Anger at all that was old was also a part of this same dynamic; the old symbolized all that they had been socialized to abhor, and it also represented a way of life that was lax and thus free of the repressive imperatives with which they had to live. Thus in the Cultural Revolution powerful, explosive forces of moral indignation were readily aimed at symbols of both authority and the presumably unenlightened past; once violent aggression was released its aim became blurred and ever wider circles of targets were hit.

Lynn White III has advanced a very insightful theory to explain the practices of ostracism and mass violence on the part of students and laborers at the height of the Cultural Revolution.[12] He argues that the critical ingredients were a widespread sense of frustration over the exaggerated promises of the regime and the slowness of actual progress, to which were added two other elements. First, there was the Communists' practice of giving everybody an indelible label, derived from what one's father or grandfather once was. There were, of course, the six Black Categories of undesirable family background—landlords, rich peasants, counterrevolutionaries, bad elements, rightists, and capitalists—and the five Red Categories of worthy families—workers, poor and lower-middle peasants, soldiers, revolutionary cadres, and revolutionary martyrs. The Chinese were in effect being squeezed into a caste system. One's prospects were determined not by one's performance but by one's rank in a rigid hierarchy based on inherited virtues and vices. There were, secondly, the mounting tensions that came from a clientalist system in which everyone's security depended upon whether or not his or her network of patron-client ties lost out to other networks. Any sense that there might be an upset in the relative ranking of such groupings could generate frantic activities either to advance one's group or to maintain the group's advantages. Finally, the spark that ignited this tinderbox was the passion unleashed by the call from above for everyone to join in the drama of mass political campaigns. The passions of the campaigns played on the intense frustration of feeling that one was the prisoner of one's caste labelling and the need to either rebel against the constraints of one's monitor or cling to the benefits of one's patron.

Many of the early eyewitness accounts by observers and participants there seemed to report some degree of political significance in the rhetoric of impassioned demonstrators.[13] Later accounts by participants make it seem that for many, if not most, of the Red Guards, the path to mass violence contained fewer political, and more mindless, considerations. Gao Yuan, for example, makes it clear that he and his schoolmates were easily caught up in the exuberant fun of adolescents who were allowed the double pleasure of skipping school and attacking their teachers. Before long he was caught up in a Lord of the Flies syndrome, in which the dynamics of youthful gang warfare escalated hatreds and every challenge had to be avenged with increasingly violent acts, until all was out of control.[14] This brings us to our second area of reassessment, the Cultural Revolution as experienced at the individual level.

Reassessing the Personal Experience

In contrast to the near silence about the deeper causes of the Cultural Revolution, there has been a flood of literature out of China telling about individual sufferings during the "ten years of great disaster." Some of the writers are disillusioned Red Guards, others were stigmatized with "bad class" backgrounds and had to endure violent physical torture and cruel humiliations, including spending many years in the countryside and in labor camps. These accounts, called by the Chinese the "wounded literature" (*shanghen wenxue*) after a Lu Xinhua story, have personalized the inhumanity of the Cultural Revolution in ways that have gone well beyond the early descriptions by Western writers. Although Karnow and Rice, among others, reported conflicts in organizations and the mistreatment of party leaders accused of being "capitalist roaders," the extent of the human suffering and deaths did not dominate the initial Western assessments of the Cultural Revolution.

The inclination to cling to the image of a benign, if somewhat misguided, Mao Zedong endured long after the evidence of his sordid treatment of old comrades had surfaced. Indeed, the most serious failure of Western scholarship in its early analysis of the Cultural Revolution was a pervasive imperviousness to violations of human rights. Self-professed liberals seemingly turned a deaf ear to reports of victims driven to suicide and of tens of thousands being sent off to labor camps and jails.

It was not that information was lacking, because almost immediately after the mass demonstrations in Tienanmen Square, China-watchers did receive reports about disillusioned former Red Guards, many of whom escaped to Hong Kong and elsewhere. We had, for example, the detailed account by Ken Ling in his *Revenge of Heaven*, and those of people interviewed by Frolic, Raddock, and Bennett and Montaperto, among others.[15] In retrospect it seems that the horrors of what was taking place in China were minimized because it was incorrectly assumed that refugees were biased. In fact, the biasing was in the other direction, because first the refugees sought credibility by modestly understating their personal troubles, and then the analysts deemed it appropriate to further tone down their descriptions. Just as Westerners intellectually knew of the existence of Soviet labor camps but required a Solzhenitsyn to give a human dimension to the horrors of the Gulag, so it took Liang Heng's and Judith Shapiro's *Son of Revolution* to make the same point about the Cultural Revolution.[16]

The reassessment of the personal dimensions of the trauma is facilitated by the present official sanctions by Beijing for speaking "bitterness" about all aspects of the Cultural Revolution. Skeptics have noted that since the authorities today approve of complaining about the evils of the Cultural Revolution, such complaints should probably be treated with some of the caution with which Mao's "achievements" should have been greeted. It is important to remember that the Cultural Revolution hit at China's elite, and in particular its intellectuals, who have been able to articulate their troubles. Far more Chinese had to endure much greater suffering as a result of the Great Leap—some thirty million probably died in the famine—but they were mainly inarticulate peasants. Still, even though Chinese culture does give considerable license to public complaining about mistreatment, the volume of the stories of suffering is so great that there can be little doubt that the times were bad for large numbers of people.

In assessing the effects of the Cultural Revolution on individuals, it is still hard to judge what the lasting psychological consequences of that experience are likely to have been. Aside from the works of a few major writers, most of the "wounded literature" contains little introspection, and mainly tendencies to resort to slogans and to blame much on "Lin Biao and the Gang of Four" and their followers. Indeed, after reading through these stories one is left unsure of whether the Cultural Revolution will have any lasting effects on the collective Chinese psyche.[17] Most of the stories document physical hardships, but the descriptions are primarily objective descriptions and nearly devoid of deep subjective probings.

It is therefore not surprising that there are mixed judgments as to the most significant lasting consequences of the Cultural Revolution. On the one hand, Merle Goldman has observed that these consequences may not be entirely negative, in that the experience has instilled in many Chinese a readiness to challenge authority and a healthy skepticism about the promises and motives of political leaders.[18] Having been taken in once and led down a disastrous trail, the victims do not intend to be again so gullible. They are even taking with a grain of salt the appeals and promises of Deng Xiaoping and his designated successors. Liang Heng confirms Goldman's view, noting that while some have called the victims China's "lost generation," they are also China's "thoughtful generation."[19] Indeed, on his trip back to China he found a variety of responses to the "nightmare," including those of victimizers who needed to expiate their guilt. He also found people who in spite of great suffering were now enthusiastically adapting to the new era.

Against such constructive judgments stands the evidence gathered by Anne F. Thurston, who through skillful interviewing has brought to light the degree to which significant numbers of victims were, according to her judgment, psychologically traumatized. Recognizing that the Cultural Revolution was comparable neither to a sudden disaster nor a holocaust, she calls it an "extreme situation," characterized by a profound sense of loss—"loss of culture and of spiritual values; loss of hope and ideals; loss of time, truth, and of life; loss, in short, of nearly everything that gives meaning to life."[21] She is convinced that many, if not most, of her informants have manifested "post-traumatic stress disorders." Above all, they express, in varying degrees, feelings of "survivor's guilt"—why should they have been so fortunate when others were not? None were able to account for what happened in large part because they tended to rely upon denial as a defense mechanism in order to gain the resilience necessary to carry on living. "No Chinese with whom I have spoken has ever pretended to be able to explain the Cultural Revolution—or in any case not fully, not completely. No one has yet been able fully to integrate that experience into his or her life."[22] Finally, by noting the tremendous hold that patriotism has on all the Chinese with whom she spoke, Thurston is able to explain the apparent contradiction of the Cultural Revolution—that is, it was a soul-searing experience, yet something they describe in shallow cliches. Patriotism makes it impossible for them to analyze Chinese society or to criticize their political system for fear of appearing disloyal.

A third possible interpretation of the effects of the Cultural Revolution is that some Chinese went through shocking experiences but came out of it with neither the trauma Thurston observes nor the political awakening that Goldman and Liang see as common. An example of this reaction is to be found in the autobiographical account by Yue Daiyun.[23*] This woman describes in excruciating detail the appallingly brutal experiences she had as a teacher at Beida. She was reprimanded and publicly humiliated even before the Anti-Rightist campaign. In that campaign she was separated from her six-month-old son and four-year-old daughter and sent down to the countryside. Then, during the Cultural Revolution, she and her husband, who was also a professor, were again brutally treated, and even after the apparent madness had ended, her children were denied for a time admittance to the universities for which they were qualified because of her political record. No matter what awful things happened to her, she remained totally incapable of questioning the Leninist system. She insists that she was not a "rightist" and therefore should not have been sent down; she gives no hint of recognizing that no human being, "rightist" or not, should ever be made to go through what she had to. Unable to recognize evil for what it is, she in the end accepts the offer to be allowed to rejoin the Party. It is hard to understand how a teacher at Beida could be as unreflective as she appears, yet she displays a strange lack of political sophistication. After thirty years of political victimization she seems not to have advanced much from being the nineteen-year-old who gazed starry-eyed at a statue of Lenin while visiting Moscow on her way to Prague as a delegate to a World Student Congress. Her notion of patriotism and loyalty seems stunted at the level of the thinking of the Red Guards.

The unchanged Yue Daiyun seems not to have the moral values of the more mature Nien Cheng, who in her autobiographical account of the tortures she experienced in the Cultural Revolution, *Life and Death in Shanghai*, tells of her need to combat evil without compromise and to debate with her interrogators about their inhuman behavior.[24] During six-and-a-half years of cruel imprisonment, Mrs. Cheng never wavered in her convictions about right and wrong. Her story is a moving testimonial to the moral courage of those educated Chinese who were able to see through the shallowness of the Red Guard version of patriotism.

Different victims (and different victimizers) have had their quite individual reactions. Individuals will interpret what happens in a collectivity in different ways, depending upon their own distinctive personalities. Hence, in the years to come, researchers will be able to collect, as Harold Isaacs has done, a rich variety of accounts even among people in similar situations.[25] Yet there is also the reality of a collective memory. What is likely to be the consensus of the Chinese people about the human meaning of the Cultural Revolution? Will it be dominated by the spirit of skepticism hypothesized by Merle Goldman? Will it come closer to Liang Heng's concern that Chinese should never forget the lesson of the Cultural Revolution, including what it teaches about the dangers of their tradition of obedience to authority and their thirst for revenge that comes from having so much "bottled up inside"?[26] Will the consensus be closer to Anne Thurston's judgment that the psychic damage was so great that it can only be overcome by the passions of patriotism, which could produce a virulent form of nationalism? Or will all the suffering be treated as appropriate to the task of making better "revolutionaries," as seems to be Yue Daiyun's pathetic conclusion?

These questions pertain to two other, fundamental questions. First, there is the question of how capable the survivors will be of reviving and making effective the institutions essential for realizing the current goals of modernization. Second, will the cumulative effects of the Cultural Revolution on the individual produce a basic change in the collective character of the Chinese with respect to what they expect of their political system? Will the Chinese have learned the folly of trusting the state—which linguistically they so easily confuse with the idea of a nurturing national family—so completely? Since the issue of the consequences of the Cultural Revolution for the individual is so closely related to the effects of that experience on Chinese institutions, let us hold off judgment until we have looked into the third area for reassessment, that of the effects of the Cultural Revolution on China's public institutions.

The Astonishing Revival of Institutions

Second only to the suffering of individuals was the damage the Cultural Revolution did to all types of institutions. Not only was the Party decimated, but government ministries and bureaus and, above all, universities and schools were left in shambles. After the storm of violence had passed, most such organizations remained in a pitiful state because they were now being run by "revolutionary committees" consisting of the "three-way alliance" of representatives of the People's Liberation Army, veteran cadres, and "revolutionary mass organizations."[27*] The stage was set for what seemed likely to be a prolonged period of factional strife with everyone out to settle scores and seek revenge.

Yet possibly the most astonishing aftermath of the Cultural Revolution was the speed with which institutional chaos was replaced by orderly hierarchies and regularized bureaucracies once the "Left" was defeated. In a matter of only a few years the skeleton organizations, which after the turmoil existed in name only, were miraculously staffed with disciplined participants. From the national research academies to the provincial and local governmental headquarters, all important organizations were rapidly manned by people who dutifully carried on their respective assignments of the day. It is true that talent was often in short supply, but no more so than would be expected in any economically underdeveloped country.

The facility with which Chinese recreated their institutions suggests some limits in the extent to which they were psychologically traumatized. They clearly had not lost their traditional readiness to array themselves in hierarchical structures of authority nor their capacity to carry out expected role relationships. Although, as we have noted, such hierarchies are not necessarily command structures but rather tend to be status arrangements, they still give the appearances of being bureaucratic formations. Moreover, the Chinese are capable of quickly adopting, at least for appearance's sake, the formal conduct expected of their assigned roles. Throughout history, the Chinese have on repeated occasions miraculously transformed social and economic chaos into seemingly disciplined organizational behavior. Just as soon as peace and order come to the land, social and economic life will almost instantly revive as everyone rejoices at the arrival of better times. The accomplishments of the Deng reforms in the wake of the disorders of the last years of Mao's rule are in fact reminiscent of the successes of the first years of the Communist regime after the confusion during the interregnum caused by the Japanese invasion and the civil war. If one compares the before-and-after statistics produced by the Chinese for the two periods, it seems that progress was more dramatic in the early 1950s than in the early 1980s—a reminder that percentage growth figures are as much, if not more, the result of the deflation of past conditions as of the inflation of current accomplishments.

The alacrity with which the Chinese can exploit the advantages of social and political order is, of course, the opposite side of the coin as the speed with which chaos ensues when order breaks down. The cultural norms are based upon responses to perceived circumstances: when the situation seems secure, purposeful, and disciplined, purposeful action becomes the rule and progress is possible; when disorder prevails passion gets out of hand, aggression surfaces, and panic is likely. The imperatives that govern the individual's behavior are geared very much to the personalized sets of relationships that provide the fabric of the larger social order. The behavior of the masses is thus largely fixed by their immediate personal ties and associations that give stability to the society, but allow for flexibility and ready bending to political currents. A few cues from above can set off mass action that will bring either ruin or tranquility to national life.

The speed with which Chinese institutions again became effective after the turmoil of the Cultural Revolution is indeed impressive for two reasons. First, in contrast to, say, the Great Leap, during which it was the masses who suffered most, the Cultural Revolution was destructive particularly of the elite, and therefore order required that power holders arrive at stable relations with each other. Second, the restaffing of organizations brought face to face people who just a few years before had been engaged in violent struggles with each other. Mortal enemies of just a few years past, both victims and victimizers, have been able somehow to repress whatever feelings of revenge and hatred they still harbor, and peacefully work side by side. What has taken place is a dramatic demonstration of the continuity of the Chinese cultural trait of separating emotions from actions by containing personal feelings and behaving according to established community norms.

It is this remarkable capacity for holding in check one's emotions and not allowing feelings to be the guide for actions that makes possible the widespread Chinese practice of feigned compliance, which we have already noted. Behavior is thus readily geared to the immediate social context, and people rountinely hide their inner thoughts. Social harmony is maintained precisely because nobody has to reveal his or her true thoughts; one need only act according to the expected norms that are supposed to govern the particular situation.

The irony, of course, is that Mao was driven to the Cultural Revolution in part precisely because he knew that the Chinese people could easily be giving lip service to the "Thoughts of Mao Zedong"; it was hard for him to know what they really believed. He therefore thought it essential to make the people bring together thought and action, and avoid feigned compliance. In the end, however, the Cultural Revolution probably worked to widen the gap between public statements and inner convictions. People who now share offices and work in the same organizations have had to mask more than ever their feelings and postpone settling scores as they fall in step with the new policies. As long as they behave correctly by carrying out their prescribed roles, it does not matter what their inner thoughts may be.

Moreover, for the public at large the new conditions created by Deng's reforms call for new norms of behavior. Conformity to ideological cues and political calculations has been replaced by conformity to consumerism and by the desire to keep up with successful neighbors—apparently to the great relief of the Chinese masses.

What does all this mean for assessing the effects of the Cultural Revolution on Chinese personality and culture? The only thing that is absolutely certain is that Mao's ambition to create a "reign of virtue," in Benjamin Schwartz's felicitous phrase, was a failure.[28] Does the quick revival of China's institutions suggest a flaw in Thurston's view of the survivors as psychic cripples? Is Goldman's notion of a generation of skeptics more consistent with the institutional after-effects? The answer seems to be that each analysis may be partially correct. The thesis of extreme shock and the hypothesis of distrust are both compatible with the idea that the Chinese have instinctively withdrawn to more traditional cultural patterns of behavior, but with norms that are now infused with greater emotional intensity than they were in the past. The survivors of the Cultural Revolution, by adapting to obligations of hierarchy and by seeking self-improvement, have in effect reverted to historical Chinese cultural behavior, even as they have followed Deng's demand that China must in the realms of technology and economics learn from the West.

The uniquely bifurcated nature of Chinese state and society meant that the Cultural Revolution had quite different consequences for state institutions and national politics on the one hand, and for the behavior of private citizens on the other. When public institutions were being shattered, private citizens turned to each other. Consequently, the inherently cellular organizations governing most people's social lives became stronger than ever. As a result of the attacks on the family during the Cultural Revolution, the family was revitalized and strengthened.

The late Chairman's vision of making a "new Chinese man," paradoxically, ended by reinforcing traditional Chinese tendencies to seek security by exploiting the advantages of inequality. The reversion to traditional practices went further than just readopting the discipline of institutional roles, for it included reemphasizing particularistic personal relationships. Thomas Gold has perceptively noted that the Cultural Revolution strengthened the traditional Chinese practices of *guanxi* and shattered the Communist ideals of comradeship.[29] Gold argues that the economic disarray and the breakdown of the social order caused by the Cultural Revolution, when combined with the arbitrary authority of "leftist" cadres who sought to dominate all spheres of life, forced the Chinese to revert more than ever to *guanxi* practices. "Through practice, young people learned that *guanxi* was supreme law."[30]

Gold's observations help to resolve the contradiction between Thurston's hypothesis about post-trauma syndrome and the speed with which Chinese institutions regained a high degree of normalcy. What seems to have happened is that Chinese behavior has been modified through personal stress, but the outcome, beyond reliance upon denial, has been the energizing of personal ties. Consequently the post-Cultural Revolution institutions may be stronger than before because personal relationships within them are now strongly invigorated by the power of *guanxi*. These personal ties may have a new dimension and intensity as a result of having been reinforced by the trauma of the experience of the Cultural Revolution. The new dimension is, it seems, a true sense of guilt for not carrying out reciprocal obligations. The Chinese seemingly are returning to their practices of *guanxi*, but they are bringing much stronger emotional charges to those relationships than in the past. Skepticism about the words used by political leaders is a part of this pattern of privatizing concerns and maximizing personal considerations. Again, the gap between state and society has widened.

The psychic effect of the Cultural Revolution has been to legitimize concern for self. This is apparent in the peculiar blend of institutional reality that Deng Xiaoping has created, which is neither disciplined Communism nor a genuine free market system. This concern is manifested by peasants rejoicing over the liberalization of the responsibility system, as well as by the sons and daughters of high cadres, the *gaoganzidi*, exploiting the pay-offs of traditional Chinese respect for hierarchy.[31]*

A Final Assessment

If we combine the results of our three levels of observation about the effects of the Cultural Revolution, the summation would seem to be a formula for a political system that is the antithesis of the one Mao set out to create. The pledge of "Never again" has opened an escape valve for dramatic systemic change. The results can be masked by the term "Socialism with Chinese characteristics"—especially when the meaning of "Chinese" is left as vague as that of "Socialism."

The personal shock the Cultural Revolution caused leaders and potential leaders has had two fundamental effects. First, it has opened their eyes to the reality of China's failures, not only during the Cultural Revolution but also during most of the earlier years of the Communist regime. Second, it may have slightly jarred the traditional sense of cultural and racial superiority that once made it hard for earlier Chinese leaders to understand foreign ways fully and to take advantage of them. Those who suffered most, such as Deng Xiaoping, seem to be the most aware that even the "early Mao's" policies were flawed; those who got off more lightly, such as Chen Yun, can still see some virtues in elements of the pre-Cultural Revolution version of "socialism." There are, of course, significant variations between individual Chinese in the degree to which they have been able to learn from the "open door policy." Many, especially those now studying abroad, are enthusiastically seeking to immerse themselves in the thoughts and ways of the modern world. Most people within China, however, are probably still caught up in the dilemma of Chinese patriotism: does love of country require blind adherence to the political currents of the day, or can the imperative of patriotism be met by achieving personal excellence as judged by international standards? Anne Thurston makes the disturbing report that many of the people who confided in her about their experiences during the Cultural Revolution now seem to have gone back to the Chinese intellectuals' abominable practice of making patriotism such a supreme value that they become uncritical defenders of the regime. They now engage in personal attacks upon those they see as less patriotic than they think themselves to be.[32] On the positive side it is well to note that increasing numbers of Chinese students now studying in the United States are finding their voices, and are learning that they should speak out in constructive criticism so as to help their country become a better place.

As for our assessment of the Cultural Revolution, the inescapable fact is that without the horrendous events of that period it is inconceivable that post-Mao China could, in terms of national policies, have deviated as much as it has not only from the Soviet model of Communism but from any known concept of Communism. If China had not been scarred by the violent turmoil of the late 1960s and early 1970s, the most likely alternative to Mao's revolutionary utopianism would have been little more than the dreary prospect of an orderly, bureaucratic form of Communism. It seems unthinkable that China would or could have adopted the bold modernizing policies of the post-Mao era.

Yet, paradoxically, the haunting memories of that chaotic period may also intimidate the current Chinese leaders and prevent them from allowing the degree of liberalization and decentralization essential for the success of the reforms in the economic realm. Chinese officials remain hypersensitive to the dangers they perceive to inhere in genuinely relaxing administrative controls. They must feel that they have been to the brink of anarchy and in looking down they saw the horrors of chaos. Memories of the disaster that followed when government lost control during the Cultural Revolution explain in part the timidity with which the government considers the prospects of adjusting the price structure, of allowing the yuan to find its worth in currency markets, of abandoning numerous subsidies, or of permitting foreign exchange reserves to decline. The great danger for China is that the current attempt to rely upon the "market" for guidance could be a disaster if prices are too irrational and too distorted by subsidies.[33]

This legacy of timidity clouds more than just economic policies. As Goldman has pointed out, China's leaders today are also haunted by the memory of how the Cultural Revolution taught people to distrust authority. The knowledge that a whole generation of young Chinese rose up and attacked all institutions of authority, including the presumably sacred Communist Party, has left the current leaders sensitive to the dangers of allowing too much political or cultural free thinking. Deng and his appointed successors want to modernize China, to turn China away from the path that Mao set the country on, but they are possibly even more concerned than Mao was about the danger that political liberalization might produce anarchy and uncontrolled change. Having seen near anarchy, they are not prepared to take chances. The extraordinary lengths to which they have gone in designating particular individuals to succeed them as assigned members of the "second" and "third echelons" is telling proof of the current leaders' distrust of any spontaneous flow of politics. This need to try to control the selection of talent for future generations is a manifestation of anxieties about the future that recall fears inspired by the "nightmare" that was the Cultural Revolution.

Thus there are, in the last analysis, two contradictory legacies of the Cultural Revolution. First, at the level of national politics, the current reforms and the open door policies could never have come about except for the trauma of that event; yet at the same time, anxieties instilled by the experience of near anarchy may make it impossible to realize fully the potential of those reforms, or to allow greater political and cultural freedoms. The result is a peculiar blend, in the attitudes of the leaders, of desiring to execute the bold move but being timid about any uncertainties. The "reforms" of Deng have indeed gone beyond any reasonable definition of reform. They constitute substantial innovation. Yet the Chinese leaders generally feel the need to cling to the structure of controls they inherited from Mao's version of bureaucratic "Communism." Their fear of uncertainty makes them want to put in place right now the next two generations of leaders, leaving nothing to chance or to the normal flow of dynamic political processes. It helps to explain their abhorrence of "bourgeois liberalization." Deng Xiaoping's instinctive reverence for discipline, which he revealed as early as when he charted the Anti-Rightist Campaign, remains strong, as shown in his attacks on the disorderly creativity of intellectuals in his "anti-bourgeois liberalism" campaign.

Second, at the personal level, the survivors of the trauma of the Cultural Revolution, having overcome their guilt for not having had it worse, and inspired by the added confidence that they they are somehow special for having survived, are now prepared to take bold gambles and deviate more from the orthodox Communist model than Mao was ever prepared to do. In their private lives they are more self-seeking than before. Much of their energies are now being directed to personal relations and their private interests. In this respect they are inclined to give new vitality to traditional Chinese patterns of behavior, thus reinforcing the bases of Chinese political culture even as national policies seem to be going in novel directions.

Given these two conflicting legacies, we cannot foresee all the lasting consequences of the Cultural Revolution, for we cannot make out any better than the Chinese can the ultimate shape of "Socialism with

Chinese characteristics." What we can be certain of as we reassess the Cultural Revolution twenty years later is that the psycho-cultural dynamics of Chinese politics, then as now, rests tenuously upon layers of latent and contradictory sentiments that are far more decisive in the flow of events than public rationalizations of political economy policies.

Although we still do not have totally satisfying explanations for the causes of the Cultural Revolution (and probably we never will, given the Chinese taboo against introspection and deep cultural analysis), it still seems that the conditions that most likely contributed to the unprecedented event no longer exist in China. Certainly the key causal factors Lynn White has identified are no longer major features of the Chinese scene. The same seems to be the case with respect to the five principle reasons that Anne Thurston believes were basic in making the Cultural Revolution possible.[34] First, she points to the excessive reverence for authority of many Chinese that made them see their leaders as demigods. Deference to authority is still there, but there is no inclination to worship any leader as they once worshiped Mao. Second, she notes that there was an absence of any moral code except the violence legitimizing Marxism-Leninism-Mao Zedong Thought. Though such is still the case, even those who espouse that doctrine have become less enthusiastic champions of violence. Third, she noted that individuals were rigidly categorized. The stress on class labels is out, but the denial of the diversity of human nature is still a problem. The fourth factor she noted was the prevalence of punishment by mob actions. This is no longer a major practice in post-Deng China, but there is still little in the way of due process or an independent judiciary. Finally, she observed that politics was the sole avenue for advancement in China. This is no longer so; more and more young Chinese see Party membership as at best no more than an instrumental way of getting ahead in other fields.

CHAPTER V

THE MYSTIQUE OF LEADERSHIP

Chinese national politics revolves around the personages of leaders. Indeed, few contemporary countries attach as much importance as China does to the mystique of the leader as the great man, the savior of the nation, the one whose will and wishes become the collective obligations of the country. Questioning such a leader is always a tricky matter, fraught with dangers, for it borders on treason. Chinese once anxiously wondered how they could hope to get along without the guidance of Mao Zedong, and then they collectively worried that their world would come to an end if Deng Xiaoping's influence should fail to long outlast him.

Elements of China's past and present ideologies reinforce each other to make leadership such a preeminent feature of the contemporary political culture. The Confucian tradition of rule by men and not by law, and the Marxist-Leninist doctrine of the preciousness of the Party (which opens the door to personality cults), when combined, as in China and also North Korea, have produced a heightened glorification of the concept of the infallible leader, the indispensable figure. Furthermore, the realities of Third World political conditions—and on this score China is totally correct in claiming to be a part of the Third World—mean that little is institutionalized and much depends upon the idiosyncratic wishes of the leader of the moment. Thus, to understand the forces that drive and guide Confucianist Leninism, we need to give special attention to the concepts of leadership that have emerged out of the blending of the two traditions. We must attend, as well, to the equally idealized views of followership.

135

Mao Zedong explicitly extolled the virtues of rule by men and not by laws, and Deng Xiaoping carried the principle to the ultimate extreme by serving as China's "paramount ruler" (as the Western press was driven to call him) while holding no formal office of major consequence beyond the modest one of chairman of the military affairs commission of the party. Giving authority to the man and not the office does allow China's supreme leader extraordinary flexibility, and absolves him from accountability. This central feature of Chinese political culture has had several decisive consequences for the character of Chinese political life. It has made the question of succession a dominant issue of Chinese politics for more than twenty years—first, in the case of Mao's succession, which began in the early 1960s and continued until after the arrest of the Gang of Four and Deng's triumph over Hua Guofeng, and then, when those battles were barely over, in the struggles that began over who should prevail "after Deng."

The Chinese stress upon rule by men and not laws has also meant that policies always have a tentative character, as everyone recognizes that in public life there is nothing binding or law-like to give permanence to decisions. With the passing of Mao came the end of his programs, and now the universal concern is over the possible fate of Deng's reforms after he dies. Pledges of enduring commitment can be made, but they are only the words of mortals, not the sacred bonds of law. Therefore much about the future is always up in the air—a situation that generates enough anxiety to make the Chinese inordinately interested in the future, and therefore consumed with wishful thinking and a compulsive need to pretend to optimism.

Uncertainty is reduced, however, in one respect: without laws to make precise the obligations of office and to fix the tenure of officials, it is universally acknowledged that leaders will hold to power as long as their prestige lasts and with little regard to senility. As a consequence the Chinese government naturally drifts towards becoming a gerontocracy—which periodically can become extreme enough to verge on becoming a foolocracy.

The Tradition of Great Rulers

The Chinese imperial tradition exalted the personage of the supreme ruler, the emperor who was the Son of Heaven and thus a semi-divine figure. Everything possible was done to make it clear to all within the realm that the emperor was the central actor who stood out above all others. Powerful ministers could rise through the bureaucracy of mandarins, but their august authority could be shattered in an instant if they incurred imperial displeasure.

The authority of all of officialdom was derivative of the sacred powers of the imperial personage. No official was allowed to rise up as an open challenger to the emperor's authority. Ministers and viceroys could glisten in their separate glories, but all would have to prostrate themselves before the emperor, and, while on all fours, strike their foreheads to the ground. Outside of officialdom no centers of power were allowed to emerge that might become legitimate sources of authority divorced from the imperial system. In contrast to the barons and city-state merchants of Europe, whose power might either challenge or reinforce the authority of the monarch, in China neither merchants nor landlords were supposed to act as conspicuous or legitimate power centers. There were short periods of time when Buddhist monasteries accumulated huge holdings of land and had influences beyond the local setting, but those were exceptional times. Nothing in China was comparable to the competing authorities of Church and State, of nobles and monarchs, in European history. The Chinese emperor did not need the support of powerful and loyal barons who in return for fealty might command their own domains unhampered from above.[1*]

The evidence of architecture and archeology speaks to the singular importance of the figure of the emperor. From the excavations of Qin Shi Huang's tomb to the awesome expanses of the Forbidden City, it is clear that everything imaginable was done to give physical proof of the bigger-than-life importance of the single supreme ruler with divine properties. In contrast, China has no remains that would testify to secondary sources of power who might act as the emperor's peers. Throughout the breadth of China there are no monuments to autonomous power centers, no Great Houses as in England, no castles on the Rhine, no grand villas as in Italy, no city castles as in Japan. After the Forbidden City there are no abodes in all of China that can inspire awe, except possibly the odd monastery. No wonder that the Chinese Communists, for all their rhetoric about the dignity of the lower orders, decided to dramatize the glories of the Forbidden City when they became the masters of the Chinese state; it stands as a great aid for teaching about the importance of government and the need to defer totally to established authority.

In imperial China it was more than just the grandeur of the Forbidden City that told people of the exceptional nature of the personage of the emperor. Equally important were the awesome

numbers of concubines—some ten to twelve thousand in the Ming and
Qing periods—and eunuchs—nearly one hundred thousand—thought
necessary and proper to serve one who was manifestly greater than
ordinary mortals.[2*]

From Past to Present

As awesome as the ancient Chinese myth of emperors was, the
connection between such traditional beliefs and the present-day belief
in the almost magical properties of leadership is not easily made. Some
historians are content with simply identifying similarities between past
and present practices and with speaking in general terms about
continuity and change. When there is no identification of the mechanism
for the transmission of continuities, these practices border on ascribing
mystical properties to a force that is undefined and only known as
History. But how does History work so that some traditions persist in
spite of revolutionary change? Too often the question goes un-
answered.[3*]

As we noted at the outset of this study, the theory of political culture
seeks to make explicit the mechanism for continuity and change by
stressing the political socialization process by which each generation
influences its successor. In some cases the transmission is a direct one,
involving initiation, discipline, and "bending the stalk to shape the tree."
In others there is a leapfrog process of rebellion and reaction, of the
interaction of mores and countermores. But the patterns of rebellion are
governed by established conventions—as, for example, in the United
States, children with an instinct for the jugular know intuitively that the
way to shatter their liberal parents is to profess conservative views, and
vice versa.

In the case of the Chinese political culture, the ideal of the
omnipotence of authority has been passed from generation to generation
by the imperative of filial piety, the rule that absolute obedience and
unquestioning deference shall be shown to one's elders and more
particularly to one's father. One learns not only that father knows best,
but that the safest course of action is always to conform to the dictates
of authority and to suppress one's personal feelings. The tradition of
filial piety in the day-to-day life of Chinese families goes far in
explaining not only the practice of conforming to political authority, but
also the peculiar Chinese concept of "revolution" as a call for a
stronger, more omnipotent, more competent authority rather than for

the abolition of authority. Filial piety appears to be at the base of the explosive anger Chinese seem to manifest when they feel that authority has not lived up to their belief in its omnipotence.[4*]

Thus, when Chinese feel compelled to challenge the authority of the leaders they have imagined to be more than life-sized, they tend to do so not by matter-of-factly presenting alternative opinions, but with aggressive passion that is a blend of derring-do, fear, and anger. This blend achieved its pure form in the actions of the Red Guards, as they directed their venom against the authorities they knew first hand in defense of the essentially abstract, idealized authority, Chairman Mao. The Party had failed Mao and therefore they could vent their anger without inhibitions. The intensity of passion that the failure of authority can arouse in the Chinese stands in stark contrast to the flatness of affect that they display in so many other situations. They expect that their commitment to conformity should be rewarded by the benevolence of a paternalistic leadership.

The Confucian ideals of leadership and followership have thus been retained in Chinese culture not just by the power of written texts but also by living practices of authority and obedience in family situations. The automatic reactions of conformity and deference to superiors have generally been well established before the Chinese child leaves home. Then, when one-time obedient subordinates move into the role of superiors, they tend immediately to expect compliance to their wishes and commands. Moreover, since Chinese social life tends to be hierarchical, many Chinese early learn to practice what has been called the "bicycle syndrome"—bending the knee to superiors and stamping on subordinates. The result is an exaggerated sense of the difference between the exalted and the base.

Seniority, Gerontocracy, and Succession Crises

The Confucian tradition of the critical importance of the benevolent ruler, when combined with the Marxist-Leninist tradition of leadership in an infallible Party, has produced in contemporary China a magnified vision of leadership. In particular, the Bolshevik concept of seniority in the Party has been compounded by the Chinese awe for the aged. The result in practical terms has been that Party members of different generations enjoy markedly different status, depending upon the date and the circumstance of their joining. The Long March generation was followed by the Yenan generation and then the Civil War generation, the Great Leap generation, the huge Cultural Revolution generation, and the much smaller generation now being recruited under the Reforms.

Over time this stress on seniority has been translated into a propensity toward gerontocracy. Respect for the aged, an ancient Chinese custom, has been legitimized in a supposedly revolutionary party by younger members who are expected to venerate the "veteran cadres." The "experiences" of the latter are presumed ones of inestimable value from which all can learn—a reassertion of the traditional Chinese concept of ruling by example, but now made even more institutional within the hierarchy of the Party. The gerontocratic tendencies in the Leninist tradition, which were so prominent in the pre-Gorbachev era of the Soviet Union and still are in all the Eastern European Communist states, have thus been compounded in Confucianist Leninism. This is true not just in China but also in Vietnam, where policies were long fixed by stubborn old men whose thinking, in the terminology of Chinese Communism, had become "ossified or semi-ossified." The Confucian tradition is, of course, also at work in Taiwan, where the Kuomintang has its near-senile Old Guard, and where it is not seen as a joke that the Youth Party should be headed by an octogenarian.

The control of subordinates by superiors that is essential to Marxist-Leninist party discipline has thus been reinforced by the cultural paralysis of the Chinese youth in challenging their elders, and more particularly fatherly and grandfatherly figures. To make matters worse, there is the Chinese tradition of enjoying old age; the aged wallow in the license to have their way, and expect everyone else to service their whims. As the Party grew older, the inevitable happened: it was dominated by increasingly older men.[5*]

Oddly, it was an aged Mao who first articulated concern about this tilting toward the old. The Chairman was astonished at how young the American officials were who accompanied National Security Advisor Henry Kissinger and President Richard Nixon on their visits to Beijing. He asked them how they did it, and suggested that it would be impossible, no matter how desirable, to advance people so young to responsible positions in China.

It was, however, left to Deng Xiaoping in the mid-1980s to tackle the problem by trying to get the most senior officials to retire. Ostensibly Deng sought to get rid of doddering comrades in order to improve the efficiency of his economic "reforms," but actually the move was a part of his three-pronged strategy for managing his own succession. The other two prongs consisted of designating Hu Yaobang and Zhao Ziyang as his heir apparents, and then identifying three echelons of officials for the lower positions.

In trying to confront the problem of gerontocracy, Deng at first merely sang the praises of elderly cadres, arguing that having served the country so well they should be *allowed* the pleasures of rest and retirement. Old officials, however, were much too wise to be taken in by mere sweet talk. The perks for senior officials had become too gratifying to be so easily abandoned. Moreover, the duties for such men were not so demanding as to require much more exertion than retirement involved. Deng next hoped to sweeten the retirement proposal by exploiting the Chinese proclivity to confuse prestige with power. He presented a plan of establishing a Central Advisory Commission made up of retired officials who would have honor and the right to communicate their ideas regarding policy to both the Party and the government. Still, senior cadres preferred the security of office to the play-acting of having a say about policy. Indeed, since most of them had reached the higher levels of power without ever having had much say in the making of policy, the idea of voicing their views about alternative policies in their twilight years had understandably little appeal. Thus even though Deng himself took on the post of chairman of the Commission he was able to attract only a few of his allies. Finally, Deng went all out, promising that those who took what might be called "early retirement, late in life" could keep all their perks—including their chauffeur-driven cars, their houses, and their shopping privileges—and their full salaries, and on the side, arrangements might be made to give their children desirable jobs.

This final offer would have greatly increased the cost of government when its ostensible objective was to increase efficiency. However, it backfired, because those who took up Deng's offer were almost without exception officials who were friendly to Deng, inclined to support his policies and fight against his factional foes. Deng quickly discovered that his pleas easily swayed his obedient allies but not his enemies. Senior figures who might have added authority to his reform policies began to fade away. Those who did not fully trust Deng, no matter how feeble they were, clung tenaciously to their posts. Consequently, Deng's own generation began increasingly to tilt against him. And given the authority and not just deference that age commands in China, this proved to be a not insignificant tilting. In early 1987, when Deng's succession plans began to unravel with the enforced "resignation" of Hu Yaobang, fourteen of the twenty-two members and alternates on the

Politburo were seventy and over. Deng and four others (all his opponents) were in their eighties. Deng could be thankful that before his troubles with Hu Yaobang surfaced, his long-standing critics Marshalls Ye Jianying, Liu Bocheng, and General Huang Kecheng had died—the first two in October, 1986, and the third in December of that year.

The problem of aged cadres dramatizes the seriousness of succession crises in Chinese politics and the uncertain consequences associated with the certainty of the leader's mortality. For more than twenty years Chinese politics has revolved around problems of succession. From before the Cultural Revolution until today China has been plagued with succession crises. The lack of any mechanism for managing orderly succession of leadership in Marxist-Leninist systems, when combined with the Confucian predisposition to revere senile figures, has insured that Chinese politics has had to march to the tune of the Grim Reaper, awaiting what would happen after Mao's death and now with Deng's passing. To the outside world the big issue has been that of whether there would be continuity or change in China's policy orientation. For those within the system, however, the foremost issue has to be that of which group of cadres will benefit and who will lose out in the inevitable readjustments in power relations that inevitably follow the death of a leader in China.

The problems of arranging for an orderly succession can be seen in the contrast between the skill with which Deng Xiaoping mastered the politics of Mao's succession and the difficulties he has had in managing his own succession. It in no way diminishes the political greatness of Deng as a leader to note that he found it easier to dominate the confusion after Mao's death than to carry out his carefully designed plans for his succession. The contrast is of more than just passing interest, for it tells much about the nature of leadership in Chinese politics.

To understand what happened after Mao's death, and what seems to be happening as Deng's passing gets nearer, it is necessary to start with the first rule in Chinese succession politics: it is imperative for the contenders to promise enough continuity to be considered legitimate successors, while holding out enough hope for change to mobilize the support of Party members by stimulating their ambitions for improving their positions. There is not much room to maneuver between these two fundamental constraints. Since Marxist-Leninist systems officially deny that individuals are the important actors in history, they must pretend that during a succession process nothing of great significance happens. Consequently, legitimacy usually goes to those who pretend, at least temporarily, to uphold the status quo. Thus, in the succession struggle, everyone must strive to claim some degree of identification with the previous arrangements in the top leadership of the Party. However, success will only come to those who can, in spite of this constraint, mobilize new support by hinting at the promise of change. The top leadership is bound to fracture and divide; the winners will be those who can draw in new support for themselves and cut off support to their opponents.

When Mao Zedong died on September 9, 1976, the baton was passed to the hapless Hua Guofeng, who had the wits to realize that his only claim to leadership was the general belief that it was Mao's wish for him to be the next chairman. His need to insist on continuity and total identification with his predecessor in order to legitimize his claim to leadership made Hua look more the simple peasant than he was. First, he had to mouth repeatedly the silly slogan of the Two Whatevers—"Whatever Chairman Mao made we must firmly support, whatever Chairman Mao instructed we must unwaveringly follow." It is a gross misreading of the nature of Chinese politics, and one that makes Hua more the fool than he actually was, to suggest that Hua Guofeng and his Whatever faction would have wanted to go back to Mao's ways of the Cultural Revolution.

Hua's ambition and that of his closest associates was probably only to enjoy the pleasures of resting securely at the top of Chinese politics, basking in the glories of being admired by the multitudes, much as their revered Chairman had done. Politics aside, Hua must have had a hard life: born and raised in Shanxi and thus endowed with an accent and dialect that was nearly unintelligible to all except other locals, he was then assigned to work for many years in Hunan, where his linguistic problems were compounded by the need to adopt a second, equally unintelligible, peasant's accent; finally he arrived in Peking, where how one speaks is often more important than what one says. Even in a circle of leaders from China's rural interior, he was a living caricature of a country bumpkin trying to make a go of it in the top reaches of society—he just wasn't chairmanship timber.

Evidence that Hua had no desire to reverse Mao's final policies and return to a Cultural Revolution situation can be seen, first, in his enthusiastic proclamation of the goals of the Four Modernizations, and second, in his conversations with the foreign leaders who descended upon Beijing to check out the new leader. It was, of course, Hua who compelled China to take up the clumsy formula of the Four

Modernizations as the way of articulating a commitment to national development. Foreign visitors found that Hua was just as versed as his predecessor in making use of cryptic code words that passed for strategic analysis in Mao's day: "the Polar Bear" (that is, the Soviet Union), "unsinkable aircraft carrier" (that is, Taiwan), "firing empty cannons" (that is, bluffing propaganda), "feinting to the East in order to attack the West" (an interpretation of Soviet strategy that would call for greater efforts on the part of the United States to apply NATO pressures on the Soviet Union).

Hua Guofeng's need to claim legitimacy by espousing continuity put him in an even more ludicrous situation after he had boldly arrested the Gang of Four. By having to adhere to Mao's dictum that "left is best," Hua ended up having to make up the patently foolish declaration that the Gang of Four were "Ultra-Rightists." Possibly Hua's counter-factual charge was in part a descendant of the classic Chinese ploy used by leaders to test the loyalty of subordinates. (The practice was for a leader to utter some form of nonsense, and then see who loyally agreed with him. If a leader only spoke common sense he would never know whether his followers were only following the dictates of reason and not blindly revering him.)

Hua soon discovered that the bulk of the Party was ready to join indiscriminately in cursing the Gang of Four as Ultra-Rightists or any other type of abomination. This formula for attacking the defeated faction thus failed to serve the second main objective in succession politics, that of mobilizing new elements of support for the new leadership. Hua's hoped-for opportunity to gain such support came in what turned out to be a poisoned gift from Deng Xiaoping. Sitting out his second exile from the top ranks of the Party in South China, Deng wrote Hua a letter pleading to be allowed to return to the service of the Party and pledging that he would be a loyal subordinate of Hua if permission were granted him to come back to the Center. The naive Hua welcomed the offer, and for a period of time Chinese officials proclaimed that the team of Hua and Deng would endure because it was based on an unshakable spirit of harmony. Chinese spokesmen took it as an insult to the honor of China if anyone even hinted that a power struggle might occur. Any questioning of whether the two leaders might not be in a factional power struggle brought the same kind of scornful denials that Chinese officials were later to use in answering questions about any possible factional basis for the campaign against "bourgeois liberalization." Some Western scholars were as naive as Hua, believing that a duo would be possible as the leadership of a Confucian Leninist system. The rest, of course, is history.

But it was not history well learned. This was to be seen when a decade later Deng anointed Hu Yaobang and Zhao Ziyang as his pair of successors, and Chinese officials earnestly proclaimed that the arrangement would be stable and lasting; once again many Western scholars who should have known better innocently believed it possible for the Chinese to avoid factional strife in a succession crisis. Deng himself seems to have forgotten what he once wrote in criticism of Mao: "It is a feudal practice if a leader chooses his own successors."[6] He probably should have said it is a "futile" practice.

This is not the place for a detailed review of Hu Yaobang's fall from grace, the rise of the anti-bourgeois liberalization campaign, and the designation of Zhao Ziyang, not as the supreme government administrator, which he was well qualified to be, but as the master of ideological and Party affairs, a no-win assignment. It is noteworthy, however, that it all began with Deng's revival, in May, 1986, of the Maoist slogan, "Let one hundred flowers bloom and one hundred schools of thought contend." The fact that it was the thirtieth anniversary of the original "double hundred" campaign should have been enough warning to Chinese intellectuals that they might be, if not careful, moving onto thin ice. For the Hundred Flowers was, of course, followed by the anti-Rightist campaign, the proposal for which was based on the "investigative report" of none other than Deng Xiaoping. (One of the unintended advantages of *pinyin* for the Chinese leadership is that it makes it hard for foreigners, especially those untrained in the Chinese language, to remember that Deng Xiaoping and Teng Hsiao-p'ing are one and the same person.)

In any case, the combination of student protests for democracy (which started on December 5, 1986, and swept the campuses of at least 117 universities, colleges, and middle schools in seventeen cities) and the rising shrillness in the criticisms of senior Chinese writers severely compromised Deng's succession plans. It was Deng's decision, whether necessitated by his opposition or because of his own change of mind, that Hu Yaobang would have to be removed from his position as general secretary of the Party. Another of the legs of Deng's plan for an orderly transferral of leadership was thus removed. The eventual appointment of Zhao Ziyang as general secretary left further questions about the eventual chances of success for Deng's succession arrangements. Hu was the one with years of close association with Deng and extensive contacts throughout the Party. Zhao, on the other hand, has always been essentially a technocrat, a leader at home with policy choices. Hu Yaobang, popular with students and the intellectuals, has long had a substantial power base of his own in the Party, and thus his removal under a challenge from the opposition was significant. In contrast to Hu, Zhao Ziyang has little in the way of a network of supporters in the Party. His only advantages are that he had been clever at policy-making and is attractive to Western businessmen.

To the extent that there was a climax in the story of Deng's succession maneuvers, it was probably the Thirteenth Party Congress, after which it was widely proclaimed that Deng had achieved a great triumph because he had ousted the old generation of leaders and put in their places younger men. Yet it was far from an unambiguous victory. Deng himself had to "retire" in order to get his elderly opponents to agree to do the same. They were replaced by a new Standing Committee who averaged sixty-three years of age, which the Chinese, bless them, declared was a victory for youth. Public attention was so absorbed with the removal of the "Old Guard" and the appointment of younger figures that little attention was given to the fact that Deng had apparently made significant concessions to his peers, as they "retired" together. Deng's accomplishment at the Congress was the not insignificant one of replacing a nearly senile generation of leaders with a generation in its sixties and seventies. Yet even he, as the master of Chinese political maneuvering, was unable to change significantly the balance of power among the new leaders at the top level of the Standing Committee of the Politburo, and thus the successors were near clones of those they replaced.

The new standing committee insured that Deng's official successors would not just be heeding his commands from behind the scene, but also responding to the wishes of other "retired" elders. Deng himself stayed on as chairman of the Military Affairs Commission. Zhao Ziyang showed that he knew that Deng was not really "retired" when he announced that, "When I come across important issues I will consult with [Deng] so I can do a better job." Chen Yun, who had repeatedly called for caution in abandoning central planning, was made chairman of the Central Advisory Commission, the body Deng had earlier established to attract elder cadres into retirement and which he had promised would have significant influence in policy-making. If the Commission turns out not to have influence on decisions, it would make Deng appear to have been a liar; if it does have influence Chen Yun will have greater legitimate access to the centers of power than technically Deng should have. Either way, Deng may have been hoisted on his own petard. Peng Zhen, who has consistently clashed with Deng over the past few years, and who appeared on national television earlier in the year to warn about the dangers of liberalization, was asked to continue to preside over the National People's Congress, China's parliament, and to serve as the chairman of its standing committee—not exactly being sent out to pasture. And of course Li Xiannian, a constant voice of caution, remained as China's president. The good news for the Reformers was that Deng Liqun, the most troublesome spokesman for ideological purity and the man who led the attack upon the intellectuals in the campaign against "bourgeois liberalism," failed to get enough votes to make even the new Central Committee, and is thus destined for true retirement.

In the drama of the transition to a new generation, attention was diverted from the fact that the significant differences of view that had existed among the retiring elite would be replicated in the new standing committee. Zhao Ziyang made it clear that his guiding consideration as the new Secretary General would be to paper over such conflicting views in the new leadership when he denied that there had been differences among Deng's generation of leaders and when he asserted that there would be continuing consensus among his subordinates on the new standing committee. In his victory press interview he said, "Some friends abroad think there is a reform faction and a conservative faction. I would say all those who base their analysis of China on this idea will make one mistake after another."

Zhao was saying that all the previous concern about Deng's having had to fight off a "conservative" opposition was fantasy and that now that he was in command he was going to be a consensus leader, not the advocate of partisan policies. However, we cannot avoid risking what Zhao called making a "mistake," for we must note that Zhao's new standing committee had essentially the same range of opinions among friends and opponents of the "reforms" as did Deng's final standing committee. Zhao Ziyang has in Hu Qili a comrade who is his equal in enthusiasm for racing full steam ahead with the economic reforms. Thus Zhao and Hu replicate the previous pair of Deng and Zhao. But the support of the other three for some features of the reforms is more questionable. Li Peng, the Soviet-trained engineer and a favorite of Chen Yun, not of Deng or Zhao, is on record as believing in the powers of administrative action for guiding economic policies. He is likely to have an instinct for caution whenever difficulties arise, and to press for bureaucratic efficiency rather than rely on the uncertainties of the market. After Li Peng was confirmed as Prime Minister by the

National People's Congress in April, 1988, he indicated in a two-hour press conference that he was aware of the speculations about the divisions of opinion among the new leadership. He was quoted as saying, "Now there is some comment in the foreign press that Zhao Ziyang is in favor of reforms and opening to the outside world, while I am in favor of stabilizing the economy. They somehow pit these two against one another. As a matter of fact there is a misunderstanding involved." To which he added the cryptic observation, "The two aspects form an integral whole and cannot be separated from each other." He then went on to ridicule the thought that he might have been influenced by his years of schooling in the Soviet Union, and concluded by saying, "If you follow that kind of logic, you may think that China will have a pro-United States government in twenty or thirty years because it now has some 20,000 students in the United States."[7] But, of course, this is exactly what most people who enthusiastically welcome the arrival of the Chinese students hope will happen.

The fourth member of the new standing committee, Yao Yilin, has never, as far as anyone knows, been an enemy of central planning, and he is known to have warned against going too fast with the economic reforms. The fifth member is Qiao Shi, an orthodox Marxist. Through his control of the Discipline Inspection Commission (which keeps Party members in line) and his associations with what the Western press has euphemistically called the security apparatus (that is, the secret police), he can be counted upon to keep in check any undue tendencies toward "bourgeois liberalization." During the past few years Qiao Shi did work closely with Peng Zhen, who has consistently been Deng's strongest "opponent." Missing from the new standing committee were Wan Li and others known to have supported Deng in his economic reforms. (Wan Li was given a consolation prize in April 1988, when he was made the chairman of the National People's Congress). Zhao Ziyang will have to establish his own relationships with those now serving with him. Not one of them owes personal allegiance to him. Hu Qili, his spiritual ally, is a long-time associate of Hu Yaobang. As the new head of the Secretariat, where he is joined by Qiao Shi, Hu Qili will have his own power base to work to become the next secretary general of the Party.

Thus, for all of his efforts, Deng Xiaoping has left behind an arrangement for his successor that is apparently not very different from the one with which he wrestled for so long. The gerontocracy has moved off the stage, but its replacements have every expectation of hanging on to power indefinitely, much as Deng's generation had. The scene is thus set for a continuation of much the same type of political process as China has had since the death of Mao. The reforms will go on, guided by pragmatism but under the cloak of the sacred Four Principles, with some leaders calling for greater speed, others demanding greater caution, and a third group mediating the differences. It is no wonder that Zhao remarked after the election of the standing committee, "I still think I'm better suited to serve in the position of premier."

The press commentators, both Chinese and Western, by focusing so intensely on Zhao Ziyang's appointment as top party leader at the Thirteenth Party Congress and by making so much over the expected appointment of younger leaders to top positions, may have missed a more important cause for hope for the continuation of the reforms. The Congress may have provided Hu Yaobang with the opportunity to emulate his mentor's feat of pulling off a resurrection from the political dead, for Hu was made a member of the Politburo. In time he could make it back to the standing committee, for he has more personal allies among its members than does Zhao Ziyang. Certainly for liberal Chinese the hope that Hu Yaobang might return to power is more meaningful than trusting in the compromise standing committee arrangement that Deng left behind. The return of Hu Yaobang would, of course, revive the possibilities of a power struggle with Zhao Ziyang.

Another development at the Thirteenth Party Congress, one that received little attention but may be extremely noteworthy, was the set of decisions made in the realm of ideology. Those who were convinced that the Chinese had become pragmatists generally dismissed the discussions about ideology at the Congress as mere window dressing. In fact, the Congress took what could turn out to have been some very important steps. First, it legitimated the doctrinal theory that China is at a "preliminary" or "primitive" stage of socialism, and can therefore operate according to the rules of a "commodity economy." By this ideological statement the Party justified the spread of market forces and the contraction of central planning. Until the Congress the official stand was that planning was dominant and the market supplementary, but with Zhao's speech, a new formula was adopted: "The state regulates the market, the market regulates firms." Second, the Congress legitimated the separation of ownership and management, which opens the way for the state to discontinue the management of what it theoretically owns. By setting aside the state's "right to operate," the theory justifies the leasing of land and the sale of bonds or shares in a factory to its workers. These ideological steps may help to settle the continuing debates as to whether China has been upholding socialism or backsliding toward capitalism. The decisions thus legitimated the reforms in doctrinal terms and may have cut the ground out from under those cadres who fear that China is moving in the direction of capitalism—exactly what many foreign observers optimistically hope is happening in China.

Although Zhao's speech helped to put the orthodox Marxists on the defensive, it was disturbingly vague with regard to the content of the next stage of the reforms in the economy. Zhao barely mentioned the key problem of price reform, and he avoided entirely the question of bankruptcies. He did say that China's "primary stage of socialism" would last for at least one hundred years after the 1950s, a welcome thought for the Reformers, but he gave no guidance as to what should be done next to solve the array of immediate problems that China faces, such as inflation, the shortage of foreign exchange, problems of rural infrastructure, the shortage of urban housing, or the determination of China's monetary and fiscal approaches in a more market oriented economy. Zhao Ziyang seemed to have abandoned his former authority as the master technocrat and was testing the waters as a politician.

Indeed, a troublesome feature of Deng's succession plans was that Zhao Ziyang had to give up administrative control of the government and assume the leadership of the party, a thankless task at a time when the problems in the ideological realm are probably unsolvable—as Hu Yaobang discovered they were when he had that role. Moreover, the announced objective of Deng's political reforms is to separate the party from the government and to reduce the role of the party in administrative matters relating to the economy—an objective that, if realized, would remove Zhao even further from the technocratic decision-making at which he is so skilled.[8*] It is hard to believe that Deng can be completely happy with what he achieved.

The task of working out a new top leadership was not the only problem Deng Xiaoping had in trying to manage his own succession. In his efforts to designate as many office holders as possible, he failed to resist the false allure of picking future leaders on the basis of their present promise rather than waiting to observe their subsequent performance. He manifested a not uncommon Chinese impatience for tidiness about the future (a weakness to which Singapore's Prime Minister Lee Kuan Yew also yielded but that Chiang Ching-kuo surprisingly resisted). Deng went to the extraordinary lengths of designating three echelons of future leaders. The first included his own generation and its immediate successor of Zhao Ziyang and Hu

Yaobang. The second echelon comprised those who were brought to the central committee at the Thirteenth Party Congress. The third echelon comprised some one hundred thousand cadres who Deng identified as the ones to occupy provincial and lower posts until called to higher office. By trying to put into place the entire succeeding generations of future leaders at all levels of Chinese politics, Deng violated the first and universal rule of patronage politics. This is that one never announces appointments until the last possible moment, because for every grateful appointee there will be a dozen disappointed, alienated candidates, each of whom will be convinced that he is more worthy. Not surprisingly, China's college students at the time of the demonstrations in the winter of 1986-87 argued for political change on the grounds that if Deng's plans were to hold, they would have little prospect of becoming political leaders; at best they could hope to be obedient technocrats.

The link between particular leaders and particular policies is not as strong in Chinese politics as many commentators seem to believe it to be. This is in part because, as we have noted, in American political culture quite a fetish is made over consistency, while in China it is taken as normal for leaders to change their views as circumstances change. It does not necessarily follow that if Deng's succession arrangements fail the result will be an end to the reforms and China's "opening to the outside world." Deng's (and Zhao's) opponents do favor a significant role for central planning, but of course Deng is not entirely against planning. Deng agrees with his opponents that outside influences are acceptable only within certain limits. Indeed, the desire to have Western technology without Western liberal values comes as close to being a consensus as is possible among the Chinese elite. The opposition rails against "wholesale Westernization," but then so do the Dengists, although in softer terms. The opposition vilifies "right deviationist ideas" and those who "slander the socialist system," but then so do Deng and Zhao. Members of Deng's leadership faction are quick to suggest that disaster would occur if the opposition were to come to power, and for exactly the same reasons that Democrats and Republicans predict doom if the other party comes to power—it would push them off the center stage. There are of course shades of policy differences, but more fundamental is the reality that power carries great pay-offs.

One of the great uncertainties in the aftermath of the Thirteenth Party Congress is the direction in which Zhao Ziyang's "pragmatism" is likely to take China. Is his pragmatism likely to lead him to uphold firmly the reforms Deng established—and thereby run the risk of appearing to be another Hua Guofeng preaching a "Whatever" slogan, this time it being "Whatever Deng said, and whatever Deng did, we must also do"? Will his pragmatism make him flexible in seeking consensus—and thereby cause him to yield to the wishes of the more cautious members of his standing committee? Or will he strike out in new directions on his own? Given these possibilities, it would seem that the odds favor change as Zhao's rule progresses.

Changes in leadership can produce profound changes in policy, but often in uncertain directions, for in China power flows in unexpected ways. Who would have predicted that Deng Xiaoping would have initiated the dramatic changes that he did with his "Reforms" (which, of course, are not reforms but revolutionary departures from Maoism)? We were alerted to expect a return to technocratic domination (such as occurred following the failures of the Great Leap) and thus to policies associated with Chen Yun and Deng's present-day "conservative" opposition, but we did not expect the extreme turn to respect for markets and the end of collectivized agriculture. Of course, the record of Mao's rule is proof that in China politics can also zig and zag without a change of the supreme leader.

One of the key reasons why both Mao and Deng had such difficulty in trying to set their successors in place is that in Chinese culture, authority tends to end at the grave. A consequence of the Chinese accent on rule by men and not by law is that old men can have amazing authority until they take their last breath, but after that their last wishes can be easily forgotten. Without a rule of law there is no mechanism for enforcing one's last will. As long as grandfather was alive deference had to be shown, but once he is in his grave the obligation is only to pacify his spirit by performing the proper rituals of ancestor worship. Practices and policies can quickly change. This is so largely because the Chinese believe that intelligent behavior is that which adapts to the situation of the moment. A change can always be rationalized with the argument that grandfather himself would have changed his wishes under altered circumstances. Moreover, the Chinese tradition of feigned compliance and respect for symbols allows rituals of respect to stand in place of actual adherence to the wishes of the dead. Formal deference to the awesome greatness of the deceased ruler is all that is required; there is no need to adhere to his precise dictates.

Hence the ease with which Mao's presumed priorities could be forgotten, and hence the limited influence Deng will have from the grave.

The Reign of the Ego

These observations about the problems of leadership succession can be summed up by the proposition that the fragility of institutionalization in Chinese politics magnifies the importance of the personality of the supreme leader. Mao's personality clearly dominated politics at the Center during the era of his reign. Evidence that the same situation prevails today can be seen in the anxieties of both Chinese and foreigners about what will happen after Deng. Whoever is the successor to Deng will no doubt follow his own distinctive leadership style and put his particular stamp on the historical evolution of China's modernization.

This fact points to a peculiar paradox in the relationship between leadership and followership in Chinese political culture; leaders are expected to have their distinctive and quite individualistic styles, while the followers and the masses are expected to be conformists. Leaders can say things that seemingly violate or belittle what are presumed to be their most cherished policies, while the masses are expected to tread a very narrow line. This is a peculiar development, given the Chinese tradition that rulers are expected to govern by example. It is even more puzzling given that conformity is such an absolute rule in the process of climbing the ladder of success in the Party hierarchy. One might have expected those who reached higher levels in the Party to have become such conformists that they no longer would have distinctive styles. Yet it is not just Mao and Deng who have such contrary styles of leadership; those who are part of Deng's first and second echelons—men such as Li Peng, Hu Qili, and Wan Li—are also distinct personalities.

There are two possible explanations for this paradox. The first is that while conformity is essential in the early stages of advancement, a point is reached when, in order to move into elite circles, leaders must take initiatives and seek out others to build the alliances that will provide them with the necessary power base. In this process they must display the distinctive qualities, in such areas as administration, ideological work, and policy formulation, necessary to make them plausible candidates for higher office.

The second explanation is that once cadres reach high office and are given leadership responsibilities, they experience such a sense of relief and security that at last they feel free to give reign to their egos. In so acting they behave in the same manner as the proverbial Chinese father, who after a lifetime of frugal living and hard work, suddenly decides in his old age that he should indulge himself rather than leave everything to his heirs, who, he suspects, would in any case dissipate the fortune.

Whatever the explanation, there is no denying the contrast between the conforming masses and the higher leaders who enjoy their status and are not afraid to manifest distinctive personal styles. In analyzing Chinese leadership it is therefore necessary to go beyond charting career paths in order to determine with which factions a leader will identify himself. It is necessary to study the individual personalities of those who are in the innermost circles and are likely to become contenders in the succession struggles. Referring back to our initial suggestion that political culture should be looked at as having different levels of appropriate analysis comparable to the three dimensions of linguistics, we can say that the study of leadership requires work at all three levels. In particular, there is a need for work at the level of "phonetics," that is to say, individual personality analysis. However, before we turn to such a review it is necessary to make a brief detour from the subject of leadership to that of followership in Chinese political culture.

Politics without Organized Interests

The key to understanding the relationship between leaders and the public in China in the past and present is the surprising fact that China is a country remarkably easy to rule. In spite of its enormous size, its massive population, its regional diversities, China has held together by the grip of its cultural identity, and not by political authority. It survived with limited governments more concerned with engaging in rituals than in responding to public needs. Europe was at one time endowed with a comparable degree of cultural homogeneity, but it split and fragmented into its multiple states when local interests were asserted against the claims of dominion by Roman empires, both classical and Holy. Even in modern times, and in spite of numerous proclaimed revolutions, China's unity has been preserved by relatively weak governments. The intensity of rule that came with the Communists was inspired by the ruler's ideology and not by any need to respond to conflicting public demands. The Communists, on coming to power, certainly could have dealt with the main public policy problems of the country, such as restoring order, fighting inflation, and reviving the economy, without establishing one of the most penetrating governments known to history. They were driven more by ideology than by necessity.

The prime reason why China has been so easy to rule is that, to a large degree, people rule themselves. China has always been a nation of participants—participants, however, not in a coherent system of national politics, but in parochial groupings. At one time such groupings included the family, clan, *bao-chia*, village, guild, and secret society, all of which looked inward to the disciplining of its members and to ideals of self-sufficiency. Today the family remains strong in spite of its battering, and there are the powerful disciplining realities of the neighborhood committees, small groups, or *danwei*, which seem in some ways to be reincarnations of comparable traditional institutions, designed to control and to meet needs so that no one should have to trouble higher authorities. To do so would be bad form—a notion that has chilling effects on people trained to conform.[9]

The fact that Chinese society has always been elaborately organized into small cellular groupings has had profound consequences on the national government. The private institutions never evolved into assertive pressure groups, organized to mobilize support to publicly change national politics. Instead, without exception, they remained essentially protective associations. While they sometimes sought particularistic favors for their members (but not in ways that might disrupt the public calm), they were mainly devoted to keeping their members out of trouble with the authorities. Government officials at the national or provincial capitals, and even at lower levels, could play their games and fight out their interests, but members of the public at large tried to avoid as much as possible having to deal with government, and they certainly did not feel that they should be demanding policies of it. At best they could publicly complain about mistreatment and hope for redress. State and society were essentially separate domains, in spite of sharing Confucianism and other values. To this day interests outside of the bureaucracy are, of course, not allowed to organize so as to compete with each other in seeking to shape public policies. There was no need in the past to try to mobilize allies and to form coalitions to challenge the policies of the authorities. If private citizens wanted to influence the government, it was better to go about it in a quiet way, seek special favors on the sly, and not make a scene in favor of any local demands. The odds favored success by corruption over public manifestos.

This tradition of Chinese politics has easily been taken up by the Communists, who in keeping with their Leninist tradition believe that all power and authority should be reserved for the world of officialdom, and that there should be no contending powers outside of the ranks of the party and government. We need to make it clear that we are speaking of interests that are autonomous—that is, outside of the government and bureaucracy. Today, as in the past, there is constant politicking among officials, and local officials today follow their predecessors' example of challenging their superiors at the center. Just as local officials once tried, for example, to reduce the tax burdens for their area and to increase the share of the revenues they could keep, so today this process still goes on. It all takes place, however, within the context of the established policies, as part of the realm of the state, not that of society.

Indeed, one of the great ironies of Mao's legacy, one that may still confound Deng's reforms, is the unintended and peculiar capacity he left provincial and local authorities for obstructing national policies. The late Chairman's obsession with self-reliance and his dream of making every province economically self-sufficient resulted in his leaving China with a multitude of local industries and enterprises that cannot economically compete if national markets become truly free ones. These enterprises are still operating today because they are being effectively protected by guarding provincial officials. The goal of Deng Xiaoping's basic industrial policy has been to reduce the powers of China's central planners and pass decision-making down to the actual managers of enterprises, with the hope that this will make the enterprises more efficient. These managers are in theory supposed to be more sensitive to the market, but in practice they are now all too frequently welcoming the shelter of the protectionist instincts of provincial and local officials imbued with the ideal of autarchy for their province, city, or region. Inefficient enterprises are being protected by provincial officials dedicated to keeping out threatening competition from the other provinces. Deng's frustration is that if he seeks to weaken these provincial and local authorities, he is likely only to strengthen the bureaucrats at the center and thereby defeat his initial purpose of limiting the scope of the planners and giving more room to market forces. In a way the various provinces are trying to practice what might be thought of as import substitution policies with barriers to protect their "infant industries." In furthering these efforts at protectionism, officials and plant managers form alliances and make quid pro quo deals.

In this sense there are, of course, tensions between the center and the provinces and localities, and local officials can get around the intentions of the national policies.[10] But just like local officials in the past, they are not inclined to organize their interests openly so as to publicly challenge the national policies of the moment. The objective is to get around the policies, not to alter them. All of this has been made easier by the Chinese skill in feigned compliance, which we have already noted. Lesser officials pretend that they are following orders, while passing up reports that may not accurately reflect local realities. Those at the center know that the world as depicted in paper reports is not likely to be the same as meets the eye, and hence the great Chinese tradition of having "inspection tours." This practice of having what, in the language of arms control, is known as "on-site inspection" does help now, as it did throughout imperial times, to smooth over the gap between the "reality" of the written reports and actual conditions. But it does so without the strains and tensions that open political combat would produce if local interests were to be autonomously organized to fight against the government, as in the history of the West. The battles in China were, and are, reserved for the realm of officialdom, and the compromises are all made in a world of make-believe, as consensus is constructed out of feigned compliance. Supposedly superior officials hate to expose their impotence, and hence are usually prepared to strike bargains that allow the pretenses to continue. Local authorities for their part are today inhibited from pushing their interests beyond acceptable limits because they have been well taught that self-interest is the same as selfishness, a sin under socialism as it was under Confucianism. But, of course, to "protect" local enterprises from "unfair competition" cannot be called selfishness.

Thus on the surface there has to be consensus. Above all, those who are not in the select world of officialdom, must, today as in the past, comply with the wishes of the rulers and also sing their praises. Indeed, under Mao China became a nation of Jonestowners, as one element after another self-destructed while singing praises to the glory of the one who might have been judged its tormentor. The bulk of China's population, its peasantry, was done in by Mao's policies, suffering grievously, especially during the Great Leap madness, and has found relief only with Deng's reversal of policies. Yet there was barely a whimper of complaint. China's intellectuals, supposedly its thinkers and articulators, were cruelly manhandled by being sent into exile in desolate habitations by policies that started with the Anti-Rightist campaign of 1957 and lasted through the Cultural Revolution and until Mao's death. Yet most of the intellectuals came out of a horrible experience unable to see the abomination that had reigned, most still professing loyalty and dedication to the "Revolution"—whatever that might be. Mao had brought the country to the brink of ruin and China's intellectuals clapped their hands in praise.

How could all of this happen? Why were the intellectuals so quick to fault themselves, protesting for example that they really were not Rightists, and so slow to find fault with their leader? It is hard to say, and eventually it is hoped that the Chinese will address the question, just as the Germans have had to grapple with how they could have supported Hitler and allowed the Holocaust. In part the explanation probably accords with Lynn White's theory, noted in the previous chapter. The Chinese people were caught up in a situation in which they were individually identified according to rigid categories with labels that carried great political weight, and their well-being depended upon holding their place in patron-client networks. Thus, their situation was easily shaken by the uncertainty of their fates and by the passions stirred up by government-decreed movements. Victims of such circumstances, they responded by ostracizing and then attacking each other. Thus, in a paradoxical fashion, the patterns of social organization that have made China so easy to govern were turned on their heads, so that instead of order there was feuding and chaos. The one who built up the fears and frustrations was, of course, Mao Zedong. Moreover, the spark that ignited the explosion clearly came from Mao's charisma. Therefore, what we need to do now is to examine Mao's leadership style, and the personality behind his demonic charisma.

Theory Gives Meaning to Facts

It must be acknowledged that Mao's mystique of leadership reached beyond the Chinese and addled the thinking of intellectuals and others elsewhere. Some Western intellectuals went so far as to elevate him to the ranks of a great philosopher when, if fact, his writings are of significance only in the parochial context of the history of Chinese Communism. Others were temporarily carried away to the point of proclaiming that Mao and Maoism might have something to teach the advanced industrial world. There were also voices raised to say that Mao's economics could be of value for other developing countries. His policies did represent something new under the sun, but fortunately few poor countries made the costly mistake of adopting them. In America at the time of the Cultural Revolution, the wonderment at the mystique of Mao was great. For example, Charles E. Lindbloom, in writing his major work in political economy, *Politics and Markets*, felt it necessary, after identifying the two universal models of a market and a command economy, to add a third one, a "persuasion economy," which he believed was the unique creation of Mao Zedong.[11] Granted, the 1960s and early 1970s were not times when clear thinking was commonplace in universities—indeed, some intellectuals were paying obeisance to African dictatorships by proclaiming them to be meritorious examples of the unique African invention of "one party democracies." Still, it was surprising how few saw that Maoism was doing immense harm to the Chinese people.

The power of the mystique of Mao's leadership to mask the follies of his policies calls for psychological explanations that go beyond the ordinary theories of charisma. How could it be that so many intelligent people, both in and out of China, could have been taken in by Mao's political rhetoric and political theater?

A good starting point in searching for an answer is Robert Robins's analysis of the combination, in the personage of the great leader, of both charisma and paranoia.[12] Robins delineates the ways in which a leader's charismatic appeal can be energized by his paranoia, which in turn the charisma helps to hide. The charismatic posturing and rhetoric, the impassioned defense of a "homeland" and the "revolution" and the "party" against devious foes, provides a cloak of respectability and legitimacy for the dark suspicions of the paranoia. The two case studies Robins analyzes are those of Hitler and Stalin. With Hitler the paranoia was of the distant variety, in which his fancied enemies fell into generalized categories, at first abstractions, but all too concrete in time: "international capitalism," "the bourgeoisie," "the Jews." In the case of Stalin the paranoia was of a more immediate variety, in that his "enemies" started with his immediate associates, but included people throughout the supposedly precious institutions of the Party and the army. According to Robert Conquest, the purges of 1936 through 1938 claimed between six and eight million victims, one third of the Party, six out of thirteen members of the Politburo, 1,100 out of 1,966 delegates to the 1934 Party Congress, three out of the five marshals in the Red Army, thirteen out of fifteen army commanders. Yet while all of this was going on in more or less public view, the mystique of Stalin and of the Bolshevik Revolution was such that substantial numbers of believers in socialism at home and abroad were unappalled.

The point here is not the clinical issue of whether or not Hitler and Stalin were paranoids—although they probably were. For the political scientist, the point is that theories of personality can be powerful tools for providing insights into political behavior, because they suggest that when certain patterns of behavior are identified, we should expect that they will be accompanied by specific other patterns of behavior. The theories tend to define syndromes, so that when some facts regarding behavior are ascertained, we should be alerted to look for specific other behaviors. What may first seem to be only random clusterings of behaviors can turn out to be established patterns known to psychology.

Returning to the case of Mao Zedong, it is clear that his charisma did have a strong infusion of narcissism, but the definition of paranoia does not provide much help in making meaningful his general behavior. Instead it seems to me that the theory of borderline personality provides illuminating guidance for understanding Mao's behavior.[13*] This is not the place to detail the borderline syndrome. What we can do is briefly demonstrate how the popular view among China-watchers that Mao had a "mercurial personality," which leaves patterns of changeableness vague and directionless, can become far more rigorously defined and predictable when the borderline syndrome is used to interpret his actions. We need to note only two features of that syndrome to illustrate our point.

First, a fundamental characteristic of a borderline personality is the need always to have an "enemy" to battle against and thereby to find a focus or purpose that can give some order to essentially mercurial behavior. The "enemy" can change quite quickly, but there is always some enemy who provides both an anchor to stabilize behavior and a purpose or goal that gives a rationale for the dominant strategy that shapes almost all calculated behavior.[14]

In Mao's case, there was no time in his life when he was not focusing on a perceived "enemy" and when he was not finding some latent pleasure in his "struggles" against whomever or whatever that enemy might be at the moment. In early childhood it was, of course, his father who was the enemy to be fought, and Mao's energies went into trying to mobilize the rest of the family against him. When he left home and went off to school at Xiang Xiang, his teacher became the "enemy," and Mao could not understand why the other students did not share his animosity and join him in making life miserable for the teacher. His explanation was that the students were "laughing at him" because of his inelegant clothing. He had the same fantasy that everyone was scorning him, looking down on him as being unworthy, when he arrived at Beijing and had the job of assistant librarian at Beida University. In the late 1960s he again thought that the cadres were scorning him. As Mao took up his political role of party leader, he had both distant categories of enemies, as Hitler did, and more immediate collegial enemies, as Stalin did. The generalized enemies included, of course, various class categories, the United States, the Soviet Union, and the "bourgeoisie who are right in the Party." Marxism-Leninism, of course, stresses class struggle, but Mao carried the idea of the permanence of class labels and the persistence of enemy classes far beyond anything known in any other Communist Party. It is noteworthy how easily the Chinese Party was able to abandon the intensity of its concerns over "class struggle" after Mao Zedong's death. Even more dramatic is the telling fact that as long as Mao ruled, China always had mortal foreign "enemies," but after his death China's foreign relations have been smoother—the country has the same national interests, but a leader with a different psychological makeup. As for Mao's perceived immediate "enemies" among his colleagues, the list is legion. Some innocently went to their doom, protesting their loyalty to him, and unable to understand why Mao should have turned against them. Others, in particular Lin Biao, seem to have sensed that, in time, Mao would inevitably see an enemy in his closest associates, and tried to take evasive, protective action. Moreover, at no time in his life did Mao have a truly close personal friend.

This brings us to a second fundamental characteristic of the borderline syndrome, an inability to make enduring emotional commitments, which is combined with a deep suspicion that the emotions of others will not be lasting. The theme of abandonment thus permeates borderline cases. The suppression of genuine feelings or expressions of affect stems from a fear of being damaged if any commitment should be made. Safety lies in abandoning others before the inevitable happens, which is that the other will turn against oneself. The result is a lifetime of acting with half-felt emotions and displays of feigned passions. More particularly, the possessor of a borderline personality may suddenly "split" with others; an apparently normal, friendly relationship can with little apparent cause become an adversarial one. Friends suddenly are seen as enemies.

In Mao's life there was a continuous series of abandonments by him of people who sought to be close to him, starting with his siblings, then extending to his wives and children, and then to colleagues. He abandoned even his own policies. Moreover, Mao's political language was obsessed with the importance of revolutionary ardor and was driven by a profound suspicion that such an emotion was not likely to be lasting among others. Yet as an orator Mao displayed little feeling, using almost no physical movements. He was then the exact opposite of Hitler, who could stir up mass passions by ranting and raving. His poetry oddly juxtaposed a mood of tranquility with the subject of warfare. Mao also seemed to exploit the borderline practice of adopting moods that were out of phase with the moods of the people around him: when others were excited, he would be calm; when others were relaxed, he would call for a redoubling of effort; when others were solemn, he would be joking, when others became informal, he would demand formality. One could never know what to expect from Mao in the way of mood or affect; one could, however, expect that whatever demeanor one adopted, he would seek to gain the upper hand by calling for another mood.

Above all, Mao's mystique of leadership seems to have been a form of charisma based upon features consistent with a borderline personality, because it called upon his followers and the public to be passionate, dedicated, unswervingly loyal, steadfast, and mindlessly persistent, while he himself practiced zigging and zagging, high involvement, and near total withdrawals—anything but consistency.

The analysis of Mao's personality and leadership does not, of course, explain all phases of his role in the history of the Chinese Communists. Situations and circumstances could be compelling, although the bias in his responses to reality had to be influenced by his personality. Fortunately, we do have abundant evidence about Mao's personality and so psychological explanations are reasonably valid in trying to understand him. There certainly are pitfalls in other approaches to analyzing his conduct as China's great leader. For example, some people have sought to chart Mao's political course by seeing him as a spokesman for China's peasantry, a man from the countryside who could speak for the peasant masses, and thereby became the authentic leader of China. Yet Mao was never actually a peasant, he displayed little understanding of the problems of farming, and above all his policies were disastrous for China's peasants, who probably suffered more under his rule than under the warlords. To write that Mao was exceptional because he was the leader of a "peasant army" is to be strangely ill-informed about Chinese realities, for in China all armies are peasant armies.

Others have sought to find the gyroscope in Mao's career by treating him as an intellectual and philosopher. Yet in his efforts to emulate Stalin and the early Bolshevik tradition of leader-writer, Mao showed that he was not a coherent thinker with consistent principles. Instead his Thoughts were a mishmash that trivialized philosophy and debased

Marxism. And, of course, through his policies he did more to damage intellectual life in China than any leader in modern times.

Others have tried to make Chinese nationalism Mao's guiding star, depicting him as a leader who brought pride to China and made its people "stand up." Yet it was Mao who went to Moscow to become the junior partner of Stalin. And what of the heroic efforts of the countless Chinese, regardless of politics, who stood up to Japan and fought a long, hard war for years without external aid? What third world country of today would fight alone against such a superior aggressor as Japan was? Indeed, politically conscious Chinese today are aware that Mao's domestic policies damaged China's international prestige and put the country behind neighbors it once looked down upon. Mao exploited Chinese nationalism; he did not create or strengthen it.

Today the Chinese seem to be more grudging in their honoring of the late Chairman, saying that the early Mao was good but the late Mao had faults. This is only Chinese rhetoric, for they have cast aside all the main policies of the so-called "good" Mao. Moreover, this is not a formula to be applauded by Americans because it was, of course, the early Mao who championed the alliance with Stalin and bitterly opposed the United States, while the later Mao denounced the Soviet Union and initiated the opening to the United States. This formula does, however, have the virtue of pointing to two important and related facts about Mao's leadership. First, it was a form of charismatic leadership that failed to provide an enduring basis for the institutionalization of his legacy. What was accomplished early was lost in the later years. Second, the uncertainty inherent in his style of rule resulted in a prolonged succession crisis of a decade or more. Mao's style of dramatizing enemies, abandoning colleagues, and playing with the emotions of the public left China with a serious erosion of legitimacy and with potential successors caught up in cynical battles of self-preservation. His legacy made it easy for Deng Xiaoping to be popular in the short run—the contrast in styles as well as policies was such a relief for the Chinese people. But in the longer run, Mao's failure to institutionalize the governing process left Deng with troublesome problems of legitimacy.

Legitimacy Problems and the Future of China's Political Culture

By the late 1980s the politics of Deng's era were also being decisively shaped by succession issues. In the actual playing out of the final rounds, Deng's succession is not likely to be as dramatic as the conclusion of the succession to Mao. No group is likely to be suddenly arrested and tried as were the Gang of Four. Yet there will certainly be a faction ready to reenact Hua Guofeng's role by proclaiming that "whatever Deng said and whatever Deng did" should be continued. Even if its members are as dim-witted as Hua was, any faction's attempt to wrap itself in the mantle of Deng's authority and claim legitimacy on the basis of continuity is likely to fail. The ultimate winner will be the one who can best reach out and bring in new elements while still appearing to be loyal to Marxism-Leninism. In the struggle to find that narrow path between advocating continuity while holding out hope for change, the main actors will have to engage in all manner of political contortions. There is likely to be just as absurd a labeling of opponents as when Hua designated the Gang of Four as Ultra-Rightists. Already the Western Press has fallen into the practice of calling those who hold to the legitimacy of Mao's radicalism China's "conservatives," an astonishing distortion of political labeling by either Western or Chinese standards. It would incidentally make it much easier for the Western public to make sense of Chinese politics if the press and China-watchers would abandon the labels "Reformers" and "Conservatives" and describe Deng's followers as "enthusiasts" or "optimists" and the opposition as "cautious critics" or "pessimists." The difference between Deng Xiaoping and, say, Chen Yun is more one of temperament and style than of basic values. The members of the opposition are generally "go slowers," while Deng's followers feel that a lot of ground must be covered fast, or at least before Deng passes from the scene.

The main problem at the time of Mao's succession was the question of ideology; the problem for Deng's successors is what to do about substantive policies. In much Western analysis of Chinese developments there has been a tendency to see the "success" of Deng's "reforms" as critical in upholding the legitimacy of his regime and that of his preferred successors. Deng himself, however, is not so politically naive as to risk such a weighty matter as legitimacy upon popular readings of the successes and failures of concrete policies. It is a fundamental rule of politics that the legitimacy of systems should never be tied to the vagaries of fortune, and especially not to popular impressions about the pay-offs of specific public policies. Policies can be adjusted, changed, given a new public face, or even repudiated; legitimacy must be anchored more deeply in the soul of a people.

The successor to Deng will be confronted with a more troublesome crisis of legitimacy than that which confronted the successors to Mao. In the late 1970s the problem was what to do with leaders who could, though defeated, claim to have had intimate associations with Mao. There was also the question of what should be made of Mao himself and his Thoughts. How far should the successor go in saying that the Father of the People's Republic of China had feet of clay, like so many other fathers of third world countries? The successors to Deng will have on their hands an even more eroded ideology and a population with far more individualistic, and hence conflicting, ambitions.

In a strange fashion Mao Zedong may have brought about a profound, but for him a totally unintended, change in the basic way the Chinese look upon leadership and government. From the dawn of Chinese civilization, it has been second nature for the Chinese to believe that the Mandate of Heaven depended upon the economic fate of masses of the people. If the people faced economic troubles they had the right to blame government, for the obligation of government was to do right so as to bring material benefits to all. Government was thus assumed to be a decisive factor in determining the state of the economy. Elsewhere in the world the myth that economics can and should be the servant of politics came much later and with far more rationalizations. In traditional China the great masses of the people believed that government could and should have a beneficial influence on their livelihood. It was only the merchants who saw the mandarins as their natural enemies and government as a hindrance to economic progress. The Confucian rulers reinforced the peasants' natural suspicions that the game of the merchant was to cheat the customer. These predispositions of traditional Chinese political culture made it easy for the Chinese to see as reasonable the Communists' claims that they could benefit the whole country by managing the economy. The Chinese had no instinctive horror of government "interference" with the economy. It seemed to them self-evident that rulers should be able to bring about good times. By the end of Mao's rule and with the successes of the early years of Deng's rule, large numbers of Chinese must have begun to rethink their basic attitudes about the relationship of politics and economics. Mao certainly taught the masses that government could be the enemy of their well-being. Prosperity came only as the Party released their hold on the economy. The Thirteenth Congress, by saying that China was only at a primary stage of socialism, formally sanctioned the view that government should be limited and scope should be given to private endeavors.

If indeed such a change has come about in the basic thinking of significant numbers of Chinese, it will constitute a profound change in the way the Chinese look to government. Instead of being a benevolent force, government will become a threat. In time this change could help resolve the crisis of legitimacy. In the short run, however, there is likely to be considerable confusion, which may make the legitimacy problem more difficult—particularly if people feel that the shift to the market has increased selfishness and corruption.

However, before we make the mistake of exaggerating these problems of legitimacy, let us remember again that China is a relatively easy country to govern because its people are governed primarily by their immediate social and community arrangements. The problem of legitimacy in China is likely to affect mainly the self-esteem of the leadership. The Chinese people at large, like people in many countries, have learned to accept as normal, and hence essentially legitimate, the fact that leaders will routinely use words that contradict reality. Widespread cynicism can be the basis for a remarkably stable form of legitimacy. The American view that corruption and lying by officials threaten legitimacy is a peculiarly ethnocentric one, and relevant only in a democracy. In many countries throughout history people have accepted various forms of corruption as being as normal as the sun rising in the East. Indeed, cynicism is more often the basis of legitimacy than the cause for its erosion. Therefore the problem of legitimacy in China is more one of what the leadership will do to satisfy its own need for self-esteem. Since, as we have observed, the rhythm of Chinese politics is not the left-right swings of Western systems but the up and down motion of tightening and relaxing controls, of centralization and decentralization, any increase in anxiety on the part of the leadership is likely to translate into a greater degree of repression. This would probably be accompanied by the regime's efforts to attain greater ideological justification.

By late 1986 such efforts were already apparent in the leaders' shrill declarations that the goal should be "socialism with Chinese characteristics" and that "bourgeois liberalization" must be vigorously opposed. The problem, as we have already noted, was that the leadership found itself inarticulate in trying to explain what was meant by either "socialism" or "Chinese characteristics." And having sent a chill through the intellectual community with its "anti-bourgeois liberalization" rhetoric, it could find little help from the people who were suppposedly the most articulate in explaining complex matters. The fuzziness of the concept of "socialism with Chinese characteristics" makes unclear not only China's goals but also the object of national pride. The slogan could easily backfire by reminding people that China's thirty-year addiction to "socialism" has not been an era of total success. Indeed, the slogan could become a symbol of national embarassment, much like the "Burmese Road to Socialism" and "African Socialism" are to other disillusioned populations.

China's identity problem, which is at the core of its legitimacy difficulties, is manifestly obvious, but few in China dare give voice to it. That problem is that China quite naturally wants to emulate the successes of its neighbors—South Korea, Taiwan, Hong Kong, Singapore, and even, but somewhat implausibly, Japan—but the Chinese can never admit to looking up to countries they have so long despised. Hence the need to assert as dogma that "socialism is superior to capitalism," a quaint nineteenth-century article of faith. In practice, moreover, "socialism" in China has come to mean a compromising of the state's monopolistic control of the economy, but not of the Party's power. The Chinese public is not likely to become agitated over where the line should be drawn between the state sector and the private sector, given the qualities of Chinese pragmatism we have observed. The monopolizing of all power by the Party, however, may become more tricky as future generations become more assertive and more questioning about the lack of democracy.

The Deng leadership has sensed this danger and issued its warnings by denouncing as unpatriotic political sins that it classifies as "bourgeois liberalism"; this term is generally understood to mean that intellectuals and students should toe the line and eschew creative thinking. "Liberalism" is understood to be the open competition of ideas, respect for the opinions of others, including those who advocate minority or heterodox views—in short, democracy in general and all of its associated civilities in particular. In denouncing "bourgeois" values the Deng leadership has, in an odd way, positioned itself as though it were opposing the almost universal desires of mankind to rise above poverty, to escape the tyranny of mindless labor, and to participate in the more comfortable life of the middle class. It may be correct in equating "bourgeois" with "capitalism," but its rhetoric shows an ignorance of both Marxism and Western experiences. Finally, in trying to make "bourgeois liberalism" seem less than a happy, almost idyllic state, the Deng leadership has sought to blacken the term by suggesting that it is related to pornography, and therefore that the idea of freedom is somehow obscene. Deng and company, in railing against such innocent pleasures as dancing cheek-to-cheek, were not just risking alienating the brightest of the younger generation in order to pacify a few crotchety killjoys in the Old Guard opposition, they were following the long-established Communist belief that among the proletariat, manifestations of joy should be limited to scenes in propaganda posters.

In spite of the Chinese leaders' Marxian earnestness, the campaign against "bourgeois liberalism" raised again questions about whether the leaders understood what middle class values actually are, and what values China will need to modernize. In the West the long established, indeed the only correct way, to *épater les bourgeois* has always been to flaunt bohemian practices, to shock the middle class with nonconformist antics. Now, however, the Chinese have come up with the astonishing idea that the way to attack bourgeois values is to make the Chinese people more puritan than the Puritans. Somehow the Chinese have taken a Western concept and turned it totally around so as to suggest that the bourgeoisie are at home with bohemian practices—a reversal of a Western concept that poses a problem in intellectual history worthy of a younger Benjamin Schwartz. (Could it be that the leaders in Beijing have been reading Daniel Bell's *Cultural Contradictions of Capitalism* on the sly, and have decided that Bell is correct and that in today's post-industrial, mass media dominated societies, the bourgeoisie can easily keep pace with the avant-garde in cultural sophistication, and therefore nonconformity can no longer shock the middle class? Maybe the Chinese have decided that although their country is still a long way from being a post-industrial society, it is not too early to worry about defenses against cosmopolitan sophistication.)

Whatever their confusions about bourgeois values in general, the Chinese have a clear grasp of what constitutes proletarian values politically: they associate such values with repression and conformity, practices they are determined not to abandon. But the issue involves deeper values, and therefore the differences are the most stark in the cultural realm. The Chinese authorities know from both their ideology and practical experiences that the dynamism of creativity in all dimensions of life comes from Western societies and their bourgeois cultures. What they have set for themselves is the task of censoring that creativity, screening from their masses all they believe to be unseemly. The process takes time, and consequently the little that is new that is allowed is what everyone else sees as passé. Thus, although the Chinese leaders crave to see their country at the forefront of innovations, they only allow their people to take up Western fashions that are on the decline. What was exciting about the innovations will have long wilted by the time the Chinese public are allowed to enjoy them. Just as the authorities now allow ballroom dancing, but not cheek-to-cheek, so maybe in time they will allow the Chinese the pleasures of elements of today's art and drama, and the stimulations of today's creative ideas—but only after they have lost their explosive impact. In the meantime, some Western observers, sensitive to the contrast to how conditions were under the heavy handed cultural policies of Mao's era, will praise the "new freedoms," but remain insensitive to the dehumanizing process whereby Chinese intellectuals come to accept the rules for being tacit propagandists of the state and the party by operating within the confines of the prescribed proletarian-technocratic culture. In this way China will be following in the path of the Soviet Union and the Eastern European countries, where harsh repression has been increasingly replaced by a process of coopting, in which intellectuals are given many favors as long as they practice conformity in their pretended creativity.[15]

The attack upon "bourgeois liberalism" in early 1987 put China out of step with trends elsewhere in the Communist world. In Gorbachev's Soviet Union and in Eastern Europe, especially Hungary and Czechoslovakia, there is an awareness that advancement into a more modern economy will call for essentially middle class, professional orientations and the abandonment of the values of the proletariat—values associated with the classical totalitarianism of Stalinism—and the acceptance of carefully screened artistic imports from the West. The European Communist rulers seem to appreciate the need to couple economic reforms with greater tolerance for diversity in cultural attitudes, while the Chinese seem to believe that attitudes can be compartmentalized so as to have economic change without other changes. There is irony here because in substantive policies the Chinese are far ahead of the other Communist states in moving away from Marxism and in recognizing the liberating forces of the market. Yet the Deng leadership seems unaware that its goals of bringing high technology to China and maintaining authoritarian values are incompatible.

Culture Wins Out

In a convoluted, clumsy way the Deng–Zhao leadership seems to be struggling to find an appropriate way of expressing, with a nineteenth-century Western vocabulary, the nineteenth-century Chinese notions of *ti-yong* that distinguished between Chinese values, which were to be protected, and Western technology, which could be safely adopted. As we have noted, Chinese reformers at the turn of the century argued that it should be possible to cling to Confucian values, which they saw as basic and profound, while accepting some Western ideas that could be treated as secondary since they were merely utilitarian. In trying to make a distinction in a domain where no clear boundaries exist, the Deng leadership finds itself in a more untenable position than did the early Chinese reformers. Today's reformers have to argue that the basic, profound values to be protected against "Westernization" are not traditional Chinese ones but the patently Western ones of an outdated Marxism-Leninism.

The great irony of China's prolonged thrashing about over its identity problems of Chineseness and socialism-communism is that China's current *ti-yong* problem is of profound consequence in the evolution of Marxism-Leninism. Its effect was not intended by the Chinese, nor is it as yet fully appreciated by them or by the Marxist world in general. Mao Zedong over the years frantically sought to leave a mark on the evolution of Marxism-Leninism, and although the Chinese still praise Marxism-Leninism-Mao Zedong Thought as though he was one of a triumvirate, any lasting contributions by the Chairman to that ideological tradition are so puny as to be close to zero. On the other hand, Deng Xiaoping has not sought to be a shaper of ideological thought, but he may have devised a formula that with a major assist from Secretary General Mikhail Gorbachev could lead to a totally new vision for Marxists. Deng did this through his formula of "Socialism with Chinese Characteristics," which says that Marxism can recognize as immutable the reality of cultures. In traditional Marxism there was no room for culture. Class characteristics were supposed to be the same the world around. The bourgeoisie and the proletariat each supposedly had the same attitudes and world views regardless of place and time. Hence the natural possibility of a "world capitalist system" and of the "workers of the world uniting" as one. Socialism and Communism were universalistic ideals, utopian conditions that would be the same for all peoples regardless of their past conditions and their cultures. It is true that Stalin grudgingly opened the door to variations due to culture by tacitly accepting the idea that there could be different "roads to socialism." But even with that formulation the idea of socialism remained a universalistic abstraction, the same for all peoples regardless of the "road" they may have taken.

After Deng announced "Socialism with Chinese Characteristics" as China's ultimate goal and Gorbachev went along with the proposition, Marxism-Leninism entered a new phase. Universal categories will now be replaced by culturally specific ones. If there can be "socialism with Chinese characteristics," then of course there will also have to be "socialism with Russian characteristics" and distinctive forms of socialism for all those who claim to be socialist countries.

This transformation in the basic orientation of Marxism-Leninism, this change in its most fundamental assumptions, not only paves the way to legitimating greater flexibility in the domestic policies of all states calling themselves Marxist-Leninist. It also eliminates the most fundamental basis for the imperative of monolithic unity among Communist states. Moscow's traditional justification for demanding compliance with its wishes and uniformity in outlook was that Marxist ideology reflected universal truths and that there was no room in that ideology for cultural differences. Armed with universal truths, the surpreme ideologists believed that they had a knowledge that was more powerful than mere parochial cultural realities. It was Deng, and not Mao, who proved them wrong.

Thus it is that Marxism-Leninism has been profoundly dented in its confrontation with Chinese culture. Thus it is that the Chinese Communists themselves have had to yield to the realities of Chinese culture. Chinese culture—in terms of basic personality, fundamental practices, and the deep and abiding values transmitted in family contexts—has endured in spite of all the efforts of the Chinese Communists to make over the Chinese in the Soviet image of the "New Man." After nearly forty years of Communist rule devoted to obliterating Chinese cultural traditions, the Deng leadership has committed itself to defending "Chineseness" against the evils of "Westernization." In doing so it has had to grapple with questions regarding its own legitimacy. More importantly it has challenged the legitimacy of traditional Marxism-Leninism.

What all of this proves is that Chinese society and its remarkable culture do have astonishing resiliency. In spite of catastrophic political problems of war and revolution, the Chinese economy, decade by decade, has made progress. There have, of course, been temporary ups and downs—the downs coming mainly from the actions of the leaders and from political turmoil—but the Chinese people operating in their immediate groupings have been able to master their circumstances and exploit with great ingenuity any moments of stability. They have the talent to bide their time when their leaders are making progress difficult and to spring into action when circumstances are propitious. There are few sillier phantoms in contemporary politics than the irrational fear of the Chinese leadership that the Chinese people are in danger of becoming "Westernized." They need only look across the waters to Japan to see how nearly impossible it is for an Asian-Confucian society to become Westernized in spirit. If it has not happened in Japan, imagine how long it will take for China to be in danger of becoming Westernized.

Therefore the moral of our story is that the genius of Chinese political culture is that it permits national rulers, in all their manifest glory, to initiate all kinds of policy changes with remarkable ease, acts which can bring to them oceans of praise; it permits local authorities to ignore when appropriate the august wishes of those above them and, through feigned compliance, to preserve consensus; and finally it allows the people as a whole to operate in their basic small groupings of family, neighborhood, and workplace, their cell-like structures that shape their personalities. The leaders have their stages on which to move about. The bureaucrats have their domains for infighting and for obstructing the desires of the great. The Chinese people have their cellular structures, which provide the comforts of the familiar if not the guarantee of security. The small worlds of the individual provide protection from the big winds of national politics, and the art of upholding consensus by gracious make-believe smooths over the gaps between rulers, bureaucrats, and citizens. Thus, political change is ceaseless, but the basic cultural patterns remain remarkably enduring. Each generation of Chinese learns how to orient behavior to the context of the immediate situation, and to look for cues from the political domain in order to avoid trouble or exploit opportunity. The Chinese with their boundless optimism that the future will be the glowing opposite of their dark past are always talking of a "New China," but of course the reality is that China endures, and changes but slowly.

I would like to end here on a personal note to justify my faith in the grass roots of Chinese society. At the end of the Pacific War I was with the 5th Marine Regiment, which was dispatched to Peking to accept the Japanese surrender. We embarked from our ship at Taku Bar during the night, unsure of what to expect, and boarded a special train that finally left at five in the morning for the eighty-odd mile ride to Peking. We did not arrive there until early afternoon. The reason we crept so slowly was that every few furlongs along the road the train would stop to let aboard delegations of Chinese from the surrounding villages and towns who were anxious to greet our commanding officer.

He was too impatient a man for such rituals and ordered me to manage the visitors with as much dispatch as possible. I immediately discovered that the delegations had an earnestness of purpose that went way beyond the formalities of cordial greetings. The principal figures in each group would bring forward documents which certified their claims to various offices such as village headman and other minor posts, and they asked that the Americans, who they expected would now be their regional rulers, place their "chop" on these papers. Some of the documents carried chops that went back to a string of warlords, as well as to the Nationalists and the Japanese puppet regime. In some cases the men looked much too young to have been in authority for so long, but they would explain that their fathers had passed the status on to them. Universally, they found inconceivable my protestations that the Marines had no "chop" nor the authority to make any political appointments. These exchanges were often prolonged and became somewhat heated before the men would fold up their precious papers and leave the train to await the arrival of the next sovereign power, who they hoped would play the Chinese game of legitimating local authority. I am sure that the upheaval of 1949 brought to an end the authority of many of these men and their families, but I suspect that the tradition of natural leadership at the local level endures, and in doing so provides stability and continuity to China's political culture. We can also take heart from the courage of the many Western-educated Chinese, like Mrs. Nien Cheng, who have remained stoutly loyal to the best in the great traditions of Chinese culture.

NOTES

Chapter I: Explaining Political Culture

1. Tiziano Terzani, *Behind the Forbidden Door: Travels in Unknown China* (New York: Henry Holt, 1986).

2. I have made a comparative analysis of the state of political culture studies among the Asian states in "Political Psychology in Asia," in Margaret G. Herman, ed., *Political Psychology* (San Francisco: Jossey-Bass, 1986).

3. In making a defense of the concept of political culture, I am aware that the pendulum has swung and there is now a significant revival of interest in this approach in political science. Samuel P. Huntington, in reviewing the current state of political development studies, comes to the conclusion that future work will necessarily focus more on political culture in seeking to explain different success rates in political, social, and economic development. ("The Goals of Development," in Myron Weiner and Samuel P. Huntington, eds., *Understanding Political Development* [Boston: Little, Brown, 1987], 21–28.) Peter Berger, the sociologist, has initiated a major project on the Confucian tradition and economic and political development. In the field of Communist studies, in addition to the work of Archie Brown, there is Robert Tucker, who is completing an important work on Russian political culture. The rapid decline in the respectability of dependency theory stems in no small part from the undeniable significance of political cultural factors for explaining different patterns of economic development in East Asia and Latin America.

4. Geoffrey Gorer, "The Concept of National Character," in *The Danger of Equality and Other Essays* (New York: Weybright and Talley, 1966), 9–23.

5. This problem brings to mind an embarrassing incident for anthropology that occurred at the end of World War II when the U.S. Navy hired a young anthropologist to study the culture of the former Japanese-controlled island of Yap, which the Navy was now

called upon to administer. The anthropologist selected a house to live in, and analyzed the activities of its occupants, on the assumption that they represented a typical living group on Yap. He worked assiduously, collecting his notes on all the comings and goings of the occupants for nearly six months before the first United States Navy ship with a large crew visited the island. On their first night ashore, with unerring instincts, the sailors discovered that the anthropologist's "typical" house was in fact the local whorehouse. Navy brass thereafter held a skeptical view of the insightfulness of anthropology.

6. A. Zee, *Fearful Symmetry: The Search for Beauty in Modern Physics* (New York: Macmillan, 1986).

7. Indeed, another peculiar twist that social scientists have given to their version of "science" is their treatment of the principle of replication. It would appear that, in the minds of some political scientists, research skills are not essential in replicating studies, and therefore anyone, irrespective of competence, should be accepted as qualified to replicate and thereby test previous research. Any study can thus be treated as a legitimate challenge of the findings of mature scholars. If the physical sciences operated under such rules, Boyle's Law would be negated at the beginning of each semester, since it is routine for nearly a third of freshmen chemistry students to fail to "prove" the law. In physics there are clear standards of excellence among experimental physicists, and the acceptance of the validity of new findings depends very much upon the reputation of the researcher. Skill in physics is exactly the same as skill in painting or music; some people are better endowed than others, experience and training count, and progress depends upon the quality of performance. The peculiar notion of replication held by some social scientists means that progress can be no faster than the achievements of the dullest practitioners.

8. A not untypical example of this use of the charge of reductionism for an indiscriminate attack on others is that of Atul Kohli's "Introduction," in his edited book, *The State and Development in the Third World* (Princeton: Princeton University Press, 1986). Gabriel Almond, by citing chapter and verse examples of the misreading of the early literature on political development and behavioralism, has exposed the errors of such misinformed critics. See his "The Development of Political Development," in Weiner and Huntington, eds., *Understanding Political Development*, 437–90; and his "Corporatism, Pluralism and Professional Memory," *World Politics* (January 1983).

9. Alex Inkeles, "National Character: The Study of Modal Personality and Socio-Cultural Systems," in G. Lindzey, ed., *Handbook of Social Psychology*, vol. 2 (Cambridge: Addison-Wesley, 1954).

10. Alex Inkeles, "Continuity and Change in American National Character," in Seymour Martin Lipset, ed., *The Third Century: America as a Post-Industrial Society* (Chicago: University of Chicago Press, 1979).

11. Gabriel A. Almond and Stephen J. Genco, "Clouds, Clocks, and the Study of Politics," *World Politics*, 29 (July 1977): 399–422.

12. The importance attached to the falsification of hypotheses came with Karl Popper's apparent solution of David Hume's problem with induction. Hume asked how we can be sure that what we learn from induction today will hold in the future. Popper agrees with Hume that it is impossible to find positive proof of hypotheses by induction; therefore Popper says that science must depend upon refutation—hypotheses, no matter how derived, that cannot be falsified are likely to be valid. Popper's solution, however, does not afford an escape from Hume's problem, for how can we be sure that what has been falsified today will remain false in the future? Although we may use the language of probability there is no denying that in practical terms both approaches depend upon the assumption that nature is law-like. The impact of Heisenberg's principle of indeterminism and of developments in subatomic physics raise the question of whether scientific theories have to be literally true to reality or whether they can be convenient fictions that lead to accurate predictions. Physicists proceed with their work without answering the question. Similarly, we can proceed to work with such concepts as political culture without deciding whether there is such a literal, physical thing or whether it is only a useful concept.

13. Although this is far from the worst example, it is distressing that Fritz Gaenslen, after an elaborate analysis of decision-making in four countries, felt he could confidently conclude from his data only that American decision-makers are more "individualistic" than Chinese, Japanese, and Russians, and that further work would be necessary to determine whether there are any differences in style among the other three. Given all the work he had done on Chinese, Japanese, and Russian decision-making, one wishes that he had felt free to share his judgments about the subject rather than remain so muscle-bound in his constrained view of the requirements of behavioralism. See Fritz Gaenslen, "Culture and Decision Making in

China, Japan, Russia and the United States," *World Politics* 39
(October 1986): 78–103.

14. Talcott Parsons, *The Social System* (Glencoe, IL: The Free
Press, 1951).

15. Clifford Geertz, *The Interpretation of Cultures* (New York:
Basic Books, 1973), 35 and 49.

16. As cited in Christopher Lehmann-Haupt's *New York Times*
(February 9, 1987) book review of Marvin Minsky, *The Society of
Mind.*

17. One of the tragedies of the Vietnam War was that the
strategic theorists of limited wars were blindly ethnocentric in
building their doctrines of "graduated escalation." The assumption
that Washington could send "signals" to Hanoi was based on the
false premise that the Vietnamese leadership perceived American
military actions in the same way as the American theorists did.
Carefully calculated American escalations designed to put pressure on
Hanoi turned out to produce more "pain" in Washington than in
Hanoi and hence failed to send threatening signals to the
Vietnamese, who had quite different thresholds of pain.

18. Aaron Wildavsky, "Choosing Preferences by Constructing
Institutions: A Cultural Theory of Preference Formation," *American
Political Science Review* 81 (1987): 3–21.

19. Myron Weiner, "Culture and Economics: A Political Science
Approach," paper for the conference "A Place for Culture in
Economic Analysis," Institute for the Study of Economic Cultures,
Boston University, December 4–5, 1986.

20. For a spirited attack upon those who feel that structural
explanations need not take into account cultural factors, see Archie
Brown, "Introduction," in Archie Brown and Jack Gray, eds., *Political
Culture and Political Change in Communist States* (New York: Holmer
and Meier Publishers, 1979).

21. In traditional Marxism, culture was dismissed largely because
so much importance was placed on universalistic considerations of
class and stages of historical development. Yet as we shall be
arguing, the power of Chinese culture has recently forced Marxism-
Leninism to make concessions to the importance of national cultural
differences.

22. Interview with Garcia Marquez by Marlise Simons, *New York
Times Book Review*, February 21, 1988, 23.

23. Graham Wallas, *Human Nature in Politics* (London: Constable,
1947, originally published 1908), 21.

24. For an analysis of how such contending themes have been a driving force in American politics see Samuel P. Huntington, *American Politics: The Promise of Disharmony* (Cambridge: Harvard University Press, 1981).

25. For an excellent discussion of theory and methodology that parallels our argument about the need to combine different approaches, see Jack Snyder's comparison of "positivism" and "holism" in his "Science and Sovietology: Bridging the Methods Gap in Soviet Foreign Policy Studies," *World Politics* 40 (January 1988): 169–93.

26. For the problems raised by the differences between available and required data and the difficulties in having to repeat qualifications for the literal minded, see Nathan Leites, "Psycho-Cultural Hypotheses about Political Acts," *World Politics* 1 (October 1948).

27. Lucian W. Pye, "Culture and Political Science: Problems in the Evaluation of the Concept of Political Culture," *Social Science Quarterly* (September 1972), reprinted in Louis Schneider and Charles M. Bonjean, eds., *The Idea of Culture in the Social Sciences*, (Cambridge: Cambridge University Press, 1973), 73–75.

28. Jack Gray, "China: Communism and Confucianism," in Brown and Gray, eds., *Political Culture and Political Change in Communist States*, 198–99.

29. Michel Oksenberg, "Getting Ahead and Along in Communist China: The Ladder of Success on the Eve of the Cultural Revolution," in John Wilson Lewis, ed., *Party Leadership and Revolutionary Power in China* (Cambridge: Cambridge University Press, 1970).

Chapter II: Psychological Roots

1. James David Barber, *The Pulse of Politics* (New York: W.W. Norton, 1980).

2. For a straight-faced analysis of the essentially ludicrous Chinese debate during the Cultural Revolution as to whether the "Swindlers," including Liu Shaoqi and Deng Xiaoping, were "Ultra-Left" of "Ultra-Right" see William A. Joseph, *The Critique of Ultra-Leftism in China, 1958–1981* (Stanford: Stanford University Press, 1984).

3. Benjamin Schwartz, "Some Polarities in Confucian Thought," in *Confucianism In Action*, David S. Nivison and Arthur F. Wright, eds., (Stanford: Stanford University Press, 1959), 50–62.

4. Frederick W. Mote, "Confucian Eremitism in the Yuan Period," in Arthur F. Wright, ed., *The Confucian Persuasion* (Stanford: Stanford University Press, 1960), 202–40.

5. There is a rich literature on the populist political culture, which sought to turn Confucian orthodoxy on its head in almost every respect. See, for example, Susan Naquin, *Shantung Rebellion: The Wang Lun Uprising of 1774* (New Haven: Yale University Press, 1981); Fei-ling Davis, *Primitive Revolutionaries of China: A Study of Secret Societies in the Late Nineteenth Century* (Honolulu: University of Hawaii Press, 1977); Philip A. Kuhn, *Rebellion and its Enemies in Late Imperial China: Militarization and Social Structure, 1976–1864* (Cambridge: Harvard University Press, 1970.

6. Jack Gray has argued that the two poles of the traditional Chinese political culture were represented by Legalism and Taoism, and that Confucianism "represented a compromise view, one might say a commonsense view." (Jack Gray, "China: Communism and Confucianism," in Archie Brown and Jack Gray, eds., *Political Culture and Political Change in Communist States* [New York: Holmes & Meier Publishers, 1979], 199.) Starting with this polarity, he found Confucianism characterized by contradictions, seven to be precise. As will be apparent shortly, we shall be arriving by quite a different route at a similar conclusion—that the intense contradictions of Chinese political culture have stimulated the Chinese worship of the value of harmony.

7. Joseph R. Levenson and Franz Schurman, *China: An Interpretive History* (Berkeley: University of California Press, 1969), 14.

8. "The Way of the Five Pecks of Rice" was named for the price that members had to pay their leader, and it was thus, as were most such movements, egalitarian in ideology but hierarchical in practice, as was Maoism. The Yellow Turbans opposed female infanticide, not for humanitarian or egalitarian reasons, but because they believed every man should have two wives, one on each side of him. (Vincent Y.C. Shih, *The Taiping Ideology* [Seattle: University of Washington Press, 1967], 341.) In most of the heterodox political cultures there was considerable ambivalence about equality of the sexes; in the case of the Taipings women were granted equal inheritance rights, but the Taipings also extolled traditional Confucian views, as in their saying,

"Should a hen desire to herald the arrival of the morning, it is one sure way of making a home miserable" (Shih, *Taiping Ideology*, 72).

9. I have examined this contradiction in greater detail in "Lethargic Officials and Diligent Masses," *The Spirit of Chinese Politics* (Cambridge: M.I.T. Press, 1968), 129–35.

10. Levenson and Schurman, *China*, 19–20.

11. Levenson and Schurman, *China*, 121.

12. Levenson and Schurman, *China*, v.

13. Wang Gungwu, *The Structure of Power in North China During the Five Dynasties* (Kuala Lampur: University of Malaya Press, 1963).

14. Shih, *Taiping Ideology*, 288.

15. Although in the novel *Shui-hu Chuan* (*Water Margin*) the concepts of loyalty and brotherhood were linked, as in the name of the Sung Chiang band's meeting place (the Chung-i T'ang or Hall of Loyalty and Brotherhood) Mao Zedong, in his campaign about the "negative example" portrayed in the novel, suggested that the idea of "loyalty" was to the emperor and not to the group itself. For details of the campaign see *Peking Review* 20 (June 3, 1977), and Merle Goldman, *China's Intellectuals: Advice and Dissent* (Cambridge: Harvard University Press, 1981).

16. Translated by Pauline Yu in Pauline Yu, *The Reading Imagery in the Chinese Poetic Tradition* (Princeton: Princeton University Press, 1987), 123.

17. Gertrude Himmelfarb, *Marriage and Morals Among the Victorians* (New York: Alfred A. Knopf; 1986), 18–22.

18. David S. Nivison, "Protest Against Conventions and Conventions of Protest," in *Confucianism in Action*, ed. Arthur F. Wright, 177–201.

19. The ideal of sacrifice in the culture of the White Lotus sect's mobilization for rebellion included the technique of "going without food" (*pu ch'ih-fan*). "Being able to go without food for ten days was known as a 'lesser merit' (*hsiao-kung*); going without food for an amazing eighty-one days was a 'greater merit' (*ta-kung*)." (Susan Naquin, *Shantung Rebellion: The Wang Lun Uprising of 1774* [New Haven: Yale University Press, 1981], 38.)

20. Paul Y. Yin, M.D., "The Search for the Peace of Heart: the Psychotherapeutic Experience of Chinese Patients," mimeographed paper, no date, 2–3.

21. Xinhua Domestic Service, January 8, 1986, in F.B.I.S., January 10, 1986, 1–6.

22. Levenson and Schurman, *China*, 120–21.

23. Philip Kuhn, "Sorcery as an Object of State Control," paper presented at the annual meeting of the Association of Asian Studies, Boston, April 10–12, 1987.

24. Lucian W. Pye, *Asian Power and Politics* (Cambridge: Harvard University Press, 1985), 203.

25. The extraordinary grip that ritual words and symbolic slogans can have on Chinese minds is evidenced by how Ding Ling, after being denied her freedom for twenty years by the Party, then finally freed, kept repeating the slogan call to "carry out the revolution" in a mindless fashion until she died—much like Chinese adherents to Amithaba Buddhism repeated the name of the founder of their sect endlessly in their hope for salvation.

26. Richard J. Smith, "Knowing Fate: The Role of Divination in Late Imperial China." Paper given at the Southwest Asian Association Meetings, Baylor University, Waco, TX, Nov. 1, 1986.

27. There is a substantial body of psychological research that supports the interpretations I am making about the Chinese view of the self in relation to the group. The evidence is to be found in such works as Michael Harris Bond, ed., *The Psychology of the Chinese People* (New York: Oxford University Press, 1986); David Y. H. Yu, ed., *Chinese Culture and Mental Health* (Orlando, FL: Academic Press, 1985); Kenneth A. Abbott, "Cultural Change and the Persistence of the Chinese Personality," in George De Vos, ed., *Response to Change: Society, Culture and Personality* (New York: Van Nostrand, 1976); Donald J. Munro, ed., *Individualism and Holism: Studies in Confucian and Taoist Values* (Ann Arbor: Center for Chinese Studies, University of Michigan, 1985). Especially noteworthy are the various works of Francis L. K. Hsu, including "The Self in Cross-cultural Perspective," in Anthony J. Marsella, George De Vos, and Francis L. K. Hsu, eds., *Culture and Self: Asian and Western Perspectives* (New York and London: Tavistock Publishers, 1985); "Eros, Affect, and *Pao*," in Francis L. K. Hsu, ed., *Kinship and Culture* (Chicago: Aldine Publishers, 1971); and *Americans and Chinese: Passages to Difference* (Honolulu: University of Hawaii Press, 1985).

28. Donald Munro, *The Concept of Man in Contemporary China* (Ann Arbor: The University of Michigan Press, 1977), 45–55.

29. When we deal with the causes of the Cultural Revolution in chapter 4, we shall have a better opportunity to give due credit to the insightful theory of Lynn White III, which identifies as a major source in generating the passions of the Cultural Revolution the

frustrations Chinese experienced from being labeled according to their family backgrounds. The theory is developed in his *Politics of Chaos: Labels, Monitors, and Campaigns as Causes of China's Cultural Revolution* (Princeton: Princeton University Press, in press).

30. The generation that now dominates Chinese public life was, of course, socialized before the establishment of the People's Republic of China, and therefore an understanding of its experiences can still be found in the works on traditional Chinese family life. These include such studies as Francis L. K. Hsu, *Under the Ancestors' Shadow* (New York: Columbia University Press, 1948); Francis L. K. Hsu, *Americans and Chinese: Passage to Differences* (Honolulu: University of Hawaii Press, 1985); Morton H. Fried, *Fabric of Chinese Society* (New York: Praeger, 1953); Maurice Freedman, ed., *Family and Kinship in Chinese Society* (Stanford: Stanford University Press); Richard Solomon, *Mao's Revolution and the Chinese Political Culture* (Berkeley: University of California Press, 1971); Arthur Wolf, *Studies in Chinese Society* (Stanford: Stanford University Press, 1975); Margery Wolf, *The House of Lim* (New York: Appleton-Century-Crofts, 1968).

For more current patterns of child raising, see two works by Richard W. Wilson: *The Moral State: A Study of the Political Socialization of Chinese and American Children* (New York: The Free Press, 1974), and *Learning to Be Chinese: The Political Socialization of Children in Taiwan* (Cambridge: M.I.T. Press, 1970); Martin King Whyte and William Parish, Jr., *Village and Family in Contemporary China* (Chicago: University of Chicago Press, 1978); William Kessen, ed., *Childhood in China* (New Haven: Yale University Press, 1975); Ruth Sidel, *Families of Fengsheng: Urban Life in China* (Baltimore: Penguin Books, 1974); and Wai-kin Che, *The Modern Chinese Family* (Palo Alto: R & E Research Associates, 1977).

31. The notion of the other that we are suggesting here has overtones of similarity with the concept of the "Other" as developed by the French school of Freudian theorists. See, for example, the works of Michel Foucault, which are effectively brought together in Paul Rabinow, ed., *The Foucault Reader* (New York: Pantheon Books, 1984); and more particularly, Jacques Lacan, *The Language of the Self*, ed. Anthony Wilden (New York: Delta Books, 1968).

Chapter III: On Chinese Pragmatism

1. See, for example, A. Doak Barnett, *China's Economy in Global Perspective* (Washington, D.C.: The Brookings Institute, 1981); Stuart R. Schram, " 'Economics in Command?' Ideology and Policy Since the Third Plenum, 1978–84," *China Quarterly* 99 (September 1984): 417–61; Richard Baum, ed., *China's Four Modernizations* (Boulder, CO: Westview Press, 1980); Michel Oksenberg and Richard Bush, "China's Political Evolution: 1972–82," *Problems of Communism* (September–October 1982): 1–19.

2. Clifford Geertz, *The Interpretations of Cultures* (New York: Basic Books, 1973).

3. One does not have to join the more extreme school of ethnomethodologists to recognize that cultural and subjective factors will limit objectivity. Our position on this problem of objectivity is much the same as that of the Nobel Laureate economist Robert Solow, who once observed, "Just because it is impossible to have a perfectly sterile environment does not mean that doctors should operate in sewers."

Richard A. Shweder, in reviewing Clifford Geertz's *Works and Lives*, sums up the current situation in anthropology with respect to objectivity as follows: "At meetings of the profession, 'anything goes' ethnographers, lacking a sense of intellectual direction, place on display the Alice-in-Wonderland principle that 'if you don't know where you're going almost any road will take you there,' while 'nothing goes' ethnographers, doubtful that any knowledge is authoritative or privileged or even possible, have convinced themselves that anything they say or write is biased or tarnished—Western imperial ideology disguised as a search for truth. The implication is that we are in need of a farm subsidy program for Western intellectuals: to avoid flooding the market with ideas, pay them not to think. A crisis of faith exists. The scientifically inclined do not write ethnographies at all. The humanistically inclined do not write believable ones or they only write about themselves struggling to write about others." *New York Times Book Review*, February 28, 1988, 13.

For discussions of the philosophical problems of objectivity see Nicholas Tilley, "Popper, Positivism and Ethnomethodology, *British Journal of Sociology*, 31 March 1980): 28–45. For ethnomethodological critiques of objective social science, see A. Giddens, *Essays in Social and Political Theory* (London: Hutchinson, 1977); P. Filmer et al.,

New Directions in Sociological Theory (London: Macmillan, 1972); Don Zimmerman, "Ethnomethodology," *American Sociologist*, 13 (1978): 6–15; and Charles Taylor, "Neutrality in Political Science," in Peter Laslett and W. G. Runciman, eds., *Philosophy, Politics and Society*, 3rd series (Oxford: Basil Blackwell, 1967): 25–57.

4. The fact that pragmatism in Britain and China is so manifestly the opposite of ideology tends to obscure the more fundamental dimension of their separate versions of pragmatism. In Britain pragmatism carries with it strong overtones of cleverness and ingenuity in self-advancement, while in China, as we shall be seeing, it is more associated with public policies in the economic realm. In the American political culture pragmatism has an ambiguous character, for it does not only involve being practical in getting the job done; it must also serve to reconcile the congeries of values in what Samuel Huntington has called the "American creed." Since American politics lacks a coherent ideological basis for giving priorities to the diverse, and generally conflicting, values of the creed, and since the creed itself contains a peculiar anti-power ethic that serves to "delegitimate" all hierarchical authority, pragmatism is called upon to cope with the often unsavory task of reconciling the inevitable tensions in an unsystematic creed. See Samuel P. Huntington, *American Politics: The Promise of Disharmony* (Cambridge: Harvard University Press, 1981). Although Americans will pay lip service to pragmatism, there is something patently absurd about upholding the values of practicality and efficiency in a political system that is designed to check and balance authority so that paralysis becomes the norm. It is no wonder that any American politician who shows signs of achieving results will instantly arouse more than the normal paranoia among his competitors.

5. In the early years of the People's Republic of China political analysts' attempts at relating Chinese culture and Communist practices often failed because culture and values were treated in much too literal a form. For example, it was argued that the two were incompatible because Marxism-Leninism stressed "class conflict" while Confucianism emphasized "harmony." (See, for example, Arthur F. Wright, "Struggle vs. Harmony: Symbols of Competing Values in Modern China," *World Politics* 6 [October 1983]: 31–44.) The point that was missed was that the tradition of harmony in fact persisted and helped to reinforce the Party's demands for conformity and consensus. The new rhetoric about the virtues of "struggle" was in practice only a revival of the traditional Confucian view that the

upholders of orthodoxy should stamp out all heterodox views, and not that challenges to orthodoxy should be allowed.

6. Alexander George, "The Operational Code: A Neglected Approach to the Study of Political Leaders and Decision-Making," *International Studies Quarterly* 13 (1969): 109–22.

7. Among the numerous Chinese articles discussing the concept of a "commodity economy," typical are Hong Guoliang, "Socialism Is Not the Highest Stage of a Commodity Economy," *Guangming Ribao*, February 10, 1985, F.B.I.S., February 22, 1985, K 11; Lu Zhichao, "Deepening a Scientific Understanding of Socialism," February 4, 1985, F.B.I.S., February 27, 1985, K 14–19; Song Yangyan, "The Key Lies in the Existence of Collective Ownership," *Guangming Ribao*, December 23, 1984, F.B.I.S., January 16, 1985, K 24–25; He Tianzhong, "Distribution According to Work and the Law of Value" *Guangming Ribao*, February 10, 1985, F.B.I.S., February 25, 1985, K 17–19.

8. Zhao Ziyang, "Advance Along the Road of Socialism with Chinese Characteristics—Report Delivered at the Thirteenth National Congress of the Communist Party of China on October 25, 1987," *Beijing Review* (November 9–15, 1987): 23–49.

9. Francis L. K. Hsu, *Under the Ancestors' Shadow* (New York: Columbia University Press, 1948); and *Americans and Chinese: Two Ways of Life* (New York: Abelard-Schuman, 1953).

10. Max Weber, *The Religion of China*, ed. and trans. Hans H. Gerth (Glencoe, IL: The Free Press, 1951).

11. Arthur P. Wolf, ed., *Religion and Ritual in Chinese Society* (Stanford: Stanford University Press, 1974); Laurence G. Thompson, *Chinese Religion: An Introduction*, 2nd ed. (Encino, CA: Dickenson Publishing Co., 1975); C. K. Yang, *Religion in Chinese Society* (Berkeley: University of California Press, 1970).

12. The phenomenal ease with which Chinese can change attitudes with a change in circumstances was dramatically demonstrated by the behavior of prisoners in the Korean War. See Alexander L. George, *The Chinese Communist Army in Action* (New York: Columbia University Press, 1967).

13. A typical example of such reifying of judgments about world politics in Jin Junhui, "Reagan's Diplomacy: An Overview," *Beijing Review* 28 (June 17, 1985): 21–25.

14. Zhou Zhonqiu's "Base Socialism on a Reality" (*Guangming Ribao*, May 20, 1985, F.B.I.S., June 6, 1985, K 11–13) is an excellent example of the Chinese practice of extolling the need to base all

"actions on reality" without giving the slightest hint as to what the realities of current Chinese politics are, beyond praising reality. The author, of course, is not so foolish as to try to spell out what constitutes reality in today's China, for he knows that all that is now called for is to signal that everyone should praise the idea of "facing reality" and "opposing idealism."

15. Bruce Jacobs, "A Preliminary Model of Particularistic Ties in Chinese Political Alliances: *Kan-ch'ing* and *Kuan-hsi* in a Rural Taiwanese Township," *China Quarterly* 78 (June 1979): 237–73. For the concept of *kanqing* see Morton Fried, *Fabric of Chinese Society* (New York: Praeger, 1953; reprint New York: Octagon Books, 1969), 103–4.

16. Barbara L. K. Pillsbury, "Factionalism Observed: Behind the Face of Harmony in a Chinese Community," *China Quarterly* 74 (June 1978): 241–72.

17. For a comparison of the various Asian systems of patron-client relationships, see Lucian W. Pye, *Asian Power and Politics: The Cultural Dimensions of Authority* (Cambridge: Harvard University Press, 1985).

18. Jacobs, "A Preliminary Model of Particularistic Ties."

19. Paul Hiniker, "Chinese Reactions to Forced Compliance: Dissonance Reduction and National Character," *Journal of Social Psychology* 77 (1969): 157–76.

20. *Psychopolitical Analysis: Selected Writings of Nathan Leites*, ed. Elizabeth Wirth Marvick (New York: John Wiley and Sons, 1977), 214.

21. George Kao, ed., *Chinese Wit and Humor* (New York: Coward-McCann, 1946), 275.

22. Stuart R. Schram, " 'Economics in Command?' Ideology and Policy Since the Third Plenum, 1978–84," *China Quarterly* 99 (September 1984): 427. Chinese leaders are, of course, not the only politicians given to contradictions in terms: Senator Edward M. Kennedy recently denounced a Republican action as "a transparent cover-up" (William Safire, "Whose Oxymoron is Gored," *New York Times Magazine*, June 2, 1985, 16).

23. Personal communication.

24. I have examined in greater detail the relationship of thought to action and the low level of procrastination in Chinese political culture in *The Spirit of Chinese Politics* (Cambridge: M.I.T. Press, 1968), 135–48.

25. *Guangming Ribao*, April 6, 1985, 1, F.B.I.S., April 12, 1985, K17.

26. William James, *Pragmatism and the Meaning of Truth*, Introduction by A. J. Ayer (Cambridge: Harvard University Press, 1975), Introduction and Chapter 1; and John Dewey, *The Quest for Certainty* (1929, reprint, New York: Perigee Books, 1980).

27. "Economic Reforms Will Continue Despite Mistakes," *Asian Wall Street Journal*, July 22, 1985, 8. It should be observed that American scholars of contemporary China regularly exhibit a strange xenophilia in that, even though they live in a country where governmental learning is miniscule, they preserve an almost unquestioned faith that the Chinese government is successfully learning from experience, as though it were a collectivity of experimental scientists.

28. For an exceptionally vivid account of the psychological trauma experienced by the victims of the Cultural Revolution, based on prolonged and skillful interviews, see Anne Thurston's two-part article, "Victims of China's Cultural Revolution: The Invisible Wounds," *Pacific Affairs* 57 (Winter 1984–85): 599–620 and 58 (Spring 1985): 5–27. By way of conclusion she cites an interviewee who displays a need for optimism by professing his faith in Deng and the Party, showing even some respect for Mao, and bowing to the dictates of Chinese patriotism—a most paralyzing constraint on Chinese pragmatism that we shall come to below. Thurston's book-length report of her research, *Enemies of the People* (New York: Alfred A. Knopf, 1987), contains more data; this, however, tends to bury her theoretical insights.

29. Hu Yaobang, "On the Party's Journalism Work," Meeting of the CPC Central Committee Secretariat, *Renmin Ribao*, April 14, 1985, 3, F.B.I.S., April 16, K9.

30. Richard W. Wilson, *Learning to Be Chinese* (Cambridge: M.I.T. Press, 1970), Chapter 1.

31. David K. Shipler, Russia: *Broken Idols, Solemn Dreams* (New York: Times Books, 1983), 5–6.

32. Harold R. Isaacs, *Re-Encounters in China*, (Armonk, NY: M. E. Sharpe, 1985).

33. "Lu Keng's Interview with Hu Yaobang," *Pai Hsing*, Hong Kong, No. 92, June 1, 1985, 3–16, F.B.I.S., June 3, 1985, W 2–3.

34. On the Chinese hope to skip over the initial industrial revolution and move directly to the electronic and biotech age described by Toffler, see Denis F. Simon and Thomas Finger, "An

Overview," special issue on science and technology in China, *Bulletin of the Atomic Scientists* 40 (October 1984), 1–15.

35. Mark Elvin, *The Pattern of the Chinese Past* (Stanford: Stanford University Press, 1973).

36. Joseph Levenson, *Confucian China and Its Modern Fate* (Berkeley: University of California Press, 1958).

37. Stanley Rosen, "Prosperity, Privatization, and China's Youth," *Problems of Communism* (March–April, 1985), 1–28.

38. For a detailed, first-hand account of the limits set on the development of political science see Kent Morrison and Robert Thompson, "Teaching Political Science in China," *News for Teachers of Political Science*, a publication of the American Political Science Association, 45 (Spring 1985), 1–3.

39. For a more detailed discussion of the problems patriotism has created for Chinese intellectuals and the way it has limited their political effectiveness in modern times—a discussion that shows how patriotism runs counter to the traditional Confucian expectation of the scholar as the key authority figure—see Pye, *Asian Power and Politics*.

40. See Liu Binyan's speech to the Fourth Congress of Artists and Writers, "Listen Carefully to the Voice of the People," Beijing, November 9, 1979, translations of which have been done by Percy Ling and Kyna Bubin, "Delving Into Life—The Chinese Writer's Duty," *New York Times Book Review*, February 22, 1987.

Chapter IV: Reassessing the Cultural Revolution

1. The impossibility of establishing exact casualty figures for such a disaster results in unproven numbers becoming accepted ones, based at best on remarks by officials who may or may not have had statistical evidence. See, for example, Li Huo-Cheng, "Chinese Communists Reveal for the First Time the Number of 20 Million Deaths in the Cultural Revolution," *Ming Pao Daily News*, October 26, 1981, 3, cited in Alan P.L. Liu, *How China Is Ruled* (Englewood Cliffs, New Jersey: Prentice-Hall, 1986), 56. Other great tragedies of modern China—the Taiping Rebellion, land reforms, the Great Leap—have been dehumanized by the unexamined repeating of the conventionalized casualty figures associated with them. On the problem of casualty figures in modern China, see Stephen Rosskamm Shalom, *Deaths in China Due to Communism: Propaganda Versus*

Reality (Tempe: Center for Asian Studies, Arizona State University, 1984). The size of China and the difficulties of penetrating the shield of secrecy that Mao's rule in particular placed around the country has meant that China's misfortunes have been largely matters of abstract discussion that have failed to elicit compassion. For example, research now is proving that the famine of 1960–3 was undoubtedly the worst in all of human history, but passed largely unnoted, in contrast to the more dramatized Ethiopian famine of the 1980s, which had far fewer deaths. It is a shame that Chinese leaders have sought pity internationally for matters undeserving of sympathy, while masking the awful tragedies of the people.

2. Simon Leys, *Chinese Shadows* (New York: Viking Press, 1974).

3. Xinhua News Service, June 28 1981.

4. Roderick MacFarquhar, *The Origins of the Cultural Revolution: The Great Leap Forward 1958–60* (New York: Columbia University Press, 1983), 207–12.

5. Robert J. Lifton, *Revolutionary Immortality: Mao Tse-tung and the Cultural Revolution* (New York: Vantage Books, 1968); Richard Solomon, *Mao's Revolution and the Chinese Political Culture* (Berkeley: University of California Press, 1971).

6. Dennis Bloodworth, *The Messiah and the Mandarins* (New York: Atheneum, 1982); Clare Hollingworth, *Mao and the Men Against Him* (London: Jonathan Cape, 1985); Ross Terrill, *Mao: A Biography* (New York: Harper and Row, 1980).

7. Philip Bridgham, "Mao's Cultural Revolution: Origin and Development," *China Quarterly* 19 (January 1967): 1–35; Stanley Karnow, *Mao and China* (Viking: New York, 1972); Edward E. Rice, *Mao's Way* (Berkeley: University of California Press, 1972); Alan P. L. Liu, *Political Culture and Group Conflict in Communist China* (Santa Barbara: California: Clio Press, 1976).

8. Byung-Joon Ahn, *Chinese Politics and the Cultural Revolution* (Seattle: University of Washington Press, 1976); Parris H. Chang, *Power and Policy in China* (University Park and London: Pennsylvania State University Press, 1975); Lowell Dittmer, *Liu Shiao ch'i and the Chinese Cultural Revolution* (Berkeley: University of California Press, 1975); Jurgen Domes, *The Internal Politics of China: 1949–1972* (London: C. Hurst and Co., 1973); Hang Yung Lee, *The Politics of the Chinese Cultural Revolution* (Berkeley: University of California Press, 1978).

9. Jerome Ch'en (in a review of Andrew Nathan's *Chinese Democracy*), *China Quarterly* 105 (March 1986): 144.

10. Ba Jin, *Random Thoughts*, trans. Geremie Barme (Hong Kong: Joint Publications Co., 1964), 76. I am indebted to Merle Goldman for bringing to my attention Ba Jin's views.

11. Svend Ranulf, *Moral Indignation and the Middle Class Psychology*, with an introduction by Harold D. Lasswell (New York: Schocken Books, 1964). In some odd respects Ranulf's analysis seems to fit Chinese culture almost better than it fits the West. The traditional Confucian ideal of the upright, virtuous person, concerned with self-cultivation and prepared to resign and withdraw into isolation rather than be associated with corrupt government, fits perfectly his idea of the pre-moral-indignation psychology. He has some problems with the wrathful Old Testament prophets who decried the evils of their day, but he insists that they were not representative of moral indignation because they were individual figures and not possessors of a collective anger that would demand criminal codes to punish all transgressors. However, the Chinese clearly have not as yet manifested the collective moral indignation that Ranulf associates with the demands for an impersonal criminal code of law.

12. Lynn T. White III, *Policies of Chaos: Labels, Monitors, and Campaigns of Causes of China's Cultural Revolution* (Princeton University Press, in press).

13. William Hinton, *Hundred Day War: The Cultural Revolution at Tsinghua University* (New York: Monthly Review Press, 1972); Victor Nee, *The Cultural Revolution at Peking University* (New York: Monthly Review Press, 1969); Neale Hunter, *Shanghai Journal: Eyewitness Account of the Cultural Revolution* (New York: Praeger, 1969); Colin Mackerras and Neale Hunter, *China Observed: 1964–1967* (London: Pall Mall, 1968).

14. *Gao Yuan, Born Red* (Stanford: Stanford University Press, 1987).

15. Ken Ling, *Revenge of Heaven* (G.P. Putnam's Sons: New York, 1972); B. Michael Frolic, *Mao's People* (Cambridge: Harvard University Press, 1980); David Raddock, *Political Behavior of Adolescents in China: The Cultural Revolution in Kwangchow* (Tucson: University of Arizona Press, 1977); Gordon A. Bennett and Ronald N. Montaperto, *Red Guard: The Political Biography of Dai Hsiao-ai* (Garden City, New York: Doubleday & Co., 1982).

16. Liang Heng and Judith Shapiro, *Son of Revolution* (Random House: New York, 1983).

17. The best translated collections of such literature include Perry Link, ed., *Stubborn Weeds: Popular and Controversial Chinese Literature After the Cultural Revolution* (Bloomington: Indiana University Press, 1983); Perry Link, ed., *Roses and Thorns* (Berkeley: University of California Press, 1984); Geremie Barme and Bennet Lee, trans., *The Wounded: New Stories of the Cultural Revolution* (Hong Kong: Joint Publishing Co., 1979).

18. Merle Goldman, "Wenhua Dageming de Fei Xiaoji Yingsheng" (The Non-negative Influence of the Cultural Revolution), in *Zhishi Fentze (The Chinese Intellectual)* (Spring, 1986), 47–49.

19. Liang Heng and Judith Shapiro, *After the Nightmare* (New York: Alfred Knopf, 1986), 5.

20. Thurston first produced an article in two installments, "Victims of China's Cultural Revolution: The Invisible Wounds," pt. 1, *Pacific Affairs* 57 (Winter, 1984–85): 599–620; and pt. 2, 58 (Spring, 1985): 5–27, and then her book, *Enemies of the People: The Ordeal of the Intellectuals in China's Great Cultural Revolution* (New York: Knopf, 1987).

21. Thurston, "Victims of China's Cultural Revolution," pt. 1, 605–6.

22. Thurston, "Victims of China's Cultural Revolution," pt. 2, 20.

23. Yue Daiyun, as told to Carolyn Wakeman, *To the Storm: The Odyssey of a Revolutionary Chinese Woman* (Berkeley: University of California Press, 1985). This book is a truly troublesome testament to the lack of political maturity of some Chinese intellectuals. Whereas one can dismiss the childlike enthusiasm of a fourteen-year-old Gao Yuan for believing that "making revolution" was nothing more than behaving irresponsibly, it is harder to accept Yue Daiyun's mindless adherence to the meaningless cliche that it is good to "make revolution." The power of revolutionary and nationalistic slogans for many Chinese is apparently so great that even intellectuals—or maybe it is especially intellectuals—seem unable to ask more profound questions about the state of their national life.

24. Nien Cheng, *Life and Death in Shanghai* (New York: Grove Press, 1987).

25. Harold R. Isaacs, *Re-Encounters in China* (Armonk, New York: M. E. Sharp, 1985).

26. Heng and Shapiro, *After the Nightmare*, 238–39.

27. The failure of Western analysts, including tour-guided visitors, to appreciate how bad the "revolutionary committees" actually were resulted in a general tendency to assume that the Cultural Revolution

had ended around 1969. For the Chinese, however, the troubles continued until Mao's death.

28. "The Reign of Virtue: Some Broad Perspectives on Leader and Party in the Cultural Revolution," *China Quarterly* 35 (July-September, 1968): 1–17.

29. Thomas B. Gold, "After Comradeship: Personal Relations in China Since the Cultural Revolution," *China Quarterly* 104 (December 1985): 657–75.

30. Gold, "After Comradeship," 669.

31. The irony of the post-Cultural Revolution mood in China is that the very responses that have energized the "reforms" have also made it possible for children of high officials to exploit their situation for material benefit. Similarly, apolitical but ambitious college graduates now routinely join the Party in order to get ahead. On the ambivalences of go-getting Chinese toward the shameless ways *gaoganzidi* lord it over the common herd, see Heng and Shapiro, *After the Nightmare*, 130–48.

32. Thurston, *Enemies of the People*, 294 ff.

33. For a summary of the problems inherent in a modified market economy that protects inefficiencies, see Yeung Wai Hong, "China's Troubling Mercantilist Bent," *The Asian Wall Street Journal*, May 12, 1986, 12.

34. Thurston, *Enemies of the People*, 284–88.

Chapter V: The Mystique of Leadership

1. Proof of the difficulties that Confucian cultures have in legitimating powerful autonomous centers of authority that might shield and reinforce the central authority figure can be seen in contemporary South Korea. In spite of the emergence of huge business combines that are major actors in the world economy, the Blue House must rule alone, unsupported by modern equivalents of loyal barons. Economic power is not easily translatable into political authority. Japan, with its feudal tradition, is more like Europe, in that its economic and other forms of power have been legitimated as participants in the political arena. I have examined the contrasting problems of legitimacy in the countries with a Confucian heritage in *Asian Power and Politics* (Cambridge: Harvard University Press, 1985).

2. The number of courtesans selected to surround the emperor reflected the Chinese desire to prevent the emergence of contending

power on the part of consort families. With so many ladies in the court, no family could expect to translate the success of its daughter into significant political collateral. The use of eunuchs, and the number of them required, were only partly necessitated by the imperative that any child conceived in the Forbidden City would have to be the emperor's so that the imperial blood line would be protected. In part it was believed that men who could not have heirs would not be interested in accumulating material wealth. This belief was utterly erroneous: the chief eunuchs routinely exploited their control of access to the emperor for handsome bribes.

3. Intellectual history, happily for its practitioners, lacks anything comparable to socialization theory as a mechanism for explaining causation. As it is, intellectual history, like political culture, must deal with subtle phenomena, but its interpretations of the influences of ideas are exempt from having to explain why some people are influenced by the reading of books while most are not. The doctrine of interdisciplinary fairness should require those who have attacked the methodological soundness of political culture to train their critical attentions more on the field of intellectual history. For as Frank E. Manuel, a master of that field, has written: "In a period when the methodology of a discipline is highly prized, the history of ideas roams through academic life like a stray cat." Manuel goes on to observe quite happily that while intellectual history lacks any widely accepted theories, it can take heart from the observation of the mathematician Jules-Henri Poincare that he " . . . was suspicious of forms of knowledge that are high on methodology and low on results." (Frank E. Manuel, "Lovejoy Revisited," *Daedalus* 116 [Spring 1987]: 125.)

4. I have elaborated on the details of the possible connections between the repressive pressures of filial piety (which prevent Chinese from expressing the most fundamental form of aggression—that of the oedipal complex) and the manifestation of anger when authority figures appear to be failures, as during the Cultural Revolution, in *The Spirit of Chinese Politics* (Cambridge: M.I.T. Press, 1968).

5. Americans, with our idealization of youthfulness and lack of reverence for those we think of as over the hill, should not be too quick to think it is only East Asian junior officials who are paralyzed in the presence of their senile seniors. The United States judiciary, including the Supreme Court, has frequently been at a loss as to what to do about doddering judges who refuse to acknowledge that they are no longer with it. A telling example is that of Supreme

Court Associate Justice Stephan Field, who became an embarassment to the other Brethren by nodding off while on the bench, garbling his words, asking non sequitur questions, and generally acting gaga. Nobody could approach him to suggest retirement until finally it was remembered that when Judge Field was a vigorous member of a lower court, there had been a similar problem with a senile colleague and he and another judge were appointed to meet with the old judge and bring up the idea of retirement. It was happily agreed that the two associate justices should remind Judge Field of what he had done on that occasion in the hope that he would take the hint and retire. When confronted and asked if he remembered the role he once played, Judge Field retorted, "Yes, I do remember. A more despicable thing I never did. I'll never be able to live it down." This case should help make vivid how hard it must be for Mr. Deng to get rid of the old comrades who enjoy their perquisites as much as their power.

6. *Selected Works of Deng Xiaoping*, pp. 305–6, as quoted in Hu Hua, "Marching on a Tortuous Road" (Paper delivered at a conference on "New Perspectives on the Cultural Revolution," Fairbank Center for East Asian Research, Harvard University, May 1987).

7. *New York Times*, April 14, 1988, A19. For an excellent analysis of developments at the Party Congress, see Michel Oksenberg, "China's 13th Party Congress," *Problems of Communism* (November–December 1987): 1–17.

8. One of the most puzzling questions about likely developments in the post-Deng era is that of whether the Chinese will be able to accomplish their goal of making "political reforms," which, as we have observed, amount mainly to administrative changes to separate the Party and government hierarchies. Given the Chinese propensity to see all relationships in terms of a single hierarchy, this may be difficult to achieve. Moreover, were the Chinese to be successful and arrive at a situation essentially the same as that in the Soviet Union and Eastern Europe, it is questionable whether this would be a significant improvement for public administration. Over the years much of the best talent in China has been systematically recruited into the Party. Thus it could be that not only will the talented Zhao Ziyang be removed from governmental responsibilities to run Party affairs, but large numbers of highly talented people in the lower ranks will also be taken out of administrative roles and consigned to Party work. Plant managers may be freed from the interference of

party cadres in their daily operations, but the capacity of the Party to throw its weight around will not be ended, particularly at the city and provincial levels.

9. For a view that interprets participation under Mao Zedong as having been more robust, see James Townsend, *Political Participation in Communist China* (Berkeley: University of California Press, 1967). During Mao's reign I spelled out my views of what participation meant in China, in "Mass Participation in Communist China: Its Limitations and the Continuity of Culture," in John M. H. Lindbeck, ed., *China: Management of a Revolutionary Society* (Seattle: University of Washington Press, 1971), 3–33.

10. For a very sophisticated and empirically rich study of the politics of alliance-building and coalition-formation among local officials dealing with different elements of the central government with regard to basic political economy issues, see Kenneth Lieberthal and Michel Oksenberg, *Bureaucratic Politics and Chinese Energy Development* (Princeton: Princeton University Press, 1987). See also Dorothy Solinger, *Chinese Business Under Socialism* (Berkeley: University of California Press, 1985).

11. Charles E. Lindbloom, *Politics and Markets: The World's Political-Economic System* (New York: Basic Books, 1977).

12. Robert Robins, "Paranoid Ideation and Charismatic Leadership," *Psychohistory Review: Studies in Motivation in History and Culture* 5 (Fall 1986): 15–55.

13. In working on my *Mao Tse-tung: The Man in the Leader* (New York: Basic Books, 1976), I was advised by psychiatrists and psychoanalysts in the Cambridge-Boston area that the evidence of Mao's behavior that I presented to them was suggestive of the borderline syndrome. In retrospect it is clear that I was unduly timid, in that I hesitated to follow their prediction that because of his personality Mao would in the end abandon Zhou Enlai, Jiang Qing, and the arrangements for his succession. They were surprisingly correct; the theory did predict exactly what was to happen in the years after I wrote the book.

14. Donald B. Rinslay, *Borderline and Other Self Disorders* (New York: Jason Aronson, 1982); O. F. Kernberg, "Borderline Personality Organization," *Journal of the American Psychoanalytical Association* 18 (1967): 64–85; P. Hartocollis, ed., *Borderline Personality Disorders* (New York: International Universities Press, 1977).

15. For what may lie ahead in China, as the state and party co-opt artists and writers who agree to accept the rewards of creativity

under conditions of conformity, see the example of what has happened in Hungary, as brilliantly described in Miklos Haraszti, *The Velvet Prison: Artists Under State Socialism* (New York: New Republic Book/Basic Books, 1987).

INDEX

Aged cadres, 140–44
Ahn, Byung-Joon, 115
Allende, Isabel, 21
Almond, Gabriel, 14, 16
Anger, and aggression, 54–58
Anti-bourgeois liberalization, 79
Anti-Rightist campaign, 145

Ba Jin, 118
Barber, James David, 38
Barnett, A. Doak, 184 n.1
Bell, Daniel, 168
Benedict, Ruth, 2, 22, 24
Boaz, Franz, 22
Borderline personality, 160–62
Borges, Jorge Luis, 21
Bourgeois liberalism, 147,
    166–69
Bo Yang, 105
Bureaucracy, 32–35

Cadres, aged, 139–43
Calvinists, 68–69
Carstairs, K. M., 24
Central Advisory Commission,
    141
Chang, Parris H., 115
Ch'en, Jerome, 118
Chen Yun, 146, 147
Chinese concept of self, 70–73

Chinese culture: acceptance of
    complaining in, 96, 97;
    acceptance of explanations in,
    97, 98; and aggression, 76;
    anti-individualistic, 59–60;
    basis of morality in, 52–53;
    concept of virtue in, 120;
    hierarchies in, 127–28; locus
    of control in, 65–66, 68, 69;
    magic, 64–65; problem of
    intimacy in, 46–49; problem
    of self-identity in, 70–73;
    realism in, 82–83; repressed
    aggression in, 72–73;
    resistance to introspection in,
    72–73, 95–96; respect of age
    in, 139–43; self-identity in,
    59–61, 62; sincerity in, 50–53;
    situation-oriented, 82, 83; this-
    worldliness of, 84; tolerance
    of cognitive dissonance, 88,
    89; unity of, 154–58; wishful
    thinking in, 65, 66
Chinese political culture:
    authority in, 138–39; authority
    figures in, 56; brotherhood
    versus respectability, 44–49;
    continuity in, 67–70;
    discounting of objectivity in,
    51–52; fatalism in, 54–58;
    humility in, 61–63; leadership

199